Bright Star of the West

AMERICAN MUSICSPHERES

Series Editor
Mark Slobin

Fiddler on the Move
Exploring the Klezmer World
Mark Slobin

The Lord's Song in a Strange Land
Music and Identity in Contemporary Jewish Worship
Jeffrey A. Summit

Lydia Mendoza's Life in Music
Ñorteno Tejano Legacies
Yolanda Broyles-González

Four Parts, No Waiting
A Social History of American Barbershop Harmony
Gage Averill

Louisiana Hayride
Radio and Roots Music along the Red River
Tracey E. W. Laird

Balkan Fascination
Creating an Alternative Music Culture in America
Mirjana Laušević

Polkabilly
How the Goose Island Ramblers Redefined American Folk Music
James P. Leary

Cajun Breakdown
The Emergence of an American-Made Music
Ryan André Brasseaux

Claiming Diaspora
Music, Transnationalism, and Cultural Politics in Asian/Chinese
America
Su Zheng

Bright Star of the West
Joe Heaney, Irish Song-Man
Sean Williams and Lillis Ó Laoire

BRIGHT STAR OF THE WEST

Joe Heaney, Irish Song-Man

Sean Williams
and
Lillis Ó Laoire

To Lorna,
Thanks for
your sensitivity
to the word!
le céim ? le
buíochas?
Ó Lillis
12/06/11

OXFORD
UNIVERSITY PRESS

OXFORD
UNIVERSITY PRESS

Oxford University Press

Oxford University Press, Inc., publishes works that further
Oxford University's objective of excellence
in research, scholarship, and education.

Oxford   New York
Auckland   Cape Town   Dar es Salaam   Hong Kong   Karachi
Kuala Lumpur   Madrid   Melbourne   Mexico City   Nairobi
New Delhi   Shanghai   Taipei   Toronto

With offices in
Argentina   Austria   Brazil   Chile   Czech Republic   France   Greece
Guatemala   Hungary   Italy   Japan   Poland   Portugal   Singapore
South Korea   Switzerland   Thailand   Turkey   Ukraine   Vietnam

Copyright © 2011 Oxford University Press

Published by Oxford University Press, Inc.
198 Madison Avenue, New York, New York 10016

www.oup.com

Library of Congress Cataloging-in-Publication Data
Williams, Sean, 1959–
Bright star of the west: Joe Heaney, Irish song-man / Sean Williams and Lillis Ó Laoire.
p.   cm.—(American musicspheres)
Includes bibliographical references and index.
ISBN 978-0-19-532118-0
1. Heaney, Joe, 1919–1984.   2. Singers—Ireland—Biography.
3. Sean-nós—Ireland—History and criticism.
I. Ó Laoire, Lillis, 1961–   II. Title.
ML420.H336W55 2011 782.42162'91620092—dc22
[B] 2010014551

1 3 5 7 9 8 6 4 2

Printed in the United States of America
on acid-free paper

But I'd filled the hall with my voice, held the crowd. They understood. And, I thought, I can do it again. I will do it again....I suppose the experience made me—giddy. But I don't know. 'Twas more than that. And 'twasn't the clapping. Like, you can talk forever, but singing. Singing, d'yeh know? The only possible way to tell people.

(spoken by the "Irish Man," a character from
Tom Murphy's play The Gigli Concert)

Acknowledgments

Simultaneously writing a book in two different countries is a challenging task, even with the use of the internet. Sean Williams (of Washington State in the United States) and Lillis Ó Laoire (of Galway, Ireland) would each like to thank the other for their mutual patience, inspiration, and sense of humor that has sustained them over their many years of friendship, writing, singing, and e-mailing in the creation of this book. We have agreed that we could not have done this without each other (or the wonders of Skype), and it has been a joy for each of us to work with such a *simpatico* partner. (Lest there be any confusion on either side of the Atlantic, Sean is female, and Lillis is male.) We also wish to acknowledge the subject of this book, Joe Heaney (also known as Seosamh Ó hÉanaí). It is not just the obvious sentiment that without Heaney's presence the book would not have been created, but rather that without Heaney's presence, our collective understanding of Irish music, culture, history, and the role of the same in America would be much less than it is today.

Liam Mac Con Iomaire researched and wrote an Irish-language biography of Joe Heaney (*Seosamh Ó hÉanaí: Nár Fhágha Mé Bás Choíche*), published in 2007 by the Irish publisher Cló Iar-Chonnachta. Liam's years of hard work, long interviews in both Irish and English (referred to frequently in this book), and his meticulous citations of articles and commentaries, have made our work immeasurably easier. We were able to rely again and again on Liam's book to supplement, reinforce, and engage our own. We offer our sincerest thanks to him and to his family.

Financial, intellectual, and general support has been generously provided to both authors on both sides of the Atlantic. We are both grateful to the good people at the University of Washington School of Music, Ethnomusicology Division (in particular Fredric Lieberman and Daniel M. Neuman), who hired Joe Heaney as a visiting artist just as Sean began her work in graduate school. H. Lorraine Sakata provided a warm and welcoming environment for Heaney during his tenure at the department, and took a primary role in focusing the attention and energy of the department and larger community when Heaney passed away in 1984.

Esther Warkov interviewed Joe Heaney at length in 1978, and those recordings were, from the beginning, an invaluable resource. Laurel Sercombe of the Ethnomusicology Archives (which houses the Joe Heaney Collection of recorded and printed materials) earns special thanks for her tireless and welcoming efforts to make the Collection continually available to all comers.

In the United States, Sean Williams was awarded two faculty summer stipends by her home institution, The Evergreen State College, to continue her work on the Heaney materials. The Irish Studies students at The Evergreen State College, together with Sean's faculty colleagues, have provided a strong resource of intellectual engagement. Sean's friends and family, especially Cary and Morgan Black, Alan and Julian Williams, Tomie Hahn, Gage Averill, Gloria Armstrong, Jim Cowdery and many others deserve her gratitude for their support and patience in waiting for the book's completion.

Financial support for Lillis Ó Laoire was provided in the form of a Senior Research Fellowship by the Irish Research Council for the Humanities and Social Sciences, and is gratefully acknowledged. IRCHSS also supported a post-doctoral researcher, Dr. Virginia Blankenhorn, to work on the materials in the Heaney archive during 2009–10. A website (www.joeheaney.org) has resulted from this research, which is now available as a teaching resource for all those interested in Heaney's work and its importance to traditional music and culture. The staff and students of Roinn na Gaeilge (Department of Irish), School of Languages, Literatures and Cultures, National University of Ireland at Galway, are a source of unfailing support in research and writing. Additionally, Acadamh na hOllscolaíochta Gaeilge, also at NUI Galway, especially at Áras Shorcha Ní Ghuairim, Carna, Co. Galway, were also unstintingly generous with their assistance. Without the assistance of the staff of the James Hardiman Library, NUI Galway, this work would undoubtedly have taken longer to complete.

Outside Galway, the staff members of The Irish Traditional Music Archive in Dublin have once again earned deep gratitude. Thanks are also due to the people of Carna for their interest in this project and for their open welcome and support of all efforts to perpetuate Joe Heaney's memory. Alert readers of scholarly work are a singular gift. These include Micheál Ó Catháin, Peadar Ó Ceannabháin, Micheál Ó Cuaig, Feargal Ó Béarra and Johanne Trew. Their incisive comments contributed to making this an immeasurably better work. Finally Lillis's thanks are due to Roy Hamilton for his understanding, reassuring care in ways too numerous and profound to mention.

The editors and staff members of Oxford University Press have been unfailing in their long-term interest in this project. Music Acquisitions Editor Suzanne Ryan helped to bring this book from idea to reality by championing it from the beginning, and her assistant Madelyn Sutton— and, later, Caelyn Cobb—helped with the day-to-day communications between authors and Oxford. Jennifer Kowing took on the task of production editor, and her careful shepherding—with the kind assistance of project manager Niranjana Harikrishnan—has resulted in the book you hold in your hands. Copyeditor Susan Ecklund deserves our profuse thanks for her meticulous attention to detail. Mark Slobin, Wesleyan University professor of ethnomusicology who also serves as Series Editor, knew Joe Heaney when Heaney came to work at Wesleyan, so the shepherding through of this project has had a personal as well as a professional dimension for him. The reviewers of this book for Oxford are among the top scholars in the world of Irish music and contributed strongly to its current form. We would like to thank Mick Moloney, Gearóid Ó hAllmhuráin, and James Cowdery for their careful reading and comments.

Contents

We dedicate this book, with gratitude,
to Micheál Ó Cuaig of Aill na Brún, Cill Chiaráin,,
whose unflagging work in producing Féile Joe Éinniú (The Joe Heaney Festival)
each May in Carna
not only honors the memory of Heaney himself, but supports and encourages
the continuous process of teaching, learning, listening, and performing
the tradition of *sean-nós* singing in one of its prime locations.
Is maol gualainn gan bráthair.
Go raibh míle maith agat.
Thank you.

Bright Star of the West

Introduction

Singing the Dark Away

Joe Heaney is probably the most famous of all traditional Gaelic singers of Ireland, and consequently the best known among followers and practitioners alike. He presented himself primarily as a narrator and singer of old-style stories and songs; the style he performed is known as *sean-nós* (old style). His recorded interviews and performances highlight his quest to extend and perfect his art beyond his native place, to the point that those not from his area could understand something of who he was and, by extension, something of his home region of Connemara. He was a larger-than-life figure to whom many laid claim during his lifetime, a fascination that continues to the present. Heaney, however, belonged fully to no one and remains elusive even to his greatest fans. There is a sense in which the more that is said or written about him, the more mysterious and puzzling he becomes. No one account can fully do justice to the complexity of Heaney's multiple human identities. Yet it is useful to try to comprehend his work and life, through his own search for recognition: for his language, his music, and his culture.

In the first place, and crucial to this understanding, is an attempt to grasp the world into which Heaney was born and in which he spent his life. His story is in some ways typical of many others of his generation, yet in certain respects it is unique because of the choices he made and the paths he followed, highlighting and emphasizing his artistic talent as he went. The fact that Heaney was born during the Irish War of Independence is an important element in coming to comprehend his story. Born when Ireland was still a colony, he matured in the Irish Free State and saw the inauguration of a new constitution while still a teenager. He was poised, then, with one foot in the colonial past and the other in the independent future, where national and personal identity were often equated.

The campaign to rediscover and reinvigorate Gaelic Ireland had gathered great momentum by the end of the nineteenth century. The word *Gaeltacht*, once a term that denoted primarily Irish speakers wherever they might be found together, translating into something like "the Irishry" or the Gaelic speakers, came during Heaney's lifetime to signify certain land areas, mostly along the western seaboard where the Gaelic language and Gaelic lifeways still predominated. Heaney was locally known as Joe (or Josie) Éinniú, acquiring the name Seosamh Ó hÉanaí much later (Ó h-Éighnigh was the school form); in fact, the English spelling of his father's name in the 1911 census was given as Heanue.[1] This spelling more accurately reflects the local Gaelic pronunciation of the name. Although the name Heaney is used here, it is an Anglicization of a Gaelic name.[2] The rediscovery and reinvigoration of Gaelic Ireland, then, represented a shift in focus that equated people with specific geographic regions, ones that would be granted statutory recognition in the emerging post-colonial state (Ó Torna 2005).

This movement also concentrated on the culture of Gaelic speakers in Gaelic regions. These people were once vilified and scorned as backward, poor, illiterate and inarticulate, not to mention savage, shiftless and dirty, as portrayed by travel writers and in the pages of periodicals such as *Punch* (Curtis 1997; Williams 2007). Gaels in the period from 1893 onward, however, became ever more exalted and revered in certain circles as a wave of cultural romantic nationalism rose among well-to-do middle-class urban dwellers. The timing of Joe Heaney's birth in 1919 placed him in a position to avail of this new acceptance and admiration, as a native Gaelic speaker, born into a storytelling and singing family in an area noted for its numerous traditional performers. The economic struggles of the new nation—by the time Heaney was in his midteens in the late 1930s—and the establishment of Irish medium preparatory colleges (1924) to educate primary school teachers became one of the few avenues of opportunity at the time.

Heaney's departure from the trajectory of advancement through education to a career in teaching, such as his close friend and fellow singer Seán 'Ac Dhonncha followed, was a life-changing occurrence. Whether chosen or forced, it resulted in a move that left his life marked by the struggle to earn a precarious living, frequently involving heavy physical work. Despite his talent—recognized early with awards—he left Ireland for Scotland. He moved later to England and eventually immigrated to the United States, where he spent much of the rest of his life. His time in Scotland and England brought him into contact with those who were interested in folk music, song, and narrative, resulting in his participation in a documentary film called *The Irishmen* (1965)—a celebration of the Irish working man's achievement in England, marked by clips of performance from Heaney.

Another opportunity for understanding Heaney presents itself through the last two decades of his life, spent largely in the United States. At a time when a majority of Irish people in America had gained acceptance under the assimilatory American category of Caucasian—invented to include non-Anglophone whites from diverse European ethnicities (Jacobson 1998)—Heaney had been celebrated for his indigenous specificity by folk music enthusiasts both in Ireland and in England. Acclaimed also for his fluency as a native speaker of Irish, his mastery marked him as divergent from the Anglo norm, linguistically almost signifying mark of color. His singing in English also attracted attention, however, for his distinctive Hiberno-English ballads, many set to untempered modal tunes. In addition, his ability to narrate reminiscences, anecdotes, legends, and tales; emblems of lifeways that many had abandoned for the comfortable amnesia of the suburbs, further imbued him with a powerful fascination for those seeking cultural alternatives to the numbing sameness of modernity. His progression through his final two decades became one of emergence from obscurity into national recognition in the United States, in Britain, and, belatedly but ultimately, at home in Ireland.

In some ways, Heaney was an anachronism in America; he was a nonassimilated, nonassimilating maverick asserting his Gaelic identity through its expressive culture. And yet, as an immigrant, faced with a rapidly changing society in which civil rights and new ideas of diversity and freedom were burgeoning, he had to negotiate and accommodate in his new environment. An examination of such negotiations can reveal much about an immigrant artist's ability to adapt and to tailor his cultural resources to his new situation. It is upon such moments that our narrative will concentrate in our attempts to provide a picture of Heaney's life and work, and above all of his success as a performer. The following paragraph serves as a standard biography for Heaney; variants of it have appeared in newspaper columns, in conversations, and in classrooms in Ireland and elsewhere, in which Heaney is upheld as the sine qua non of the old-style (*sean-nós*) singing.

Joe Heaney was an Irish singer and storyteller of the old style. He was born in 1919 in the parish of Carna in Connemara, where he grew up among Irish-speaking extended family and neighbors. He became nationally known as a singer in the early 1940s when he first began to appear onstage and won the prestigious award as finest *sean-nós*, or old-style, singer at home in Ireland at the Oireachtas competition. He later immigrated, first to Scotland and later to England, and finally to the United States. After years of working as a doorman in New York City, he made an appearance on the Merv Griffin television show that relaunched his career as a performer. He was hired as a visiting artist at Wesleyan University and ended his days at the University of Washington in Seattle, working with graduate students and local audiences by telling stories and singing to them about the lifeways of his people. As an Irishman who found a measure of success in America, and as a multifaceted symbol of Ireland's rural past and contemporary ambiguity over what that past represented, Joe Heaney was many things to many people at home and abroad.

As Fred McCormick noted, "To the crowds at American folk festivals, he embodied an Ireland where the cottage door was always open, and the kettle was always on the turf fire, and the *poitín* still bubbled merrily and secretly nearby" (2000:10). Heaney was enormously popular among certain American audiences, and he came to represent an Ireland of the historical present that they had never known and could not know. Joe Heaney's residency as visiting artist at the University of Washington resulted in many hours of oral history, songs, and stories preserved on tape in what is now the Joe Heaney Collection at the UW Ethnomusicology Archives. These archives are an essential resource for scholars and singers alike.

In each performance or interview, Heaney took it upon himself to reveal aspects of Irishness that reflected well upon himself and upon the members of his community at home. Because of his own cultural formation, influenced by the ideologies of the Gaelic League and Irish Ireland, Heaney's understanding of Irish identity differed considerably from American—particularly Irish American—norms. Consequently, he also deliberately thwarted standard American icons of Irish identity with their images of shamrocks, shillelaghs, and leprechauns. Instead he showed an entirely different—and not always welcome to American or Irish audiences—version of the Ireland that he wanted to remember (and to have others remember or learn for the first time) from his days as a young man from the rocky west coast of Ireland.

This book came about for several reasons. Joe Heaney's life and artistry had a strong impact on singers and scholars in both the United States and Ireland. His many performances enhanced his influence as he became, for some people, highly symbolic of either the Ireland they abandoned or the Ireland to which they longed to return. In exploring issues of exile, famine, (re)presentation, masculinity, song, and other key features of Irish and Irish American experiences, Joe Heaney is located here in a milieu that has shaped both Irish and American history. It is our further intention to critically examine the ways in which Heaney's life, songs, stories, and sheer presence served to simultaneously galvanize aspects of the American folk music community and create sometimes difficult dividing lines among Irish and Irish Americans.

A critical biography differs from a chronological biography in several ways. This critical biography focuses on *how* Heaney did what he did, *what choices* he made in drawing from his exhaustive repertoire of songs and stories, *why* he made those particular choices, and *what impact* those choices had not only on himself and his career but also on the people who came to work with him and to know him. His is not the story of someone who hummed quietly to himself as part of a daily routine of work on land and sea, or who sang exclusively for small groups of kinfolk and neighbors in intimate settings; Heaney commanded audiences large and small, held them spellbound, and lived an existence that was, in many ways, larger than life, as befits a preeminent performer.

This is a deep study, focusing almost exclusively on Heaney's life and works. Other characters appear briefly in this text; however, the close focus on Heaney should not blind the reader to the fact that Heaney was part of a much broader musical and cultural trend, which characterizes Anglo-Celtic culture in the mid-twentieth century. The interest in vernacular cultures and languages outside the mainstream was part of a great democratizing impulse deriving from the Romantic reaction to the Enlightenment, the growth of new nations, and the desire for ethnic distinctiveness. A study of Heaney's life and works, then, illuminates "larger issues through smaller situations" (Slobin 2000:10). While characters such as Lead Belly, Norman Kennedy, and Jean Redpath appear only briefly, they also are part of this movement, performers who rode a wave of interest that brought many of them fame and success. Heaney's quest for recognition as an Irish song-man is our primary concern.

All performers present an illusion, based on deep cultural knowledge and everyday experience. In common with all art, performing must be molded to the needs of a particular time, situation, and audience. Therein lies a contradiction for Heaney, who always asserted that the culture not be changed, even as he himself adapted it for his own purposes in performance.

The forces that drove Heaney's life and art—including his early valorization in competition, the desire to achieve recognition both for the art form and, by extension, for his language and culture, and other elements of his life experience—form the core of this exploration.

The authors would be remiss if an existing book about Joe Heaney's life by the Irish scholar Liam Mac Con Iomaire went unmentioned. Titled *Seosamh Ó hÉanaí: Nár Fhágha Mé Bás Choíche* (Joe Heaney: May I Never Die), it is an Irish-language biography of Heaney, rich with anecdotes from Heaney's friends and acquaintances (many transcribed in English), together with extensive quotations from articles and reviews. It is an essential companion volume to this one (Mac Con Iomaire 2007). We acknowledge and celebrate Liam Mac Con Iomaire's book as an exciting and enduring addition to the collective knowledge about Joe Heaney's life, friends, and work.

The Scope of This Book

This book divides logically into several sections: an introduction to the man and the style of singing for which he was known; an analysis of specific types of songs; an exploration of issues surrounding masculinity and singing; and a discussion of his work in the United States. In this introduction, we explore who Joe Heaney was. We also contextualize his work in both the nineteenth and the twentieth century. As products of a man of the twentieth century, Joe Heaney's attitudes and cultural horizons nonetheless drew heavily from ideas, cultural patterns, and ideals prevalent in nineteenth-century Connemara, Ireland in general, and the United States. A central feature of the nineteenth century—and, indeed, of Irish historical memory—is the Famine of 1845–50. We discuss the most basic aspects of the Famine here to set the stage for a deeper discussion in chapter 3. The Famine has loomed large in Irish and Irish American imaginations particularly since the commemorations of its 150th anniversary in the 1990s. This has led to accusations of multiple wrongdoing from nearly all parties, a charge that complicates and intensifies memories and expectations. The Famine has remained a skeleton in the cultural closet of

Irish America, and for many of those among Heaney's audiences who wished to make sense of vestigial memories passed on to them by their elders—through conversations, family letters, and old stories. An understanding of the Famine's effects on Irish American memory—and hunger—is crucial to situating Heaney as a representative of authentic Irishness in an American performative context.

Chapter 1 has as its focus the overall nature of *sean-nós* singing—songs in the old style. *Sean-nós* singing is deeply linked not only to Joe Heaney but also to the land from which he came. This chapter highlights some of the salient features of the genre, controversies surrounding its performance practice, and its current status in Ireland. It also examines the Oireachtas, a yearly competition not just for the finest and most representative singer of *sean-nós* but also for storytelling, comedic recitation, children's singing, and other Irish-language treasures. Joe Heaney was an early winner of this competition, an honor that gave him some of the cultural authority that he carried with him his entire life.

Anyone who asked Heaney about the secret to his extraordinary gift for melodic decoration of songs was usually treated to a curt reply: "There's nobody living who can tell anyone where to put grace notes into a song; you just do it." And yet chapter 2 attempts to do just that: to offer at least a few possible keys for understanding how Heaney's songs and their melodic ornaments are affected by the use of Gaelic or English as the chosen language of performance. Chapter 2 also includes a discussion of some of the poetry of the song lyrics, some musical analysis, and works with the idea of how the Connemara style—as represented in Heaney's singing—has been lionized in competition and how that lionization has had an impact on general performance practice of *sean-nós*.

We come to the Famine in chapter 3 to look specifically at several songs that engage the event musically. The first, "Johnny Seoighe," is noteworthy in connection with Heaney's repertoire in that he consciously chose *not* to sing it. Instead, he selected "Come Lay Me Down," a song that he himself adapted from the Scottish love song "I'll Lay Ye Doon, Love," to reference the Famine effectively for American audiences. The chapter also includes a close examination of the vaudeville song "Muldoon, the Solid Man" by Ned Harrigan, which also has links to "Come Lay Me Down." We explore these songs in order to highlight the continuing debate on the music about the Famine, the thorny issue of song composition by someone who claimed explicitly that he never wrote a song, and the importance of the presence of the audience in the presentation of songs. Songs about the Famine continue to reveal contested territory even as they illuminate divergent points between history and memory (Beiner 2007).

Joe Heaney was well known in Ireland for the performance of three religious laments: "Caoineadh na dTrí Muire" ("The Lament of the Three Marys"), "Dán Oíche Nollag" ("The Poem of Christmas Eve"), and "Amhrán na Páise" ("The Song of the Passion" [of Christ]). These laments form the heart of chapter 4, in which we explore Heaney's role in the gradual professionalization of what had previously been a role primarily associated with women: assuming the responsibilities for expressing the grief of a community through keening (ritualized mourning). We also discuss Heaney's own relationship with formalized religion, the clergy, and the kind of vernacular spiritual tradition that was so important in his formative years and those of his neighbors and family members.

No discussion of the life of such an influential vocalist would be complete without an in-depth reading of several iconic songs. Chapter 5 explores the lyrics, melodies, and contexts of the songs "Seachrán Chearbhaill" ("The Rambles of Cearbhall"), "Eileanóir a Rún" ("Eileanóir My Treasure"), and "Eileen Aroon" (an English-language version of "Eileanóir a Rún"). These songs—attributed to the seventeenth-century poet Cearbhall Ó Dálaigh—are melodically similar versions of the same basic idea, but each one works in a specific performance context. The iconic song "The Rocks of Bawn"—a Heaney favorite—is examined in some detail, including the reasons for *why* it became so important to Heaney himself. The chapter closes with songs about emigration that Heaney was quite fond of singing at his performances in the United States. As some of Heaney's favorite and most frequently performed material, all these songs illustrate his priorities, how he chose to represent his tradition, and the sheer excellence of his artistry.

The subtitle of this book—*Joe Heaney, Irish Song-Man*—is an indication of important issues having to do with masculinity and musicianship in Irish culture, past and present. In chapter 6 we contrast the popular media image of the classic Irish tenors of both the past and the present with the strikingly different image of the male *sean-nós* singer in the body, voice, and spirit of Joe Heaney. In making this comparison we draw out the ways in which Irish notions of masculinity appear on- and offstage in Ireland and the United States. Chapter 7 continues the theme of masculinity through an analysis of the songs "Morrissey and the Russian Sailor," "Bean a' Leanna," and "I Wish I Had Someone to Love Me." These songs illustrate the ways in which Heaney came to personify rural masculinity; they also allow us to analyze Heaney's use of the Irish concept of *gaisce* (warrior deed) to reveal the great deeds celebrated in his songs and in his own masculinized performance of the songs.

Chapter 8 covers aspects of Heaney's life in the United States, from when he left Ireland until his death in 1984. He was raised in rural Connemara but also spent time working in the urban centers of Dublin, London, Glasgow, and other areas as a laborer. Upon moving to the United States, he performed at the 1965 Newport Folk Festival, worked as a doorman in an upscale district of Manhattan, worked with the avant-garde composer John Cage in a triumphant performance of *Roaratorio: An Irish Circus on Finnegans Wake*, traveled extensively, and was celebrated with the National Heritage Fellowship in 1982. We discuss how Joe Heaney eventually found himself working as a respected visiting professor at several American universities in the 1970s and early 1980s. Heaney's death from emphysema in 1984 closes the chapter; it had an impact on the ways in which Irish people regarded one of their most famous musical sons.

Chapter 9 covers the ways in which a single man became, for some, the sole representative not only of historical Ireland but also of a lost nation of sons and daughters. Through Heaney's work not only in American performance venues but also in American universities, he successfully and almost single-handedly placed the entire genre of *sean-nós* singing on the world music map. Ethnomusicologists began to use his recordings in their classrooms, and new generations of Irish Americans and Irish music enthusiasts came to learn of *sean-nós* through Joe Heaney's artistry alone, even as recordings of other *sean-nós* artists became available. This chapter also includes a critical examination of the reasons that Joe Heaney as living man and living treasure was rejected by so many Irish Americans, particularly on the East Coast. The problematic nature of Irish and Irish American reactions to symbols of the rural past is a crucial part of this examination. In addition, we examine why it was that both folk music enthusiasts and academics focused so strongly on Heaney's work, and how they came to adopt him as a peerless icon of authentic Irishness.

Throughout this book, we draw from the rich resources of Joe Heaney's recorded interviews and performances at the University of Washington Ethnomusicology Archives, as well as Liam Mac Con Iomaire's biography of Heaney (2007). Heaney was an eloquent man, given alternately to expounding bitter truths and wild hyperbole, depending on his audience, his expectations of them, and their expectations of him. He was perpetually ready, with a single steely glare from under his bushy white eyebrows, to scorn anyone brave enough either to pull out a guitar in his presence, to serve him tea that had been made from a tea bag (instead of loose tea), or to innocently request a weepy rendition of what they considered a "real" Irish song like "Danny Boy."

To enlarge and diversify the context of this book, we include a photo essay of fifteen images relevant to various aspects of our work. A recurring, implicit theme of this book is place. Although our main focus here is on Heaney in America, the contrast between modern, urban landscapes on a regulated grid and Heaney's childhood terrain remains a constant source of fascination. The leading image here is the portrait on the cover of the book. As we discuss later (chapter 6), comments about Heaney's artistic presence again and again drew attention to his face. They likened it repeatedly to the rugged, chiseled territory from which Heaney came. The magical sobriquet "Connemara" projects images of romantic grandeur and primitive savagery that intrigued many commentators long before Heaney's time. Identifications between the physiognomy and the place whence it came therefore carry that genealogy of imagery. It is entirely appropriate, then, that we include several images characteristic of the Connemara known intimately by Heaney, whose face was said to invoke its stark features so powerfully.

As a counterpoint to the images of mountains and moors, we also provide some pictures of working locations, the building where Heaney went to primary school and the pier where he worked as a fisherman. A study of all these images enables us to contemplate how chain links of associations combine in producing compelling and mythic narratives that both help and hinder a full understanding of the man behind the face. We also include a press photograph taken with Cáit Ní Mhuimhneacháin after the Oireachtas competitions of 1942, from which they both emerged triumphant. The picture provides a salient reminder that Heaney was also once a young man, and that this picture was taken at a moment that decided the course of his life afterward.

The image of the gravestone deserves special attention because it proclaims, with the force of a period, the finality of Heaney's end. The monument's elegant severity suggests Heaney's achievement as an artist. Yet like the landscape, it is remote and austere, representing Heaney's well-known hauteur and self-belief. The small plastic items placed around the foot of the tombstone, however, tell a different story. They link Heaney to the popular antiauthoritarian Catholicism that emerges from his sacred songs, resembling items deposited at a holy well. They reveal the care taken by kin in their own terms in maintaining Heaney's memory, a memory that mitigates and humanizes the stern starkness of the tomb. The contrast is eloquent, suggesting differing constructions of Heaney, the very tensions that form the greater part of the narrative of this book.

Heaney was part of a community, and it is important to remember that he was the first among equals in many senses. Annie Devaney O'Brien from the Carna area, dancing to the exuberant and unique flute music of Séamus Tansey, provides a salutary reminder that this culture is for enjoyment and entertainment, for the fulfillment of deep-seated human needs. The singer Dara Bán Mac Donnchadha (1939–2008), from a family raised a stone's throw from the Heaney household, relished the accolade he had received from Heaney all his life. Having heard Dara sing, when visiting the family home with the Clancy brothers, Heaney pronounced emphatically, "This man is better than myself." Dara Bán claimed to know 500 songs, some of which he said could be sung publicly, adding wryly that some could not. The photo of Dara Bán also includes Micheál Ó Cuaig, an acclaimed modern poet and teacher who is the main organizer of the Joe Heaney Festival, known in Irish as the Féile Joe Éinniú, and a prominent custodian of his legacy to whom this book is dedicated.

Taken together, a study of all these images enables us to contemplate how chain links of associations combine in producing compelling and mythic narratives that both help and hinder a full understanding of the man behind the face.

The Context of Sean-nós Singers and Songs

An essential contributing factor to the milieu into which Joe Heaney was raised is the Famine, almost a character in its own right on the national stage. Certainly Ireland is much more than what happened before, during, and after the Famine. Yet the Famine continues to have a lasting impact on Irish religious behavior, political currents, and social trends. It was not until the opening of the Irish nation's first Famine Museum (1994), 150 years after the event, that the disaster became a focus of public discussion.[3]

> The Great Famine has been the unseen guest at every Irish dinner table since the mid-nineteenth century. Despite long familiarity with famine conditions—there were five periods of major famine conditions in the eighteenth century and eight in the nineteenth century prior to 1845—the Great Famine stands by itself as one of the worst catastrophes of modern Irish history....Few had the resources to flee the disaster, and the scene of their emaciated dying bodies lying by the roadsides remains vivid in the folk memory to this day. (Harris 1999:2–3)

Outside the discussion in chapter 3, it would be both challenging and repetitive of significant excellent sources on the subject to discuss the events that led up to the Famine.[4] In the context of Ireland in the nineteenth century, however, it is essential to our understanding of the region that produced Joe Heaney and so many other fine singers that we examine what happened in Ireland and the United States in the decades *after* the Famine.

Ireland's population plummeted to half its previous level in the decades following the Famine. Those who survived became increasingly occupied with progress and social advancement, exacerbating social and cultural divisions. Such rifts developed on both sides of the Atlantic as Irish communities reestablished themselves into a more overtly Catholic, parish-based set of societies. Whereas in Ireland, many of these parishes were rural, in North America the parish system was nearly 100 percent urban, set up in enclaves dominated by the social and calendrical rhythms of church, school, and union. Class divisions became more sharply drawn—particularly in the United States—resulting in characterizations such as "shanty Irish" and "lace-curtain Irish." The shanty Irish were those who failed to achieve the desired transition into the middle-classes in the American economy, whereas the lace-curtain Irish were those who could pass. English-language skills were one of the significant tickets out of the world of the shanty and into that of the lace curtain. While this trend was taking place in the United States, Ireland was facing no less significant developments as well. The struggle for independence, the task of nation building, and the emergence of a new English-language poetic voice in the works of the national literary movement of W. B. Yeats and Lady Gregory (and others) all contributed to social and class divisions at home.

The usage of the word "dark" in the title of this introduction is a multi-faceted reference. References to the darkness of Irish culture abound in poetry and literature; for example, in the 1938 poem "The Statues," Yeats (Finneran 1989: 336) situates the word as follows:

We Irish, born into that ancient sect
But thrown upon this filthy modern tide
And by its formless spawning fury wrecked
Climb to our proper dark, that we may trace
The lineaments of a plummet-measured face.

While the filthy modern tide is perhaps the most famous phrase in these lines from "The Statues," it is the reference to darkness that locates "we Irish" in a late nineteenth-century Romantic and Celtic Twilight–era consciousness. In a post-Famine context, darkness represents an older, Gaelic era whose loss Yeats and the other Celtic Twilight writers, scholars, and artists lamented through the medium of the *English* language. And in a reference to the psychological darkness of the Famine and the nationwide tendency to avoid discussing it, singing the dark away brings up the idea of changes in Irish society that served not only to reinforce messages of the Famine but to distance the descendants of Famine survivors from the reality of the experience. The continuation and legacy of this distancing resulted, a century later in the United States, in the near-outright shunning by many of people like Joe Heaney, whose very presence was for many people a painful reminder of a dark past they hoped to forget.

Ireland underwent a shift in religious practices following the Famine. Church attendance grew as some members of the rural population drew back from vernacular religious practices, and the church came to have an increasing influence on daily life. Simultaneously, the use of English, which had already spread rapidly in the previous half century, increased exponentially to the point that by the end of the nineteenth century, Irish was in use by only a fraction of the population. In the twenty-first century, Ireland's two national languages are English and Irish-Gaelic (referred to generally throughout the present volume as Irish), with the latter spoken as a native language by about only 6 percent of the population and used in daily communication outside an educational context by as few as 70,000. Nearly all of Ireland's business, political, literary, and musical events are held in English, and most native speakers of Irish are, of necessity, fluent or competent speakers of English as well.[5]

Consequently, due to these unfavorable conditions, a legacy of colonial heritage, the burden of communication falls upon bilingual Irish speakers, forcing them to converge toward the English-speaking majority. This is a common feature in the power dynamics of bilingual communities sharing a prestige and a low-status language (Balcazar 2008:27).[6]

The English language came to Ireland by the twelfth century but long remained concentrated in small enclaves. It coexisted with other languages, including Norse, Norman-French as well as Irish, but it was not until the sixteenth century that the English made significant inroads along political lines. The complexity of the conquest of Ireland by the English is often reduced to strict Protestant/Catholic divisions, in which—in an inexorable and steadfastly linear manner—an English-speaking Protestant minority came to dominate an Irish-speaking Catholic majority (Barbour 2000:36). The reality is such that several languages were in use during the second millennium, and language use did not fall out neatly along sectarian or republican lines.

The British Ordnance Survey of the 1830s accelerated the practice of renaming Irish locations with English-language equivalents, or in Anglicizing the sound of the Irish name, with Uachtar Ard (upper height) becoming Oughterard, and Áth Fhirdia (Ferdia's Ford) becoming Ardee.[7] Such Gaelic place-names "succinctly married the legendary and the local" (Heaney 1980:131). Connections such as these are often erased by this Anglicization. As Hyde noted, people began to translate their names into English, often attempting to conceal their Irishness (1986:162–65). The discarding of Irish-language names for places and people presaged the discarding of Irish names for objects and abstract concepts as well, even though some cosmological ideas and terms were more effectively expressed in Irish than in English.

John Campbell (d. 2006), the noted storyteller-raconteur, told a story that illustrates this point humorously. When he was stopped by a British soldier in his native South Armagh, the soldier asked where he was coming from and where he was going. Campbell answered, "I'm coming from Killnaman, and I'm going to Killmore."[8]

This sense of domestication of the Irish spurred the development of the Gaelic Athletic Association in 1884 and the Gaelic League in 1893. The nineteenth-century Romantic movement, leaning on the legacy of eighteenth-century philosopher Johann Herder and on preceding scholarly antiquarian activity, came alive in Ireland. The richness of Irish folklore, oral narrative traditions, folkways, and songs in rural Ireland formed the backdrop for the later work of the Celtic Revivalists, but with the stark conditions of the post-Famine evictions, large-scale emigration, and successive failures associated with the efforts of the Land League, the survival of the language and its concomitant traditions seemed bleak indeed. In the post-Famine period, the Gaelic League was well placed to celebrate and perpetuate the development of the Irish language and traditional Irish culture in all its complexity. It also provided a type of intellectual and artistic venue for the development of an array of rules governing the production and performance of music and dance, many of which are still followed quite closely today.

One issue confronting those involved in nation building in the late nineteenth and early twentieth centuries was that the development of a contemporary Irish identity was already happening through the medium of English; that development (through English) has continued to evolve into the present:

> In contrast to many other languages of subject nations, by the time
> Irish became a focus of interest for a local intelligentsia it was already,
> numerically, in a clearly minority position; a Catholic middle class
> sympathetic to Irish did not develop until the late nineteenth century,

by which time famine, emigration, and education through English had very seriously depleted the number of native Irish speakers. (Barbour 2000:37)

The authors Tymoczko and Ireland point out that the language was in a difficult position vis-à-vis the eventual construction of nationhood, that after partition "Ireland was faced with the task of constructing an autonomous culture just when the bulk of the Irish country people had abandoned the Irish language in favor of English. Thus, the constructions of Irishness proceeded largely in English, in tandem with the Irish-language movement spearheaded by the Gaelic League" (2003:10).

By the start of the twentieth century, Ireland's population was still in decline. Connections between the United States and Ireland were firmly in place, as thousands of Irish immigrants and their children continued to support the people at home even as they themselves sought lives outside the usual jobs on railroads and construction sites for men, and as maids and cooks for the women. Though birthrates remained high in Ireland, so many children immigrated to England, Scotland, and North America that the overall population on the island remained stable for decades. On the American side of the Atlantic, the non–Irish Americans (particularly of the American East Coast) carried a powerful array of stereotypes about the Irish—which we discuss in detail in chapter 9—that had not quite disappeared by the turn of the twenty-first century. The growing development of the Irish-American middle class was assisted by the arrival of new waves of immigrants from Scandinavian and Eastern European countries. In accepting jobs for menial labor, the new immigrants nudged the Irish slightly farther upward on the track to acquiring lace curtains and all their accompanying symbolic status.

It was into this colonial context that Joe Heaney was born: in the wake of the First World War on an island itself on the brink of partition and bitter civil conflict, in a small townland called Aird Thoir on the south coast of Connemara, into an Irish-speaking extended family, in a community where Gaelic language, song, and story were a vibrant, everyday reality. That he should have become such a significant figure in the United States by the late twentieth century, simultaneously revered and reviled for what he came to symbolize, forms an essential part of this book's inquiry.

Joe Heaney Presents His Upbringing

Anyone who had the chance to meet Joe Heaney was immediately swept into his past, whether he was on- or offstage. His commanding presence, his rich and melodious voice (whether speaking or singing), and his self-referential performance of his life tended to draw listeners in immediately. Listeners learned quickly about his history, which he often presented—with some minor variations—in the following words:[9]

Well, I was born in a very remote village in Connemara, Galway, where there was hardly anything but rocks, and very little soil on the rocks or between the rocks. And the people usually make their living from the sea. And up to the 17th century there was very little...anybody living in that area until Oliver Cromwell decided that he'd get the people to Hell or Connaught. Now, my ancestors was born living in Meath, in the richest part of Ireland, when Cromwell came, and because they wouldn't give in to his whims, he said "To Hell or Connaught." That means, at that time he thought, that anybody who went to Connaught would die of starvation. So instead of killing them, he reckoned he could give them a slow death by sending them to Connaught. So they put all their belongings on their back, that's all they were allowed to take, and made their way to Connaught, and built their houses near the sea, because their only hope was the sea, the fishing.

Now that area is so remote that when Alan Lomax was back there in 1945 he couldn't believe how anybody could exist in that area, because at that time when I was growing up, there was hardly any industry at all, there was nothing except what you struggled hard to get. And when I was a boy, and before we went to school we had to row a boat, a three-oar *curach*, three miles out and three miles back, and lift about forty lobster pots. And at that time a dozen lobsters was about two and six, about 30 pence I suppose would be in your money or less, and they had what they call a baker's dozen, they had thirteen lobsters in the dozen. But now, Gael Linn came back in 1955 and they built a factory in that particular area, and they paid the fishermen by the pound. They paid them so much a pound for every fish they caught, and nowadays it's thriving now as it never was before.

Now at that period I'm talking about when I was growing up there was no radio. Naturally, there was no television. And the only radio was in the parish priest's house, or the local TD, they were the only people who could afford it. As a result, all we had is what we grew up with, our parents and our grandparents. And they had a depth of material that goes back, I suppose it goes back to the Middle Ages. Songs about the crucifixion of Christ, Fionn MacCumhaill, all these handed down to them in the Gaelic language, there was no English translation to these and still isn't. Never will be, I suppose.

The village of Carna—where Heaney was born and raised—lies about fifty miles west of Galway city, but it is a long drive from the city on often narrow, difficult roads that skirt lakes and bogs. The entire region is famous for its wealth of songs in both Irish and English; many of Joe Heaney's family and people from neighboring areas served as important sources of songs and stories for the Irish Folklore Commission, for later song and story collectors, and for radio and recording company agents.

When Joe Heaney was young, he played the melodeon, the ten-key single-row instrument that preceded the two-row button accordion. He mentioned that he gave it up when he became too busy, but he also noted that the song was of primary importance in his area, contrasting it to the more prominently instrumental traditions of east Galway and Clare. He claims that he began singing at the age of five, and mentioned that some of his first songs were "Morrissey and the Russian Sailor" (see chapter 7) and "The Rocks of Bawn" (see chapter 5), but did not sing publicly until he was more than twenty years old.

Heaney initially studied to become a teacher, attending three years of a preparatory college in Dublin starting in 1934, with a scholarship. The reasons for his cessation of school remain murky, with various explanations being offered by Heaney at various times. His most common story about it was that he was expelled for smoking. He discusses this point in his life:

> When my father died then I left school, you see, and came home. I don't know why I left it but I left it that's all, there was…not much happening for me in school after that, I don't know why. [I studied] everything. Every subject. General subjects, I just wanted to be a teacher, you know. I never followed it up, you know, and I didn't go into what they say training or anything, but I used to then, when I went to England I used to do a little bit of teaching Irish [to adults], you know, here and there, and that's held me good, you know, gave me a good way how to do it.

Mac Con Iomaire (2007:76–81) convincingly suggests, based on accounts from other contemporary pupils, that Heaney may have run afoul of and rebelled against a particularly harsh teacher, which was enough to seal his fate. What is not in dispute is that when he came home from the college after being expelled, he arrived at the moment of his father's funeral in 1937; word had not arrived in time to alert him. The abrupt way in which he learned of his father's death can only have been a severe shock, given the fact that he had his own piece of bad news to impart to his family.

Because he had not completed his education, Heaney's options were even more limited than they might have been. Prevented from going into teacher training, as his parents had intended for him, and with few other openings available, he worked primarily at fishing in the Carna area for the following ten years, "scallops, lobster, every kind of fish," as he said himself. It was during this period that his reputation as a singer was made, first locally, reputedly at a regatta in Roundstone, and later consolidated nationally at Oireachtas na Gaeilge, the Gaelic League's cultural festival, in 1942. Not surprisingly, living as he did in an economy where ready cash was scarce, the prize money made a strong impression on Heaney. He commented: "The prize at that time was big money, mind you. The first prize money was three pounds. That'd be about six dollars of your money. At that time three pounds was a lot of money, and that was the prize." However, despite this one-off windfall, steady material reward remained elusive, and the meager earnings from his fishing activities were sorely needed. He and his brother attempted to go to England during this time, but they turned back because they did not have the boat fare.

Heaney also underwent surgery in June 1946 and had his collarbone removed (uí Ógáin 2007:329). Mac Con Iomaire suggests his ten-year sojourn in Carna provided him with access to musical materials he never would have had had he continued his formal education. Despite this, Heaney had to leave eventually, to enable his brother Máirtín to marry and start his own family on the family holding. He set off for Glasgow in 1947. He lived in the district of Clydebank, where relatives and neighbors had ventured earlier, in the familiar pattern of chain migration. These people provided an important support system for him and other recent migrants. He was in Scotland from 1947 to 1951, marrying Mary Connolly, whose family on both sides were Carna people but who had been raised in Scotland. After the marriage produced four children (Jackie, Patricia, Barbara, and Michael), Heaney left the family to pursue further work in England and, eventually, the United States. He visited his wife and family in Clydebank only sporadically, and according to all reports, he never returned to Scotland after the early 1960s, including after his wife passed away in 1966. Clearly this is a chapter of his life that he neither referred to directly nor spoke of in public (Mac Con Iomaire 2007:261), even when pressed for details. He did refer to the anti-Catholic sectarianism prevalent in Glasgow as one reason for leaving Scotland, and his preference for working in England, where such prejudice was not evident (Mac Con Iomaire 2007:128). In England, Heaney worked as a laborer at first, like many of his fellow countrymen. Later, he began to frequent singers' clubs and found work in the coastal city of Southampton, making visits to Scotland and home to Ireland as time and resources allowed:

> I started performing less than when I went to London, then I forgot about it. I never sang for fifteen years. And then again the urge came on me, I had to do what was in me, I had to do it. Although I used to sing, I put a couple of songs of Folkways Records for Ralph Rinzler in London 1957 or '58, I think, with Maggie Barry and Michael Gorman. Other people, I think Seamus was on it too, Seamus Ennis. And, but that was the loose singer around the pub you see, at the time the English folksong scene was only starting, and there was hardly any clubs, especially there was nobody singing unaccompanied in the clubs. Now there are hundreds of people doing it, you know.
>
> I suppose I was one of the first with MacColl and Seeger and Bert Lloyd you know started the folksong clubs. I was a resident singer at the Singers', the Irish resident singer of the Singers' Club that time. That's when they were starting, you know. At that time there wasn't much of maybe. Everything you sang there, it was, well, seven pounds was the standard fee for everybody. Of course it's much more than that now, I'm sure, seven pounds wouldn't get you two packs of

cigarettes now. But it used to be beautiful, lovely, I used to love it, you know.

Another compelling attraction of England over Scotland for Heaney was the large number of new immigrant communities there. Between 1940 and 1970 a huge influx of Irish migrants, mainly from the western counties of Ireland, settled in the urban areas of England, creating Irish enclaves and maintaining their Irish identity and culture in various ways. One of the most significant of these was music making in Irish pubs. This created a lively musical scene in which musicians were able to perform regularly. Some managed to eke a living from their music, others simply supplemented the income from their main employment. Performers such as Michael Gorman, Margaret Barry, and many others, including Tommy McCarthy, Bobby Casey, and Willie Clancy from Clare, met and played together in these sessions. Heaney was a welcome addition to these gatherings; indeed, Ralph Rinzler's recordings from the Bedford Arms on *Irish Music from London Pubs* (FG3575) bear out Reg Hall's rich description of the performance situation there:

Working men from the West of Ireland, dressed uniformly in blue serge suits, white shirts, dark ties and polished shoes stood drinking pints of bitter or half-pints of bottled Guinness with their friends. Tough men at work they might have been, but in the pub they were commonly shy and self-effacing, polite to strangers and generous to a fault.... The resident musicians Michael Gorman and Margaret Barry and one of two others sat in the far corner of the small, shabby public bar, huddled on a tiny stage constructed of beer crates and lino. Michael Gorman led the band, selecting the material, setting the pace, welcoming guests to join in, handling the occasional abusive drunk and evading inappropriate requests. The music was acoustic,... and it is listened to and appreciated above a hubbub of conversation and laughter and the sounds of the chinking glass and the cash register. Knowing nods of the head and occasional cries of "Good man!", "Fair play t'yer, now!", "More power to yer elbow!" or "Up Sligo!" were standard acknowledgement for musicians. Singers were received quite differently. Margaret Barry stood up several times during the evening, introducing her songs only by a punch tremolo statement of the air on the banjo and singing in her loud, street-singer's voice with her broad Cork City accent. Her presence and performance commanded attention and the room fell silent broken by a cheer and clapping as she came to the end of her song." (Hall 1995:9)

Such an attentive and appreciative atmosphere for his singing would clearly have appealed to Heaney, providing an additional incentive for him to go to England.

The longer story of Joe Heaney's life is that he was unable to make a living doing what he did best until his final years in the United States. Though he had been in training to be a teacher, it was a hard fact of life that only one child could inherit the family holdings, and Heaney left to make room for another of his siblings, Máirtín. Unlike some of his other siblings, he did not have many options. While he was working in England, Heaney was connected to large numbers of other Irish laborers and found a place for himself in the migrant community there. Once he arrived in the States, an even larger community of Irish immigrants was already well established in the large East Coast cities: "Music is credited with powers of bringing people together and engendering the moral cohesion of the community, evoking collective and private memory. Place, for many migrant communities, is something which is constructed through music with an intensity not found elsewhere in their social lives" (Stokes 1994:114).

As an unquestioned celebrity among select audiences and singers, Joe Heaney quickly came to represent more than himself. Well aware of the ways in which many people looked to him to signify something of their past and present identity, he often tailored his stories and shifted his emphasis to reflect what his listeners required of him. In his construction of the Famine for American audiences through the performance of the song "Come Lay Me Down" (see chapter 3), he presented the image of an honest and stoic peasantry that requested only a drop of water and a decent burial to be happy. Using a combination of songs, stories, anecdotes, and opinions, he alternately admonished, instructed, and guided his audiences, acquaintances, and friends on a path that led directly to an idealized Ireland.

Bright Star of the West

The title of this book derives from the song "Erin, Grá mo Chroí" ("Ireland, Love of My Heart"), whose lyrics celebrate the Irish homeland from the standpoint of someone far away:

> Oh Erin, *grá mo chroí*, you're the only land to me
> You're the fairest spot my eyes did ever behold
> You're the bright star of the west, and the land St. Patrick blessed,
> You're far dearer than silver or gold.
>
> At the setting of the sun when my daily work was done
> I rambled to the seashore for a walk
> I being all alone I sat down upon a stone
> To gaze on the scenery of New York.
>
> The turf will burn bright on the hearth at home tonight
> The snowflakes will fall fast on a winter's day

St. Patrick's Day will come, and the shamrock will be worn
In my own native land so far away.

It broke my mother's heart when from her I went to part
Will I ever see my darling anymore?
Not until my bones are laid in a cold and silent grave
In my own native isle so far away.

In this book, we envision Joe Heaney himself as the bright star of the west. As a man from a small community in the west of Ireland who gained international fame and renown through his performance of the traditional arts he absorbed in that community, he shone brightly, and remains a permanent exemplar in traditional song. Yet there is a contradiction in this particular song. It is an emigrant song, looking back through rose-colored glasses at the land left behind, but what is not spoken or even hinted at here is the reason for leaving.

"Erin, Grá mo Chroí" sums up the pain and contradiction of Heaney's life as an immigrant. The air (figure 0.1) is a Gaelic one, variants of which have also served as the air for two love songs in Connemara: "Bean Dubh an Ghleanna," "Nóra Ní Chonchúir Bháin" (Mhic Choisdealbha 1990:141), and "Nancy Walsh," a song by the poet Raftery in praise of a young woman.[10] Consequently, this can be seen as a song musically rooted in the Gaelic tradition and sung using an English text. It is a hybrid revealing a process of adaptation: the erotic love underlying the lyrics of the three Connemara songs has been replaced by a profound longing for home.

If sean-nós is widely recognized today, Joe Heaney is one of the main reasons for that recognition. He is a permanent, canonized part of the discourse of sean-nós, and singers frequently work with his recorded legacy in an effort to absorb some of his style. When Heaney emerged as a singer in the early 1940s, sean-nós was not widely known or understood in Ireland or anywhere else. The majority of Irish people would have found it strange and perhaps unmusical. In fact, Nicholas Carolan, from County Louth in the east of Ireland, the director of the Irish Traditional Music Archive and a man involved from his youth in traditional music, has mentioned his

Fig. 0.1: The air to "Erin, Grá mo Chroí"

feeling of puzzlement on first hearing songs in the *sean-nós* tradition, which eventually gave way to a "better understanding and liking" (2005:13). In what Carolan refers to as the modern metacommunity, connected in multifarious ways by mass media, the Internet, and other media, that level of discovery is almost inconceivable, and yet it is important to remember that this is how it was in the days of emerging media technology.

For many, Heaney was part of that wave of first encounters with traditional music and song that reached into thousands of individual homes across Ireland. Understanding the process through which Heaney has become a household name is an important element of the history of culture in general, and of ethnomusicology in particular. Furthermore, exploring how performers such as Heaney presented themselves and created new audiences with the aid of the media is central to this inquiry. Heaney provides an excellent example of someone who engaged intensively with those processes, and whose experiences as a performer were profoundly shaped by the cultural and political currents of Ireland in the 1940s and 1950s. In studying Heaney's life and performance repertoire, therefore, we can grasp the politics and poetics of how we encounter media today, and the processes that influence that engagement and consumption.

Sean-nós is now broadcast nationally on Raidió na Gaeltachta and on the television station TG4 (both broadcast in the Irish language). TG4 also broadcasts live and on the Web from the annual Oireachtas celebration (see chapter 1), which has grown considerably, into a festival attended by some 10,000 people annually, since Heaney was a regular attendee in the 1940s. Irish music has gone from something to be ashamed of—in Heaney's lifetime and its immediate aftermath—to a source of celebration on an international scale, with performances by the folk revival groups, the many manifestations of *Riverdance*, and thousands of video clips of both professional and amateur players from all over the world on youtube.com. Heaney made an influential contribution to that development, which was a part of the larger Irish cultural nationalist agenda.

Younger *sean-nós* singers continue to emerge, tour, and make recordings; the tradition has changed and will continue to change. It has become more experimental and more professionalized, but despite complaints from conservatives, that too has become acceptable in the current climate of musical revitalization. Such experimentation would have been roundly condemned as contamination in the cultural and economic milieu of Heaney's lifetime. Indeed, Heaney's opposition to the guitar reveals his own views on the matter. Whereas it was nearly impossible to make a living as an Irish musician prior to the late twentieth century, the influence of global marketing of Irish music and dance has resulted in a cadre of professional Irish musicians, among them some *sean-nós* singers.

The cultural and political climate into which Joe Heaney was born was radically different from what any singer—*sean-nós* or not—would encounter today. Postcolonial Ireland has experienced a stunning economic upswing and subsequent destabilization, and in the process it has lifted many (but not all) boats. With the newfound prosperity (reaching its peak at the turn of the twenty-first century) came the tendency to collectively forget or put away as inconvenient certain aspects of the past. At this juncture, in a deepening recession, it has been our task to attempt to remind our readers of the legacy of history and memory, both in the life of Joe Heaney and in his music. Paul Ricoeur's claim that "human lives need and merit being narrated" (1984:75) is nowhere more true than it is about Joe Heaney's life—lived in a sometimes larger-than-life way in the public arena of the American folk revival—and deserves not just its own story but an interpretation of that story. As a song-man who struggled against almost overwhelming odds, Heaney achieved wide recognition for the small, excluded voice, appreciated by only the few, one that was, in fact, his own. As a result, his singing is today revered within Ireland and beyond. This narrative explores the way in which Heaney achieved this parallel status in two nations. Moreover, it is a sincere attempt to understand the life of someone who has been and will continue to be an important figure in the renaissance of traditional arts in Ireland and elsewhere.

Part I

⚜

Sean-nós Singing

This first part, comprising the first two chapters of the book, introduces the concept of *sean-nós* singing. Many writers claim *sean-nós*
singing as crucial in Irish traditional music, and this book explores the
intimate connection between an individual singer and the genre. Joe
Heaney's name was synonymous with the style and repertoire; because of
his international profile, Heaney exerted a formative influence. He made
the term known in places where it might otherwise never have been heard.
Notwithstanding the development of Heaney's reputation as a storyteller
in America, he was known primarily as a singer. Consequently, that aspect
of his performance practice is highlighted here.

Chapter 1 explores how the term *sean-nós* came to be widely used and
what it has come to represent. It also describes the use of the genre in
competition, as an identity marker, and as a badge of authentic Irishness.
The development of *sean-nós* was also part of a larger movement in re-
Gaelicizing Ireland. Even as Ireland moved inexorably toward
independence, the leaders of the Gaelic League regarded song, music, and
other traditional forms as a way to instill a sense of pride in what it was to
be Irish at the end of the nineteenth century. *Sean-nós* later came to represent something of the hard times Irish people had experienced in their
history, and—outside Gaelic circles—its public appeal, though never widespread, waned.

Chapter 2 goes into the practice of *sean-nós*, and how Joe Heaney's technique of melodic ornamentation connected with the poetic rhythms of the
lyrics he sang. Covering such topics as metaphor, bilingualism, and vibrato,
the chapter considers some of the specifics of musical analysis that have
not been examined elsewhere. Even as Heaney himself denied any connection between the lyrics and the ornamentation (other than as a decorative
feature), an examination of his performances suggests otherwise.

Because of Gaelic song's importance as a culturally distinctive expression, certain elements of the repertoire of ornamentation such as melisma

assumed greater importance as song embarked upon a second life beyond the communities where it was a major form of entertainment. The uncertain ground of aesthetic interpretation of songs has become crucial in Irish competitions. Importantly, Heaney's own immeasurable skill in ornamentation was an aspect of singing that he refused to reduce to simply a matter of vocal proficiency or technique. For Heaney's students there were no shortcuts to master *sean-nós*; a prospective singer must engage deeply and holistically with a song. Chapter 2 combines his words and his songs to shed light on how performance and pedagogical practice worked.

1

Sean-nós Singing in Theory and Practice

The name of Joe Heaney is deeply connected with the term *sean-nós*. Heaney attended the Gaelic League's *sean-nós* competitions regularly from 1940 until the late 1950s, a period of almost twenty years. In fact, from his early youth, as well as in informal domestic contexts, he had been exposed to music keyed to a competitive framework (Cowdery 1990:36). Heaney's association with *sean-nós* is no accident, and it is important to explore the close link between him and the development of this form of singing. The term began to gain currency as a name for old-style traditional Gaelic singing during the period immediately preceding his birth and was consolidated by the time he reached maturity. This chapter shows how the term *sean-nós* was conceived and how it came to prominence in the cultural nationalist movement. Such a summary will help us understand Heaney's engagement with this musical genre and his stubborn, unswerving adherence to its principles throughout his life.

Anyone who goes below the surface of Irish traditional music knows the term *sean-nós*. Until very recently, it referred mainly to the unaccompanied, monophonic, solo style of singing the melodies that carry old songs in the Irish language;[1] additionally, it refers to the repertoire of those songs itself (Breathnach 1971; Ó Riada 1982; Ó Canainn 1978; Shields 1993; Carson 1996; Ó hAllmhuráin 1998). The term *sean-nós* also carries with it a highly contested and intractable politics of authenticity. Arguments develop about which singers and which regions possess the true or best *sean-nós*, and singers who depart from the norms of this art form may be severely criticized. Not surprisingly, then, references and definitions of *sean-nós* abound. Some are contradictory or represent an idealized form of singing that may never have existed in Ireland. Nonetheless, the translation of *sean-nós* is "old way, manner, custom, or style," and with such translations may be felt the inheritance of the wave of nineteenth-century Romanticism that swept Europe and rooted deeply in Ireland. Johann Gottfried Von Herder, an eighteenth-century German philosopher, was a strong proponent of folkways as a key to a nation's authenticity (Bendix 1997:16). Mediated through figures such as Thomas Davis and Douglas Hyde, the Romantic Nationalist movement that burgeoned in late nineteenth-century Ireland adopted many of Herder's precepts and applied them to the insular context, so that the longing for the pure and genuine as represented by folk music and musicians persisted unabated. So it is with *sean-nós* singing: musically it may represent a kind of pristine, premodern Irishness, a connection to an idealized precolonial past.

The term *sean-nós* dates perhaps to the sixteenth century but was not yet used in a musical context (Nic Dhonncha 2004:80). The phrase was reinterpreted in the late nineteenth century and has gained greater currency throughout the twentieth century under the auspices of the Gaelic League's first Oireachtas festivals dating from 1897, and continuing unbroken since 1939 (Ó Súilleabháin 1984). Despite its widespread adoption, the term was controversial and remains so. In the 1940s, for example, those involved in a symposium to discuss the genre and the term deplored its use, unanimously preferring *amhránaíocht dhúchasach* (native or traditional singing) instead (Nic Dhonncha 2004:44). Nevertheless, the label stuck and has proliferated. Nowadays, for better or worse, it is the main term used to refer to unaccompanied traditional singing.[2]

To some, *sean-nós* represents an idealized form of traditional singing that exhibits an unbroken continuity with the Gaelic past. As such, *sean-nós* carries a powerful symbolism for a sense of Gaelic cultural cohesiveness. It is one emblem of that imagined community (Anderson 1983) of an idealized Ireland espoused by Eamon de Valera—the Republic of Ireland's first president—in his famous speech "The Undeserted Village Ireland" (1943):

> That Ireland which we dreamed of would be the home of a people who valued material wealth only as the basis of right living, of a people who were satisfied with frugal comfort and devoted their leisure to the things of the spirit—a land whose countryside would be bright with cosy homesteads, whose fields and villages would be joyous with the sounds of industry, with the romping of sturdy children, the contests of athletic youths and the laughter of comely maidens, whose firesides would be forums for the wisdom of serene old age. (de Valera 1991:748)

In this speech, widely known and heavily critiqued, not to say ridiculed in Ireland and abroad, lie the next steps—post-Independence—of an idealized, reauthenticized Ireland, in which traditional arts, crafts, and particularly language would be celebrated as an expression of a kind of economic flowering of the new nation. Its visionary idealism, however, was not borne out in reality. The failure of de Valera's vision on a national scale over the following two decades does not detract from the fact that in some parts of Ireland, including in Joe Heaney's milieu, *sean-nós* singing and traditional ways of working and living were still active, and even thriving. It was these regions that added some validity to de Valera's vision. While de Valera did not anticipate the economic troubles and severe toll that emigration would wreak on Ireland, he at least had a sense of what Ireland could be if it adhered strictly to the vision of the Gaelic League. Indeed, the speech focuses primarily on reviving the Irish language and was presented at the fiftieth anniversary of the founding of the Gaelic League. Thus, a tight constellation of authenticity, language, *sean-nós* singing, Gaelic sports, Irishness, and Catholicism was already fixed in place before de Valera ever codified it publicly.

Music in Ireland generally carries inordinate burdens around ideas of identity, and arguably, this identity function marks *sean-nós* as an important cultural icon, beyond its purely musical status. This is obvious because of the position accorded *sean-nós* song in the Oireachtas competitive festival organized by the Gaelic League and first held in 1897. Calling for the de-Anglicization of Ireland in a famous 1892 address, Douglas Hyde placed music and song as second only to language and literature in the achievement of this project (Hyde 1986:156).

Irish music and song were under threat from the industrialized, popularized music of the music halls both at home and abroad. In these music hall songs, the Irish were often presented as foolish, lazy, and/or drunken, all of which were directly in contrast with the goals of the Gaelic League. Such an infiltration of popular song had to be resisted with an adherence and a loyalty to the native traditional Gaelic music. Consequently, a powerful binary was reinforced, setting up traditional music in direct opposition to modern, popular, and indeed, it must be added, classical forms. The Gaelic movement took up Hyde's exhortation and championed a hitherto unrecognized style of music in terms of a resistance to hegemonic state and market forces (Hebdige 1979:17). Consequently, this style could be viewed as a coded critique and consequent rejection of such powerful trends in the shaping of musical taste. It represented a turning away from such forms of music, a rejection of Yeats's "filthy modern tide" in some sense, in favor of an idealized rural precolonial Gaelic vision. The paradox was that such a view was predicated upon the emergence and preeminence of the modern (Ó Giolláin 2000:12, 20, 54–57).

Directly influenced by the folk song movement in Britain, Irish enthusiasts adopted descriptive characteristics outlined in works such as *Sharp's English Folk Song: Some Conclusions* (1907). These characteristics were developed to create a new performance aesthetic, calculated to oppose dominant vocal performance models (bel canto vocal style, for example) promoted by musical conservatories, and the popular forms of the music hall, one seen as promoting the colonial hegemony, the other a representative of a tawdry, contaminated modernity. Gradually, however, and despite arguments to the contrary (Pearse 1906), these recently identified descriptive characteristics were to become entrenched as essentialized markers of authenticity in some eyes, a sine qua non of traditional Gaelic folk song style (Henebry 1903, 1928; Hardebeck 1911). Although these traits were first marked in this way at the beginning of the twentieth century, significantly, they resurfaced as dogmatic, prescriptive definitions in the 1960s.

As a basic working definition, *sean-nós* singing is characterized by unaccompanied vocal performance in the Irish language, often in relatively free rhythm, although rhythmically regular items also form part of the repertoire (Ó Canainn 1978). Depending on factors such as region and personal preference, singers may include significant vocal ornamentation (melismas, turns, etc.) or may use subtler techniques that distinguish their singing as traditional. Now that Ireland has moved into its post-Celtic Tiger period, and a larger audience begins to encounter *sean-nós* singing, these regional and individual differences are becoming better understood and more welcomed than in the past, when—during Heaney's era in Ireland—certain regions were given pride of place as the main producers of authentic *sean-nós*. The process by which the melismatically rich styles of singing have been accorded preeminent status as most authentically Irish deserves some comment here, together with an explanation of the powerful influence exerted by one man, and what he stood for.

Seán Ó Riada and Traditional Music

Seán Ó Riada (1931–71), a young, classically trained Irish composer, became increasingly drawn to his own traditional music background in the late 1950s and early 1960s. As an influential public figure, and one who worked for the national broadcaster RTÉ, his radio series *Our Musical Heritage* (1962) broadcast in 1962 and published in part in 1982, was an important landmark in achieving popular recognition for traditional music.[3] Ó Riada had absorbed much of the thinking of his contemporaries with regard to the style of traditional music and song, and he reformulated it according to his own often trenchantly expressed ideas. His views on *sean-nós* singing sum up the thinking of the time on the subject while also promoting a rather dogmatic and monochromatic view of the correct style of singing. These rules, complete with musical examples both oral and transcribed, dictated a bare voice, no vibrato, no use of dynamics, individual use of ornamentation, nonmetered singing, performance with soul, an emphasis on the consonants *l*, *m*, *n*, and *r* to add a droning resonance, a nasal sound, music being more important than lyrics, the use of nonlexical supplementary syllables and glottal stops, lack of accompaniment, variation in melody from one verse to the next, and performance in the Irish language (Ó Riada 1982; Bodley 1972–73; Ó Canainn 1978).

As an important presence in the Irish media scene in Dublin—and as a trained composer—Ó Riada was frequently in the right place at the right time. He brought traditional instrumentalists and singers to Dublin to perform and record as part of his *Our Musical Heritage* series, including many of the top singers of the *sean-nós* style (Ó Canainn 2003:79). His choices were conservative, and his writing highlighted that which he believed to represent Irish musical traditions at their ancient best. As a result of this work with Irish media, Ó Riada contributed to the establishment of a canonical style and approach that gratified many in a conservative musical tradition. In taking existing regional standards in performance practice, Ó Riada disseminated these standards to a national audience, thereby reinforcing his preferred norms of influential traditional musicians. With regard to singing, Ó Riada also helped to codify and buttress certain stylistic preferences, and his groundbreaking radio series ensured that the views he expounded were widely disseminated and heeded. In the context of drastic differences between regions, individual performance practice, and community support, the style that corresponded most closely to the benchmarks promoted by Ó Riada came to be the dominant one, and singers who could do what he stipulated won the first prize repeatedly at the Oireachtas song competition.

Ó Riada held up certain performers as beacons of excellence, and Heaney was among those whom he praised. For example, his pride in the outstanding achievement of Nioclás Tóibín of Ring in Waterford is palpable. He particularly celebrated the great melodic range and length of the Munster airs that, he argued, represented a greater compass than those of other regions. In contrast, he regarded Connemara melodies as being more compressed, in that he felt they had a narrower musical compass. Interestingly, this regional hierarchy, with Munster holding top place for its possession of airs with the greatest range, was current before Ó Riada expressed it in the sixties.

Séamus Ennis, when engaged in his first fieldwork trips to Carna, commented favorably on the singing of a select number of families in the Carna area, Heaney's among them. He remarked: "It was in their possession I found the most complex airs on the Connemara coast—they resemble more the good music of Munster as Cáit Ní Mhuimhneacháin and Labhrás Ó Cadhla have it" (Uí Ógáin 2007:72).[4] Cáit Ní Mhuimhneacháin (1918–49) was the singer who shared the accolade with Heaney at the Oireachtas in 1942, and Labhrás Ó Cadhla (1889–1960) was a pioneer for the recognition of *sean-nós* singing some forty years Heaney's senior. In view of the attitude that valued the music with the widest melodic range as the best, Ennis's judgment of Heaney's repertoire is significant.

However, despite the exceptions noticed by Ennis, general opinion relegated the airs of the Connemara region to a secondary position. It was certainly something of a value judgment, and one that antagonized (and continues to antagonize) some musicians and singers (Ó Riada 1982:33; Ó Canainn 1978:16). Ó Riada's reinforcement of this attitude and his close alignment of region and style do not factor in individual ability, nor does his recognition of the great and unique talent of a singer such as Nioclás Tóibín. Ó Riada overlooks this important consideration when he claims that Tóibín's use of intervallic variation would be inconceivable to a singer from Connemara. Arguably, such variation might have been equally inconceivable to Nioclás Tóibín's predecessors, neighbors, or siblings because none of them had been blessed with the singular gift bestowed upon him. In any case, as Ennis noted, treating even Connemara as a single homogeneous unit risked missing variation within family and individual traditions in this relatively small area.

Ó Riada argued strongly for the idea of what he termed the variation principle—the ability to endlessly improvise within the strophic musical structure of the stanza. To him, the ability to continuously re-create the music within the constraints of the strophic structure was an essential feature of *sean-nós* song. Those singers who, he considered, were able to do this constituted the pinnacle of the musical achievement of *sean-nós* singing. Those who did not were clearly inferior and, he argued, inauthentic. Again, this idea came about as a result of musicological analysis of the melodies of traditional songs, and it foregrounded that element in a way that was unusual in the traditional communities that practiced *sean-nós* as a form of entertainment. This is not to say that listeners were unaware of the musical component of their songs, or that they did not appreciate them. What it does claim is that the discourse that would allow a discussion of such improvisatory impulses was largely inarticulate in terms of conventional literate musical theory.

Following on from the folk song movement at the turn of the twentieth century, which had discovered and identified the modes and celebrated the subtle richness of folk song style for the first time, Ó Riada expressed these ideas in musical terms for a public unused to thinking about traditional music as sophisticated or complex. His interest in other forms of music, notably jazz, of which he was a regular and enthusiastic player (Ó Canainn 2003:15), almost certainly also provided an additional perspective on the variation principle as he termed it. In any case, Ó Riada's ideas were memorably expressed and became widely accepted as a standard way to judge good *sean-nós* singing, especially by literate middle-class aficionados of the art. Of course, such views eventually influenced the communities in which *sean-nós* singing was highly developed, to the extent that such ideas are now standard, and, for many, are believed to have always formed an explicit part of the way the music of the *sean-nós* was understood (Coleman 1996; 1997:33).

As might be expected in such a Romantic Nationalist construction, Ó Riada found the tradition in decline in most of its heartlands, believing that the influence of modern recorded and written music had corrupted the tradition and that most of the singers had forgotten how to vary the music of the songs. He even pointed to examples of faulty ornamentation drawing from a singer whom he did not name (1982:16). Despite the gloomy prospects, however, he identified a number of exceptions, such as Darach Ó Catháin, a singer from the Leitir Móir area of Connemara, and Seán Jeaic Mac Donnchadha, from Aird Thiar, Carna, Connemara, significantly a near neighbor of Joe Heaney, someone he performed with at Oireachtas competitions and whom he regarded as among the best male singers he had heard (Mac Con Iomaire 2007:108–26).

Heaney was also singled out for special mention; established as Heaney was, this accolade from Ó Riada reaffirmed his ascendant position as a leading exponent of *sean-nós* singing. The tremendous musicality of these singers marked them out as exceptional and, consequently, reinforced the claim of their region to be considered the most authentic in that the true art of traditional singing had best survived there. In other words, the fact that these individuals were excellent singers and that they were recognized as such served to consolidate an overall concept and practice of regional authenticity in a national context.

In accordance with the norms of cultural nationalism, this region could henceforth be marked as the most authentic, and its acclaim could also reinforce the region's supremacy so that it achieved the status of national standard, to be emulated by other areas. Therefore, the highly ornamented melismatic musical style of Connemara achieved preeminent status in a way that other regions could not hope to match. The singling out of one style from a heteroglossic diversity to act as a model for best national practice is a characteristic of revivalist programs in cultural nationalism and can also be identified in other aspects of culture, including instrumental music and sport (Whelan 1993:29–35). It is almost as if a national revival program needs to simplify matters, to choose one style from the myriad that proliferate in a living tradition in order to organize culture into what it considers a coherent and presentable form. This form then becomes the gold standard to which all others are bound to conform if they are to achieve recognition. Such a drastic pruning of style, rather than encouraging further growth, effectively narrowed the range of musical choices for *sean-nós* practitioners.

The anomalies inherent in this selection process are abundant. Addressing the problems created by such a prescriptive system, Pádraig Ó Cearbhaill (1995:44–45) identifies five characteristics that are nowadays seen as salient and uncompromising features of traditional song in the Irish language. These are (1) that the voice quality uses no appreciable shift in dynamics, (2) that rhythmic and rubato songs are distinct categories, (3) that the singers do not use vibrato, (4) that it is thought that words precede music in importance, and (5) that the melodic phrases must not be broken. He then gives examples from traditional singers and others that contradict these supposedly categorical rules. Arising from those contradictions, he suggests that rule makers ought to be very careful when formulating any kind of rule about *sean-nós*, and that categorical statements such as those made by Ó Riada and others tend to lose their potency because of their inherent rigidity. As with isolating one style to predominate over all others, enforcing strict rules about performance practice has not necessarily served the genre of *sean-nós* well.

It is certainly worth noting that many, if not most, *sean-nós* singers incorporate varieties of vibrato and dynamic change into their singing. In addition, unless it is an important occasion like a competition, many singers simply break phrases as they run out of breath, though some attention is paid to continuity of phrasing. Nonetheless, it is the singers themselves—including Joe Heaney, one of the strongest advocates of Ó

Riada's rules—who passionately discuss the importance of adhering to what they perceive as an older style, even as they themselves bend or break through the stylistic outlines of the genre.

Ó Riada may have disseminated these ideas widely and cast them in a new mold, but versions of them had been around since the beginning of the twentieth century at least (cf. Henebry 1903, 1928; de Noraidh 1964; Hardebeck 1911; Nic Dhonncha 2004; uí Ógáin 2007:72). Therefore, it is reasonable to suppose that, since Heaney was a dedicated attendee at Oireachtas competitions, and since he achieved a degree of national recognition through this arena, such thinking influenced him directly. Additionally, none of the competitions has ever taken place in a social or cultural vacuum. Participants attend at least as much for the socializing and discussion (the *craic*) as for the singing, and a lively topic of conversation continues to be the rules—the criteria for what constitutes a good performance—in both the minds of the judges and the ears of the judged.

The foregoing summary provides a context for understanding some basic concepts about *sean-nós* singing, together with Joe Heaney's engagement with it. It shows the cultural processes that influenced the development of *sean-nós* as a canonic genre, with special emphasis on repertoire and musical style. What about Joe Heaney himself as a *sean-nós* singer? He had a strong bass voice with a fairly wide range, straying down as low as C-sharp below the bass clef on songs like "Róisín Dubh" but usually bringing the entire song upward by a half step between its beginning and end. He was a compelling performer, shifting moods easily while watching his audience closely and—in contrast to traditional performance practices—glaring if anyone stirred.

An unobtrusive vibrato is noticeable in all of Heaney's recordings and performances. It should be pointed out here that all singers perform with varying degrees of oscillation. The vibrato to which most Irish singers refer (sometimes with derision) is likely the Italianate opera-influenced vibrato associated with nineteenth-century parlor music, the bel canto tradition, and Irish tenors. The oscillation of that vibrato is often quite wide; intervals as wide as a major third or even a perfect fourth can be heard between its upper and lower pitches. While *sean-nós* singers often sing with vibrato, the breadth of oscillation is usually much narrower, along the lines of a quarter step at most. It is easier to imagine a singer disclaiming an oscillation of such a small degree.

While Heaney's singing came to represent the exceptionally melismatic and celebrated style of Connemara ornamentation, he often reserved those melismas for the first verse of a long song, paring back the ornamentation to turns and rolls in subsequent verses, a feature noted by Ó Riada (1982) in other singers. Heaney spoke of his favorite English-language songs (especially ones that followed the same linguistic rules as the Irish-language ones) as *sean-nós* also, even though by linguistic definition—and by the most casual understanding of the rules of *sean-nós*—they lay (and continue to lie) outside the boundaries of the style. In spite of all his rule breaking, however, few questioned his excellence as an exponent of the genre except, perhaps, Joe Heaney himself.

Joe Heaney's performances were never limited to just one song. Instead, he developed over the years a particular style of performance that incorporated puns, autobiography, short and long stories, references to Connemara customs, children's songs, emigration songs, drinking songs, and, yes, a few *sean-nós* songs (see the final chapters of this book). Many of his performances (in Ireland, England, and the United States) were almost exclusively in English. It is quite revealing to picture such a symbolic and influential figure—who so powerfully represented much of Gaelic Ireland to Irish and Americans alike—performing English-language drinking songs that he picked up during his days as a laborer in England. This mingling was necessary for successful performance at the most pragmatic level in front of audiences that were not deeply versed in Gaelic tradition and who understood little Gaelic. Such was the aura of his natal heritage, however, that it allowed all these various strands to be heard as if they had emerged in one piece at the dawn of time in a pure Gaelic-speaking haven.

At home in his community in Connemara, of course, Heaney was free to speak and sing exclusively in Irish; it was an opportunity he cherished because of having to spend most of his adulthood speaking in a language that was foreign to him. It must also be remembered, though, that his community was bilingual and enjoyed English-language songs as well, although the language spoken was invariably Gaelic (Bourke 2007). However, Heaney's visits home were infrequent and fraught with contradiction. His repeated assertions, during his performances in the States, that "back home they all sing like that," were readily acknowledged as truth in immigrant, academic, and folk music communities. In Carna, his home, only a few singers could be said to have achieved a similar stature or level of grand achievement as Heaney himself. In fact, Séamus Ennis, when working as a collector there in the 1940s, identified the Heaney family, their neighbors Seán Choilm Mac Donnchadha and Seán Jeaic Mac Donnchadha, and the Mac Donnchadha family of Fínis as the leading exponents of traditional style and repertoire in an area replete with such performers (uí Ógáin 2007, 72). When Heaney claimed such a skill level for all the members of his community, he was claiming a rock-solid authoritative pedigree and identity for himself.

The Oireachtas

Up to this point *sean-nós* and its cultural context have been discussed here as if they were dominant forms and discourses of Irish culture during the twentieth century. Although there is no doubt that these discourses were influential, they must be seen in the light of other competing forces at work in Ireland. As a result of colonization and culminating in the catastrophe of the Great Famine (as mentioned in the introduction),

Ireland experienced a major language shift in the nineteenth century. This linguistic change was exacerbated by the Famine and its effects: mortality through starvation and disease and greatly accelerated emigration. The Gaelic League's program, then, was a response to these changes, which had in practice been largely effected by the end of the nineteenth century. That is to say, those places where Irish remained the dominant language were few and far between. Additionally, the Irish language was stigmatized by its associations with backwardness, poverty, ignorance, and hidebound conservatism. All those who wished to improve their lot in life used the English language to do so, jettisoning the Irish language, seemingly without compunction, along the way and investing their identity more fully in the resurgent reformed Catholicism of the post-Famine period.

The Romantic Nationalists tried, in their way, to counteract centuries of entrenched negative associations accruing to Irish with little more than a cultural agenda. This cultural program, however, soon became identified with separatist political nationalism. As part of the new establishment of nationhood, Irish scholars and political leaders alike sought to develop a contemporary identity that was nonetheless part of the larger current of Romanticism. Developing this identity required highlighting Ireland's unique qualities and focusing on folklore, songs, and native mythology in ways that would have made Johann Herder proud.

The Gaelic Athletic Association, established in 1884, was a part of this movement, and the Gaelic League, which began in 1893, carried it forward to celebrate and perpetuate the development of the Irish language and traditional Irish culture in all its complexity. Although economic improvers were also active, their programs were not specifically language-linked. To be sure, the sight of well-dressed, middle-class enthusiasts on the roads of Irish-speaking areas during summer vacation times had a certain beneficial influence on local attitudes toward Irish. But summers passed, and the visitors, like the swallows, departed for more comfortable climes, leaving those who had no choice but Irish in the grip of often-dire economic circumstances. The old truths of Irish being an exclusively local, familial language died hard. Seasonal migration, emigration to England and America, and poor living conditions were difficult to contradict by means of culture alone. Consequently, the two discourses—economic and cultural—were in competition. The cultural looked back at the high glory of the Gaelic past, whereas the economic realities pointed to the acquisition of English and its benefits of progress (Ó Giolláin 2000:144):

> Minority and "low prestige" languages, even in modern Europe, are often characterized as being conservative and backward-looking, particularly by speakers of majority and high-prestige languages. Such characterizations are especially evident in postcolonial contexts where the privilege and status attributed to high-prestige languages reflect the social status, political power, educational opportunities, technological advantages, economic well-being, and public standing of their speakers.(Tymoczko and Ireland 2003:4)

These are some of the dilemmas and debates that informed life in the west of Ireland and the lives of those who were born in Irish-speaking communities. Joe Heaney was born into such a community; it must be acknowledged that these debates were a part of his life, particularly as one who chose the Gaelic path as opposed to the English one (Mac Con Iomaire 2007:82–108). Consequently, an exposition of the workings of the Oireachtas has much to reveal about Heaney's preoccupations, obsessions, and principles.[5]

Oireachtas is an old Gaelic word brought to the fore during the cultural revival of the late nineteenth and early twentieth centuries. Originally it meant "a king's assembly," held on the high festival days of Samhain or Bealtaine, where people would gather from all parts of Ireland to meet, transact business, resolve legal disputes, make matches, and enjoy storytelling, music, and other entertainment. In referring to this royal gathering, the organizers hoped to imbue its contemporary manifestation with that same high status. A counteractive impulse attempting to diminish the debilitating effects of long-term Gaelic economic impoverishment is clearly noticeable in this turn to the past.

Not only do Irish-language singing competitions confirm and reinforce regional stereotypes to the non–Irish speakers of Ireland, but they also serve, paradoxically, as a vehicle of exceptional solidarity for the Irish-speaking communities of Ireland and abroad. Nearly all of Ireland's business, political, literary, and musical events are held in English, and almost all native speakers of Irish are fluent speakers of English as well. Ireland's uneasy relationship with its original language has led to deep divisiveness within the country and among the Irish in the internal and external diaspora. More colloquially, as several native Irish speakers recently opined, they are just not yet "cool" enough for the majority of the Irish population.

In 1921 Ireland was partitioned: Northern Ireland, which remained part of the United Kingdom, under British rule, and the Irish Free State. The existence of a largely English-speaking, Protestant majority in the North guaranteed the ability of the English to maintain a political presence, and the largely English-speaking but primarily Catholic majority in the South established an autonomous state mostly free of political domination by outsiders. After partition, a commission was set up to discover the extent of Irish-speaking communities. The commission drew boundaries around these in 1926 and designated them Gaeltacht—Irish-speaking areas. Regions where 80 percent or more of the population spoke Irish daily were called *Fíor-Ghaeltacht* (true-Gaeltacht), and those with less than 80 percent were called *Breac-Ghaeltacht* (speckled-Gaeltacht). In general, these Gaeltachtaí are areas in which the Irish language is expected by the government and by others to be the medium of communication in daily life. In practice, the actual use of the language varies widely by location, and large areas within the designated confines are today primarily English -speaking. This signifies that language decline was well advanced by the time the boundaries were drawn, so that the older generation of Irish speakers were practically replaced by largely monolingual English speakers.

Towns have always been Anglicizing centers in these regions. Other locations contain isolated pockets of Irish speakers among a larger English-speaking population. The Irish Language Regional Authority, or Údarás na Gaeltachta (established 1980), describes these Gaeltacht areas as "the unbroken link with a past that saw Irish as the main language in Ireland. The area is a vital lynchpin for the transmission of Irish as a community language to the next generation and a cornerstone in the development of a truly bilingual society in Ireland. The Gaeltacht, Ireland at its most Irish!" (www.udaras.ie). The implication here is, of course, that the English-speaking regions of Ireland—which constitute most of the nation—are not particularly Irish. This promotional blurb also hides the fact that English is also spoken in these areas, and that the language shift completed elsewhere in Ireland is still working itself out here. The sense of alienation of the Irish-language culture from the mainstream—English-speaking—culture goes back hundreds of years.[6]

The term *Gaeltacht* is an abstract noun, originally applied to people who were Gaels and who followed Gaelic ways. The 1926 statutes, however, effected a change. Thenceforth, Gaeltacht in Ireland referred primarily to geographic locations, largely in the rural west of the island. The Gaeltacht symbolically functioned as a type of deep Ireland. However, it was conveniently located far from the centers of power, where the actual struggle for independence had been carried out, and where people were more aware of class tensions and differences. In some ways, the Gaeltacht represented an iconic utopia where the contested politics of socioeconomic status were suspended.

Although this development of Irish-speaking districts was intended to guarantee the protection of the language and related aspects of expressive culture of these regions from extinction in the face of continuing pressure from English, the state machinery continued as before the establishment of the Free State. That is to say, a largely English-speaking and unsympathetic bureaucracy continued to perform its duties primarily in English to deal with the public, so that there was an anomaly between theory and practice. Historically, the Gaeltacht regions have been among the least economically developed parts of the country, and some of the most discriminated against for their association with premodern Ireland. They were lacking in natural resources, but faced both heavy densities of population and high rates of out-migration. The attempts at protection frequently served to increase already entrenched negative attitudes; many believed that Gaeltacht inhabitants benefited unfairly from governmental economic subsidies designed to shore up a weak infrastructure. Moreover, they pointed out that impoverished English-speaking areas were just as needy, and that the grant mentality fostered a lack of initiative.

The English-language achievements of the Abbey Theater, of Yeats, Synge, and Lady Gregory need no rehearsal here. It is to their enduring works that many Irish people at home and in the diaspora gravitate in search of an identity. This is a testament to what Tymoczko and Ireland have noted: "Ironically, Ireland was faced with the task of constructing an autonomous culture just when the bulk of the Irish country people were giving up the Irish language in favor of English. Thus, the constructions of Irishness proceeded largely in English, in tandem with the Irish-language movement spearheaded by the Gaelic League" (2003:10). The Gaelic League's attempts at developing its cultural program coalesced around the idea of a literary and cultural festival, borrowed from similar events held in Wales and Scotland. The Oireachtas, first held in 1897, was the first of its kind in Ireland, following the call of Douglas Hyde for the development of a modern literature and the safeguarding of traditional music and song. Hyde was the son of a (Protestant) Church of Ireland minister in County Roscommon who had learned Irish from older neighbors in the 1860s and who, later in his life, became a noted folklorist and the first professor of Irish at University College Dublin. The literary side of the competition concerns us less than the performative aspect. A major difficulty for the organizers was that no standard of performance existed because no such gathering of Irish musicians had happened since the harpers congregated in Belfast in 1792. Cultural expression had been largely local and vernacular, without any national framework for organization.

Songs in the Irish language comprised two elements most saliently Irish, that is, the Irish language itself and, second, Irish melody. Consequently, it is not surprising that they were singled out for special attention. Over the years, people discussed the merits and disadvantages of various forms of presentation. These included choral singing from printed sheet music, issues of monophony or harmonization, and the place of the solo singer hailing from an Irish-speaking community. The older unaccompanied Irish-language songs were held to be the highest standard of Gaelic expressive culture. At the time none of these issues were set in stone, and debates quickly developed around them. As part of the push toward preservation and maintenance of at least the nineteenth-century past, certain members of the Gaelic League focused on keeping Irish-language songs away from elements of modernization, such as harmony singing and piano accompaniment (Ó Súilleabháin 1984). Proponents of this school of thought won out, so that the unaccompanied singer from the Gaeltacht region, singing alone in Irish, became imbued with more-than-ordinary gravitas. By the time Joe Heaney was born in 1919, this discourse was well established.

The Oireachtas was also connected to the folklore movement in Ireland, and Hyde was intimately connected with folklore. In many respects, the Gaelic Revival and folklore went hand in hand, and folk song was integral to that. The establishment of the Folklore of Ireland Society (1927) and the Folklore Commission (1935) gave folklore a disciplinary and institutional identity, however underresourced and precarious, establishing folklore collection on a systematic basis, specifically linked to the project of nation building (Briody 2007). Heaney's family were directly involved in this set of efforts; in fact, his brother Seán was an early contributor to the archives. In 1931, during the Christmas holidays, at the age of eighteen, he wrote down a considerable amount of folklore from his father. An examination of the manuscript reveals his high level of literacy and familiarity not just with the materials themselves but also with the principles of folklore collection. Clearly, then, Heaney's life was profoundly influenced by these movements—nation building and language revitalization, both linked intimately with the collection and preservation of folklore—from the beginning.

The Oireachtas continued as a festival until 1924; because of disruptions caused by the War of Independence and its aftermath, it was discontinued for a number of years until 1939, a year in which no competitions were held. Competitive events began again in 1940, and Joe Heaney, at nineteen, was among those present. Heaney continued to attend the Oireachtas regularly over a period of twenty years, exhibiting steadfast loyalty, and thriving on this touchstone to reinforce deeply held cultural convictions. It is even more impressive when one considers that he was a resident abroad in Scotland and in England for at least half of that time. He said himself that the Oireachtas was what kept him alive (Mac Con Iomaire 2007: 159).

It is not surprising that Heaney exhibited this loyalty to the festival. He himself comments that very few Irish speakers had sung songs in Irish outside the Gaeltacht before the reestablishment of the festival in 1939. Given what we have said about the politics of language and culture in the mid-twentieth century, such validation was a significant event, an honor that was likely to remain memorable for the one who received it. Heaney had sung at Feis Charna (a competitive festival in his native town), which functioned as a qualifying competition for the Oireachtas. He received a prize there, which was to go compete at the Oireachtas in Dublin. His talent was quickly recognized. Two years later, he took the gold medal in the men's competition—the highest prize then awarded any singer—sharing it with Cáit Ní Mhuimhneacháin, who received the gold medal in the women's competition.

Although the events of the Second World War were raging elsewhere, Ireland remained neutral. Officially, the war was referred to as "The Emergency," and in a stagnant economy of little else happening, the Oireachtas was a major national festival. It was widely reported on, particularly in the Irish nationalist newspaper the *Irish Press*, and Heaney's photograph was published in the paper as well (Mac Con Iomaire 2007:96). This was a significant distinction for a previously unknown young man from a small Irish-speaking country town land. The award, together with the public recognition that accompanied it, established for Heaney an essential sense of self-respect and pride that remained with him, and that became an abiding obsession, for the rest of his life. It drove him to seek validation in different venues, from the folk clubs of Scotland to the pubs of London, and finally to the festival and university circuit in America. In retrospect, it can be seen that Heaney's early recognition both stimulated and prefigured a search for his final and greatest accolade, the United States National Heritage Fellowship in 1982, exactly forty years later.

Joe Heaney: The Recordings

One way of understanding Joe Heaney's representations of self, region, and nation as a singer is to look at the recordings he made and the items that appear on each of them. Heaney was first recorded commercially in the late 1950s by Gael Linn for its Ceolta Éireann series, which produced a number of 78 rpm records of recognized traditional vocal and instrumental musicians from various parts of Ireland. By and large, the instrumental musicians tended to be from English-speaking Ireland, and the vocalists tended to be Gaeltacht (Irish-language) performers. As befitted Gael Linn's mission as an organization promoting the Irish language, no English-language singers were recorded, nor were Irish-speaking singers recorded singing in English. Heaney made multiple recordings in this series, including "Bean a' Leanna," "Is Measa Liom Bródach Uí Ghaora," "Caoineadh na dTrí Muire," "Neansín Bhán," "Currachaí na Trá Báine," "Amhrán na Páise," and "Sadhbh Ní Bhruinneallaigh." Each recording included a *sean-nós* song on one side and an instrumental track on the other. Heaney and his friend Seán 'ac Dhonnchadha each recorded seven tracks, making more recordings in this series than any other singer, clearly indicating the high esteem in which their own singing was held, as representative of their region.

Heaney's early Topic recording (*Joe Heaney: Irish Traditional Songs in Gaelic and English* [1963]) contains both English- and Irish-language items. Among them are (in English) "The Rocks of Bawn," "The Wife of the Bold Tenant Farmer," "The Trees They Grow Tall," and "John Mitchel." The Irish-language songs include "Casadh an tSugáin," "Peigín is Peadar," "Cunnla," "Caoineadh na dTrí Muire" (see chapter 4), "An Tighearna Randal," and "Bean an Leanna" (see chapter 7). The one macaronic (bilingual) song is "One Morning in June," though Heaney often sang "Cunnla" in both Irish and English. Significantly, this record was produced in England for a proposed audience of English speakers, and all of these songs were quite prominent in his American performances twenty years later. The importance given to songs in Irish is impressive and reveals the prestige accruing to Heaney as a bilingual singer in the early 1960s. Given the strength of anti-Irish sentiment in Britain at the time, the pride of place given to the Irish language on this recording demonstrates an appreciation among folk song enthusiasts belying the general negative trend.

Like the songs in the Ceolta Éireann series, Heaney's two solo LP recordings for Gael Linn again contain only Irish-language material, specifically material regarded as indigenous to his native Carna. For the Irish-language activists and enthusiasts who supported these projects, this was Heaney's true métier, a rich vein of Gaelic poetry and melody that could be traced at least to the seventeenth century or even earlier in some cases, one that remained productive with local poets still composing songs in a similar style well into Heaney's own time. Here, Anglicized Ireland could perceive what they regarded as the seamless continuity with the glorious Gaelic past unbroken, uncontaminated, and uncompromised. Indeed, this belief is still shared by many of Joe Heaney's fans today.

It must be said that these two albums do show off the Gaelic gems in Heaney's repertoire to excellent effect, and the two recordings—recently re-released as a two-CD set—are widely acknowledged as representative of Heaney's skills at their height. However poorly they were understood by his English-language audiences, these songs must, in fact, be regarded as classics with regard to the items themselves, their musical configuration, Heaney's inimitable performance style, and the pride he clearly felt in this heritage. The point is, however, that the agenda in these recordings crosses into the bounds of cultural politics as much as it remains in the realm of musical art.

The *Say a Song* recording released in 1996 by the Ethnomusicology Archives at the University of Washington contains both Irish-language and English-language items. Significantly, some of the Irish-language material on this recording derives from the school curriculum. In contrast to the Gael Linn classic recordings, *Say a Song* reveals that Heaney underwent the formal education process like any other Irish person of his generation. The material that he absorbed there would not be regarded as valuable from the point of view of the folk song aesthetic, being learned from books and teachers, those individuals whose credentials as bearers of tradition were suspect because of their literacy and education. In these recordings we get different impressions of Heaney the singer. A listener familiar with the distinctions between the items in the repertoire might wonder at the inclusion of some such as "Óró mo Bháidín" or "Óró Sé Do Bheatha 'Bhaile"—songs widely taught in Irish schools throughout the twentieth century. Although these items are in Gaelic, they are products of the Gaelic Revival, not ones for which he first gained fame and recognition at the Oireachtas festival in 1942.

For most American listeners, however, these criteria would not apply. Americans would not necessarily recognize that "Óró Sé Do Bheatha 'Bhaile" was any different from "Eileanóir a Rún" or "An Buinneán Buí." The song is in Irish and therefore valid for inclusion. Heaney sang this song for his American audiences, although it is questionable whether he would ever sing such a song for an Irish-speaking audience in Ireland. Having been culturally formed in Ireland, absorbing such prejudices along the way, he would certainly have been careful not to transgress them at home. In America, however, unfamiliarity with the Gaelic repertoire released Heaney to some extent from the authentic/spurious bind. Consequently, when in need of new items for teaching and performance, he sometimes chose to avail himself of material acquired through the formal schooling process. No one from Ireland was present to disapprove of such choices, and his need for variety and novelty in his material helped him to overcome his own reservations. Furthermore, the largely uncritical acceptance of whatever he chose to present to his academic audiences enabled him to select simpler, easier Irish-language songs to teach his students or offer to audience members.

Joe Heaney/Seosamh Ó hÉanaí: The Road from Connemara was produced in 2000. The two-CD set features an array of Irish-language songs and some of his favorite songs in English as well. The set also includes some examples of Heaney's stories, as well as his spoken introductions to songs. Based on a series of recorded interviews at the home at Ewan MacColl and Peggy Seeger in Kent, England, in 1964, the resulting recording not only is quite revealing of Heaney in his unguarded moments but also reflects one instance of what happened to Heaney's recordings after he passed away—and therefore had no control over what was released. The exceptionally detailed liner notes include lyrics, translations, an introduction by Liam Mac Con Iomaire, and a long article by Fred McCormick.[7] The omission of "The Rocks of Bawn" and "Caoineadh na dTrí Muire" is notable, and perhaps is due to the desire to concentrate on other, less-well-known, songs.

The content and the liner notes of this recording offer valuable insights into Heaney and his milieu in ways that the other recordings do not. A number of the songs reveal the extent of Heaney's repertoire, including some he knew only partially. It is doubtful whether Heaney would have approved of the release of all the material on this record, since he set such store by excellence in performance. Furthermore, in the interest of thoroughness, MacColl elicited the item "Whiskey Ó Roudeldum-Row" during the recording sessions. The song, a vehicle for extempore composition, contains some bawdy references in Heaney's version. As a song probably performed exclusively in a single-gender context, its sexual content effectively crosses a once-forbidden gender boundary in its current availability to anyone with access to iTunes. Given Heaney's public reticence about sexual matters, it is likely that he would have preferred that this item not be publicly available. Indeed, the Carna community and Heaney's relatives there were unhappy with the publication for this reason.

Consequently, we can see that each recorded unit constructs a different image of Heaney's repertoire of song. The Gael Linn recordings recognize only the Irish-language material that was local to his Carna home. Certainly, some of these items are known from printed versions and some of them were taught in differing formats under the school curriculum. But the versions sung by Heaney on the Gael Linn albums conform closely to the idea of the self-contained organic community unspoiled by outside influence, the rural utopia espoused by de Valera's "Undeserted Village Ireland." The selection of only Irish-language Carna material for Gael Linn promotes the image of a Gaelic community surviving intact despite the ravages of famine, emigration, and want into the twentieth century and Irish national self-realization. Here is the image of the *sean-nós* in a pristine, prelapsarian condition, free from contaminating Anglicization or decadence (Ó Riada 1982:29). As such it is an important cultural statement and reveals much about the cultural concerns of the architects of the Irish Free State and budding republic.

In the Topic recording the material is more widely cast. Here Irish-language material alternates with English and macaronic material.

Despite the mixing of languages, however, the material here again is pure unadulterated folk, that is to say, drawn from the oral nonofficial tradition and calculated to please a folk audience. Whereas the Gael Linn recordings imply that Heaney's milieu is entirely Irish-speaking, the Topic recording (which came first) makes no such claim. However, other potential musical influences, such as ballad broadsheets and popular, school, or other songs, are ignored. *Say a Song*, published posthumously, arguably problematizes the others. Here we have the Irish-language material characteristic of Carna, but we also have material that reflects Heaney's experience of schooling. The English-language material likewise does not follow the pure contour of oral folk material alone. It reveals more popular items, giving us a broader picture of Heaney's musical repertoire and one, perhaps, that might not have been in his own interests to reveal while alive.[8]

All his recordings reveal Heaney's ability to present different aspects of his repertoire and how astute he was in the choices he made. Gael Linn, as an organization that promoted the Irish language and Gaelic Ireland, focused on Heaney's Gaelic material. Indeed, the reputation of his native Carna as a place rich in this material and of his own family as custodians of it undoubtedly helped to promote his own talent, leading to his first break: the Oireachtas gold medal. Later, others such as MacColl and Seeger—while acknowledging the importance of the Gaelic material—tended to focus more on the English language repertoire. Heaney had grist for all mills and quickly learned how to respond to demand. It is difficult, however, not to believe that his regard for the Gaelic material, despite his lack of opportunity to perform much of it in the United States, was foremost for him. The care and preparation he took with the Gael Linn records provide ample testimony for that (Mac Con Iomaire 2007:263). As a professional, however, he had to cater to audience demand, and by the end of his life he had become a master of stagecraft and presentation. Despite the lack of props and the verisimilitude of his performances, it would be a mistake to think that their success was not based on careful and meticulous planning (Mac Con Iomaire 2007:306).

Perhaps the most interesting aspect of Heaney's recordings is their entanglement with issues of authenticity: Whose authenticity? As we discuss elsewhere in the present volume, Heaney developed multiple performance personae to serve his personal mission of musically exploring his heritage, his influences, and his long set of experiences. The recordings reveal an Irish face to an Irish audience (the Gael Linn recordings), a consistent set of hits targeted to two different foreign audiences (the Topic recording, for English and American audiences), and his work as a dedicated and deeply engaged teacher (the *Say a Song* CD and its story-containing companion, *Tell a Story*). At the last (some of the *Say a Song* items were recorded during classes he offered in his final months), he essentially went over his entire history, bringing out songs and stories that he had allowed to languish for years. He needed little prompting and in fact seemed deeply pleased to explore and reminisce in considerable detail about all aspects of his tradition, ranging from childhood games and Christmas customs to obscure stories, legends, and songs.

This particular collection of songs and stories recorded in his final years at the University of Washington, from which the *Say a Song* and *Tell a Story* recordings are largely drawn, may represent Heaney at his most introspective and certainly, in English-language terms, his most intimate. Listening to these recordings, it is clear that they are among his most effective. Although they have not all been published, they contain a remarkable record of the pinnacle of his achievement as a teacher and performer.

2

ensreobserved

The Performance of *Sean-nós* in Connemara

Someone listening to *sean-nós* singing for the first time would probably comment on the rather highly-ornamented melodic outline of the song and, in so
doing, would pinpoint what is possibly the most significant musical aspect of
the art. (Ó Canainn 1978:71)

This chapter explores both the musical features of Joe Heaney's
performance practice and the seeming obsession among members
of the folk revival with melodic decoration of one form or another.
Comparisons of theory (as described orally and discussed in print) with
practice must take into account Heaney's own interpretation of the musical
features of *sean-nós* singing. The reader is already familiar with Seán Ó
Riada's discussion of his rules for correct *sean-nós* singing from chapter 1;
his student and colleague Tomás Ó Canainn published an interesting and
compelling discussion of song lyrics and a further explanation of the
music of *sean-nós* in a chapter of his book *Traditional Music in Ireland*
(1978).

These two texts provide fascinating insight into *sean-nós* musicality.
Such theories emerge from a familiarity on the part of Ó Riada and Ó
Canainn with standard European notation and musical theoretical principles. Joe Heaney, on the other hand, was primarily an oral musician and
originally had no such theoretical grounding, relying on what he had
absorbed from his long familiarity with the tradition and from conversations with others. There is no doubt that he felt the lack of more training
in this regard, though it was a deficiency he would be unlikely to admit.
Rather, using all the resources at his command, he formulated his own
theory of *sean-nós*, comparing it by turns to lovemaking and to engaging
in battle. He also clearly accessed theories and terminologies of folk music
current among enthusiasts and scholars during his lifetime. Significantly,
however, he was always likely to attribute them to his father's teaching
and, strategically, to omit any overt references to book learning! In
exploring *sean-nós* as sung in Connemara, we acknowledge the primary
position occupied by that regional tradition in the hierarchy of *sean-nós*
singing. Connemara is recognized as the foremost region in Ireland where
traditional song in Gaelic is sung. Connemara singers and those who sing

in that style have taken the major prizes year after year at the Oireachtas and other competitions. This is a testimony to the vitality of traditional arts and especially song in the region. It may also be viewed as an endorsement by cultural nationalism in one form or another for a regional variety that best exemplifies the principles of an organic, living folk culture.

Many features combine to make *sean-nós* singing such an extraordinary art form, from subject matter to storytelling to melodic, rhythmic, and linguistic features. While *sean-nós* is sung exclusively in Irish under the most traditional circumstances, singers are nowadays generally fluent in English, although they may be dominant in Irish. Many know and perform songs in English while others sing only in Irish as a deliberate choice. The English-language songs that show up in performance are often melodically ornamented in ways familiar to singers in Irish and exhibit the same types of regional variation that Irish-language songs do. Although each singer ornaments songs in an individual way, larger stylistic differences— particularly the use of melismatic ornamentation—appear to separate Connemara *sean-nós* from the singing of some of the other areas. Defining the characteristic aspects of *sean-nós* vocal ornamentation in both Irish and English will, ideally, further the development of a grammar for stylistically correct melodic ornamentation in the Connemara style.

During Joe Heaney's time in the United States, his greatest difficulty as a teacher was in getting his students to understand the correct ways of performing vocal ornamentation. His usual explanation of correctly ornamenting a song included statements like "There's nobody living who can tell anyone where to put grace notes into a song; you just do it." Although Heaney claimed no explicit understanding of melodic ornamentation in *sean-nós* songs, he often spoke of it in metaphoric terms or in terms of feelings about the underlying meaning of the song. He stated that "putting ornamentations into a song is like when you're courting a girl with your two arms around her. You're not going to do it the other fella's way. You got to do it your own way" (interview, February 24, 1978).

Heaney's simile is apt. He emphasizes the personal, almost private nature of ornamentation, its delicacy and intimacy, suggestive of correct deportment and execution, of the unforced assurance that characterized his own singing and that turned it into such a mystery for his American students. Heaney insisted that the art could not be taught in a clinical, analytic fashion such as other aspects of musical proficiency might be, but that it must be acquired by familiarity with the material, by feeling and by desire. Consequently, he communicated the human dimension to his students, urging them to immerse themselves in the music and the language so that they might eventually succeed in their quest.

Steve Coleman—himself once a student of Heaney's—notes, "Scholarly inquiry into the '*sean-nós*' tradition has quite consistently focused on ornamentation. Likewise, the popular media in Ireland as well as the folk and Gaelic revival movements have taken ornamentation as a sign of the uniqueness, antiquity, or 'other'-ness of the tradition. This had led some critics to comment on the 'fetishisation' of ornamentation" (1997:49).

While ornamentation is indeed only one of many dimensions of *sean-nós* singing to explore, it does happen to be an issue that looms large in aesthetic decisions about a particular performer's skill (cf. Ó Laoire 2000).

Melodic ornamentation is influenced both by syntax and by poetic stress patterns, and depends on the language in which it is sung (Williams 2004:122–45). Songs in Irish are often ornamented on unstressed syllables. Similarly, songs in the English language that use Irish syntax and stress are ornamented on unstressed syllables whenever possible. English-language songs that do not follow Irish patterns of stress and syntax are more strongly influenced, in terms of ornamentation, by melodic contour rather than by stress and syntax (Hogan 1927:54).[1] An issue that is explored later in this chapter is that melodic ornamentation differs between songs sung in English and Irish. *Stylistically*, however, it is not only possible but quite common to perform an English-language song in *sean-nós* style. Heaney did it himself as a normal part of his performance practice.

The political and cultural upheavals of the seventeenth century are identified with Oliver Cromwell in Irish oral historical narrative. Popular tradition also remembers the aphorism "To Hell or to Connacht" and holds that many residents of fertile inland areas were displaced and moved to more inhospitable areas on the coasts. Statistics show that the province of Connacht did indeed contain the greatest numbers of Catholics in proportion to Protestants (Courbage 1997:173–74). Heaney's oral history attributed this to the Cromellian upheavals and he drew frequently on these traditions in his narratives, crediting the richness of Gaelic song in his native area with these movements of population. He asserted that what is now referred to as the *sean-nós* repertoire and style had emerged from such turmoil and disorder. According to Heaney's view one musical result of Cromwell's violent evictions of the Irish from their homelands to the barren rocks of Connacht[2] was that multiple song forms were thrown together, leading to the development of what is now referred to as *sean-nós*. Although it has been speculated that both the topics and meters of what are now *sean-nós* songs have existed since the thirteenth century (Bergin 1937:281; Breathnach 1977:22), almost no mention of them can be found in medieval Irish literature. The poems preserved in the manuscripts were mostly in praise of chieftains and their families, paeans to their bravery and their munificence. Bardic praise poems were composed in syllabic meters, quite unlike the stressed meters of what we now call *sean-nós* songs.

Paradoxically, the decline of the aristocratic tradition in the seventeenth century spurred a greater interest in these songs, allowing them to appear more frequently in manuscripts and eventually in print. Professional mendicant harpers carried these songs and performed them for their patrons down to the end of the eighteenth century. Some among them, famously Turlough O'Carolan, for instance (1670–1738), composed new music and lyrics in this style. Occasionally, these became included in popular song tradition, carried on by nonprofessionals in informal settings. In a bilingual society, it is not surprising that English-language songs gradually also became part of the repertoire. All of this varied accumulation of music and its associated narratives formed part of Joe Heaney's heritage, enabling him to perform songs in both English and Irish during a single evening's performance. Despite his deep affection for his Gaelic songs, it was expeditious for Heaney also to claim the authenticity of the English-language tradition, especially when confronted with non-Gaelic-speaking audiences.

Poetic Rhythm in Song

The use of English in Ireland has a lengthy and complicated history; what follows is a very brief account of the relationship between the two languages and how they work in song performance. The Irish language often stresses the first syllable of each word; exceptions to this rule tend to occur with foreign words or when nouns are compounded. Contemporary speakers of English in Ireland may stress the first syllable of English words that normally are not stressed; it is one indication of how strong the Irish language remains in English-speaking Ireland. English has been recorded in poetic manuscripts in Ireland from as early as the thirteenth century (Hogan 1927:23). As English eventually reached into the remotest coastal areas, English songs were also adopted together with an unusual combination of English vocabulary and Irish syntax. However, no main English dialect came to dominate Ireland; differences in class, location, and other features have resulted in a diffusion of linguistic varieties across the island (Hickey 2007:4).

Many of the songs in English from the bilingual period exhibit certain features of the Irish language. In Connemara, English lent itself awkwardly to local speech patterns, even though it had been spoken in the region for decades. Songs performed in English were certainly understood, but they underwent alteration as each Irish-speaking area reworked songs to fit local ways of singing. One of the most distinctive indicators of an English-language song that has been localized is the use of the verb "to be" at the beginning of a line. This feature in Irish occurs in the forms of the verbs *is* and *tá*, both of which are used for "to be" in different situations, not unlike the Spanish verbs *ser* and *estar* (Zimmerman 1967:100; Joyce 1991 [1910]:10). *Is* especially may be used as an emphasizer in a linguistic strategy called "fronting." Any part of the sentence the speaker wishes to stress is brought to the front and placed beside the copula (*is*). For example, the song "A Stór Mo Chroí" (discussed in detail in chapter 5) includes the phrase "And *it's* many a time by night and day that your heart will be sorely grieving." Heaney's performance of the song "Going to Mass Last Sunday" includes "And *it's* down in yonder valley, she is my heart's delight."

In Irish, present and present continous are distinguished by separate forms, *tá* and *bíonn* respectively. Whereas a standard English speaker might not distinguish "he is here now" from "he is here every week," Irish uses *tá sé* for the first and *bíonn* sé (translated literally as "he does be"), marking the difference with specific verbal forms. English-language songs often include a variety of examples of Gaelicization, among them the concept of disagreement in gender, number, and tense (Joyce 1991 [1910]:84). Another example would be the use of the possessive for verbal nouns (when someone is standing, in Irish, he is said to be *ina sheasamh*, or "in his standing"—hence the use of the possessive). Two other Irish forms occur in the use of consonants. The first is referred to as metathesis, or the reversal of internal consonants (which occurred frequently in Heaney's speech); the second is the interjection of supplementary syllables between consonants.[3] Heaney often used supplementary syllables in both his English- and his Irish-language songs, as discussed by Hugh Shields (1973: 62–71). The song "The Green Linnet" includes the phrase "In a soft voice she murmured, my green linnet he's [a] gone," while "Anach Cuain" includes "Daon mhac [a] máthar dar rugadh ariamh" (62–71).

One important indicator of the differences between Irish and English metric systems is that English-language folk poetry is often in iambic form. That is, in a two-syllable metric foot, the emphasis falls on the second syllable, such as the word "delight." Irish-language folk poetry, in contrast, is primarily trochaic, which means that the stressed syllable occurs *before* the unstressed syllable, as in the word "mountain" (Preminger 1974:285). Knowing these poetic terms is useful because the Irish characteristics of an English-language song may be illuminated, in part, by an examination of the song's metric structure. For example, Heaney's performance of the song "Please Restore My Baby Boy" demonstrates its Irish influences on the language through its trochaic structure. In the following example from the third verse, emphasis occurs on the first syllable of each metric foot:

> "Please Restore My Baby Boy"
> *O'*er the/*moun*tain,/*through* the/*wild*wood/
> *Where* in/*child*hood he/*long*ed to/*play*/
> *Where* the/*flow*ers are/*fresh*ly/*spring*ing/
> *There* I/*wan*der,/*day* by/*day*.

Contrast this example with one in iambic meter, and the result bears little resemblance to the Irish. Such an example is "The Trees They Grow Tall," another song frequently performed by Heaney in the United States. Although the first line appears to be anapestic (grouped in threes with the emphasis on the first syllable), it is turned into an iambic phrase when sung using half notes and dotted quarter notes of the melody as additive tools for iambic scansion. Otherwise, its basically iambic structure is made clear in the following outline of the first verse:

> "The Trees They Grow Tall"
> The *trees*/*they*/grow *tall*/and the *grass*/*it*/grows *green*/
> The *time*/has *come*/and *passed*/my *love*/since *you*/and *I*/have *been*/
> It's a *cold*/and *bit* -/ter *night*/my *love*/that *I*/lie *here*/alone/
> For/my *bon* -/ny *boy*/was *young*,/*but*/he's *gone*/

The last and possibly most interesting aspect of song composition in English is that Irish poets seem to have consciously or unconsciously imitated the assonantal patterns found in the early Gaelic poetic meters. One technique referred to by early Irish poets as *aicill* is the device of rhyming the last word of the first line with the first word or a word in the middle of the next. In "Please Restore My Baby Boy," this phenomenon is clearly demonstrated at least twice in the first verse alone:

> "Please Restore My Baby Boy"
> A mother came when stars were *paling*
> *Wailing* around the fairy spring
> Thus her tears were softly *falling*
> *Calling* on the fairy king.

These examples demonstrate the ability for speakers of Irish to make English-language songs their own by adding certain features that originally belonged to the Irish language (Shields 1993: 6–7). Although the translation of songs is generally not a feasible means of adaptation to Irish forms, Heaney himself proved that adaptation can be done gracefully and in a stylistically correct and aesthetically satisfying manner.

Metaphor in Sean-nós Singing

According to Heaney, the best songs do not spell out exactly what is taking place. By leaving much to the imagination, the singer compels the audience to think about what is being sung by the text and to speculate on what hidden meanings may be illuminated by further thought. Indeed, the twelfth-century Welsh scholar-traveler Giraldus Cambrensis wrote of the Irish in their harping that "that which is concealed is bettered—art revealed is art shamed" (Rimmer 1977:29). In essence, either telling a story or performing something without recourse to decoration or metaphor is to disappoint one's audience; weaving a tale or song with twists and turns is an invitation to participate in understanding its hidden meanings. Joe Heaney mentioned that his English-language songs contained only a fraction of the metaphors used in the Irish-language songs, and that the Irish songs were clearly more rich and descriptive for this reason.

Like any text, *sean-nós* lyrics are polysemic, and may be understood in disparate ways. Gaelic songs, because of their oral basis and their frequently allusive nonlinear structure, lend themselves well to multiple and often contradictory meanings (Shields 1993:58–83). One way of calling attention to the presence of a secondary meaning is the use of melodic ornamentation. Multiple examples of the use of metaphor occur in the *sean-nós* repertoire. In using metaphoric terms, the *sean-nós* singer projects images and subtle emotional content rather than concrete statements. As an example, metaphoric love songs to Ireland as a young woman are well known in the song tradition, including "Cáit Ní Dhuibhir"

("Kate O'Dwyer"), "Cáitlín Ní Úallacháin" ("Kathleen O'Houlihan"), "Róisín Dubh" ("Little Black Rose"), and "Gráinne Mhaol" ("Grace O'Malley"). The gendering of Ireland as feminine occurs in early Gallic literature, and later, in English-language, poetry, music and plays; it became part of a constellation of images surrounding the idea of the nation as subjugated female. These images became much more complicated over time (Davis 2006:221), but the Gaelic repertoire from which Joe Heaney drew was, for the most part, older than the late nineteenth century.

The idea of Ireland as a woman goes back to the earliest literature—the Book of Invasions, in fact, when the three goddesses (Banba, Fodla, and Eriu) promised the land to the Sons of Míl (Cross and Slover 1936: 14–27). The idea changed and developed over time, to the point that in the seventeenth and eighteenth centuries, Ireland was seen as a languishing woman under the yoke of a foreign usurper waiting for her true lover the Stuart king to return and claim her. In explaining the use of metaphor to sing about Ireland, Heaney noted that the singers and audience "clearly feel for the plight of Ireland because no one would lament so strongly about a woman." Rather than pointing in particular to any type of ornamentation or other clue that might indicate a metaphoric song, Heaney let it suffice to say that the very presence of elaborate ornamentation in a *sean-nós* song about specifically named women indicates metaphor. This trope and its application to the Indo-European myth of kingship pervade the whole of Irish history from the beginning.

In the traditional context that Heaney presented, however, every member of the audience would know and understand each song at multiple levels. In a sense, there was no uninformed audience at home, such as would constitute the majority of his performances in North America or England. Without the need for explanation, Heaney could go directly to the song and allow the song to stand in, as it were, for the nation. In North America, however, he always included the story of the song—*údar an amhráin*—and almost always selected "Róisín Dubh" as his metaphoric song about Ireland (Shields 1993:77–79). Taking it even further, Heaney would explain directly to his audiences that he was using metaphor to convey deeper nationalist meanings and, in so doing, would break open the code for his audience to follow.

According to Heaney, all of his songs—especially the Irish-language songs—demonstrated a deeper meaning through the use of ornamentation. Isolating the text as indicator of song type and ornamentation as indicator of feeling or meaning in a song provides an explanation of more local criteria for performance. Heaney always classified songs by the story they told (broken-token songs, laments, supernatural songs, and others), not by melody type. In other words, his audiences might (with repeated listening) recognize that he was choosing a similar air for two different songs, but he did not point this out to them. His assumption, even among a crowd of ethnomusicology graduate students, was that performing a song was *all* about telling the story. Heaney did not invent these taxonomies. Rather, the grouping of songs under these categories points to his association with Ewan MacColl, Peggy Seeger, and others in the British folk revival before his U.S. days. Appropriating their more academic terminology, he grafted it seamlessly onto his own understanding of song as narrative, cannily availing of established systems to his own advantage, the jargon an affirmation of his credentials.

By frequently citing the phrase *abair amhrán* (say a song) in his classes, Heaney demonstrated that communicating the plot with feeling was more important than (for example) having a specific type of voice for singing *sean-nós* songs. In every case the song's story, to Heaney, was at least as important as the melody or air. That the relationship could be heightened, and the meaning intensified, through the use of melodic ornamentation was something he pointed out frequently.

Performance Practice

Those who perform *sean-nós* songs (and those who write about them) often list important features that characterize a good performance. Among these are clarity of articulation, nasalization, staying on pitch, and conveying a sense of emotional depth of understanding of the song, its context, and its relationship to other regional songs and song families. These important features, however, vary from place to place, which is one reason any emphasis on rules is problematic and ill-advised. A particularly difficult point of discussion in *sean-nós* singing is the issue of melodic ornamentation; its regionalism is clear to its practitioners, but for various historical reasons (including the fame of Joe Heaney himself), a regional practice came to dominate national norms until fairly recently.

The frequency and density of melodic ornamentation used in performance vary dramatically from one region of Ireland to the next. Since melisma came to be seen as a specifically Irish trait (Henigan 1991:97–104), it tended to be rewarded above other ornamental or variational features. Since the singing of the west is characterized by both of these principles, awards consistently tended to go to singers from Connemara and the Aran Islands. This is not to say that the winners did not deserve their prizes. From the beginning of the 1990s, a younger generation of singers from other regions have won awards periodically.

In this chapter, the focus *is* on Connemara—specifically, Joe Heaney's Connemara—performance practice, which means that melismatic ornamentation specific to Heaney's region is discussed in order to clarify not just the magic of it but also the fetishization of it. *Sean-nós* songs from many regions in Ireland can be performed slowly in a rubato style, and many individual singers from regions outside of Connemara can bring melismatic ornamentation into their singing. Additionally, a song can be performed in a relatively straightforward meter (as in ¾ time) and still be described as *sean-nós*.

On a larger scale, those songs most strongly celebrated by Heaney were those with many verses, melismatic ornamentation, and a rubato style of performance. Heaney prefaced his performance of songs like this by warning the audience that he was going to give them "the real thing, now," and his translation of the songs was very detailed. In reacting to Heaney's explicit celebration of the big songs, then, his audiences came to know and value them over the others—above the comic, bawdy, and drinking songs, and above the English-language songs as well. The big songs became important to Heaney's American audiences because, quite simply, the songs were important to him. Seoirse Bodley reinforces this ideal by noting that "The tradition of *sean-nós* is above all else a personal matter. It is a way of singing in which the choice of notes and ornaments is largely guided by the singer's own preferences and musical ability" (Bodley 1972–73:44–54).

The feeling of making a song one's own by singing it one's own way is very strong (Cowdery 1990:31). At the same time, prohibitions against crossing any of the circumscribed boundary lines (unwritten but implicit) permeate the community. This set of conventions points to a distinctive grammar for performance; each individual is expected to make a song his or her own and to do it one's own way, yet only within the boundaries of what is considered appropriate by the community. For example, *sean-nós* is supposed to be a solo tradition. Yet one sometimes finds family members singing in unison, including closely modeling each other's ornaments (O'Crohan 1951). That such a practice would be considered unthinkable (Breathnach 1977:102) is a clear example of how customary usage became transformed into a rigid norm. The heterophonic group singing in communities such as Tory Island (Ó Laoire 2007) also shows that solo performance was never the only way to sing. Despite this, however, although Heaney sometimes ignored other rules, he steadfastly upheld the norm of solo performance, even as he deplored the idea of adding accompaniment. One also finds members of the community singing along on choruses. Such rules appear meant to be broken in genuine practice; Heaney himself often broke his own rules, though he never relented on his condemnation of the guitar in the accompaniment of *sean-nós* songs.[4]

Many *sean-nós* singers perform with a strong nasal tone. This tone was described by Heaney as an attempt to reproduce the sound of the uilleann pipes. His own long friendship and rivalry with the piper and song collector Seamus Ennis was at least partly the impetus for his discussion of vocal nasality in this manner; he often mentioned Ennis when nasality came up in conversation. Breandán Breathnach mentions that nasality occurs in singing more than in speaking, while others see the use of nasal tone as a means for providing continuity between verses and for aiding in the implementation of melodic ornaments (see Breathnach 1971:105; Bodley 1973:46; Ó Canainn 1978:74). Joe Heaney referred to this effect as a way of providing a quiet drone in his head to keep him on pitch.

Heaney described nasal tone by the term *neá* (cf. Breathnach 1971:101). *Neá* is an onomatopoeic term that, according to Heaney, represented the sound of the Irish pipes providing both musical and emotional support.

This support was necessary not only for each song but in a sense legitimizing his entire tradition by backing him up during the course of a song:

> Well of course the pipes, you know, is borrowed after vocal style, the drone of the pipes, you know, and all that.... This is the way they handed it down, you see, this is the way they used to do it—through their nose mostly, you know, and humming—and slave working in the fields and all that, this came about: [hums softly on one pitch] hmmmm, hm-hm, like when you start up the bagpipes, that's the first note you'll hear, you know the, first thing you'll hear is that sad lament. (Cowdery 1990:36)

Claiming to hear the drone at all times, even when not singing, Heaney explained that every good *sean-nós* singer had the *neá*. He also tied his traditional song forms to Native American and East Indian vocal genres in that he felt they had the *neá* as well (Cowdery 1990:38). The audible manifestation of the *neá* takes the form of a slightly nasal hum at the very beginnings and sometimes at the ends of phrases. The resonant quality produced in the head of the singer, using the bones of the skull and jaw as resonators, is generally not perceived by the audience as anything but a nasal tone. Often a *sean-nós* singer will hum the *neá* pitch for a fraction of a second before actually beginning the song. No word is attached to the *neá* pitch; occasionally it is slurred into the first pitch of the song, however, and a word will arise from the humming sound.

Although Heaney had a resonant voice, resonance in singing is not necessarily an important criterion for a good performance. Some of the best *sean-nós* singers have very thin voices, according to Heaney, but they have the *neá* just the same. The importance of ornamentation over resonance is reinforced by Seoirse Bodley in that "where fast runs have to be negotiated in rapid succession, it is obviously not possible to have great resonance" (1973: 46). The *neá* affects the vocal quality, which allows the singer to produce the kinds of ornaments that are characteristic of *sean-nós*.

While vibrato has been an important aspect of Irish parlor songs of the nineteenth century (and the contemporary success of the "Three Irish Tenors" in the United States reveals the attraction of modern audiences toward vibrato), it appears in *sean-nós* performance practice only sometimes, depending on the individual singer (see chapter 6 on differences between the Irish tenor and the *sean-nós* singer). While many writers have asserted that lack of vibrato in *sean-nós* songs is an essential characteristic (Ó Riada 1982; Zimmerman 1967:114; Bodley 1972-73:46), a natural understand vibrato may not only be common but accepted:

> The *sean-nós* singer does not use vibrato...the song is allowed to speak for itself with a minimum of artificial intrusion or histrionics on the part of the performer. (Ó Canainn 1978:75)

The use of vibrato, of dynamic and dramatic effects, is absolutely foreign to the traditional manner, a characteristic which is also shared with plainchant. (Breathnach 1971:101).

Vibrato is a contentious issue in *sean-nós* style, considered by most of the major writers on the topic as "absolutely foreign" (Breathnach 1971:101). Ó Riada seems to have thought it had originally been a stylistic trope in *sean-nós* but that it had died out. The use of vibrato was described by Joe Heaney as "knockin' hell out o' it"; his insistence on the absence of vibrato in his singing is consistent with his general agreement with Ó Riada on the rules. However, generally, a voice without vibrato, using a vocal timbre similar to that of early music, or to some other non-Western styles, for example, is generally preferred. The human voice must vibrate in order to produce sound, but vibrato in this context refers to the wide vibrato of classical opera and bel canto singing. The requisites of ornamentation preclude such vocal production. Although a subtle vibrato may be discerned in Heaney's singing, and indeed in the singing of other *sean-nós* performers, it was important for Heaney to disassociate himself from the very idea of bel canto because the employment of such a schooled vibrato would put him directly in conflict with Gaelic League ideals of authenticity, which he had appropriated and made his own.

Like vibrato, dynamics, that is to say, the raising or lowering of the volume of music in performance, vocal or instrumental, is considered a contaminating nonnative element in traditional Irish music. It is thought to reveal the influence of classical and popular music, and therefore is usually avoided. This style excludes dynamics in vocal effects, to the point that singers who use them are not considered worthy of the title *sean-nós* singer. To be blunt, the use of dynamics raises an instant red flag (Breathnach 1971; Ó Canainn 1978; Ó Riada 1982). Clearly, this aversion centers on both the desire for purity and the fear of polluting the tradition, which so deeply inform much of cultural nationalist rhetoric, and the study of folkloric forms that constitute a part of it. Whether or not it was completely absent from the music is a matter that has not been widely researched.

Considering this theoretical aversion, it is all the more striking that Heaney was given occasionally to softening his tone for effect. A subtle use of what might be described as diminuendo may be heard, for example on his version of "Caoineadh na dTrí Muire" on the Gael Linn album. Heaney dropped the volume of his voice by almost half to sing the final verse of the song (in which Jesus urges his mother not to mourn his death). This judicious use of dynamics is directly contradictory to the words of Breandán Breathnach, who notes the following: "*Crescendo* and *diminuendo* are terms for which one finds no use in the notation of the music, and this rule applies equally to singing and to playing. The use of dynamics betrays the non-native" (1971:90). Clearly Heaney was a native, and an authority; Breathnach would not question Heaney's right to perform as he saw fit. Rather, what this conundrum reveals is that rules cannot be unilaterally

applied in *sean-nós*, and that individual singers use their own idiosyn-
cratic combinations of aesthetics and appropriateness to engage a song's
meaning. Although this is clearly outside the bounds of conventional theoretical precepts as expounded by the main writers, no one has called
attention to Heaney's departure from the norm, at least in writing. Heaney's
use of the device is subtle and well judged, despite its transgressive potential. Heaney knew the rules as well as anyone. His reasons for this departure
cannot be known, but it is likely that this technique met some of his own
performance needs. It increased his effectiveness as a performer and was
therefore acceptable, according to his own definitions of technical and
aesthetic propriety.

A final device commonly used to end a song is speaking the last phrase,
mentioned by many writers (Shields 1993:121; Breathnach 1971:105;
Zimmerman 1966:114; Ó Canainn 1978:80) and easily seen in performance.
While speaking the last phrase of the song does not occur in every
performance, it appears often enough that the participants at the gathering know to join in the final words. Certainly the audience knows the
song, and they always know what to expect from a familiar singer's rendition of a song. All the essentials of good participation, according hospitality
to each singer through attentive listening, and a warm reception following
a song done well are a part of a comprehensive reciprocity that permeates
every aspect of local behavior, including musical performance.

Bilingual Ethnopoetics and Melodic Ornamentation[5]

Although some are strongly rhythmic, those considered true *sean-nós*
songs are usually performed in free rhythm; the rhythm of the song is
independent of any regular beat, and the words do not necessarily have to
fit into any specific time frame.[6] The songs are instead regulated by a
pulse that corresponds to the poetic meter of the language in which
the songs are performed. Joe Heaney himself used the term "pulse," and
its application here is fitting to describe the rhythm of language. Ornamentation or embellishment of the melodic line by the use of melismatic
passages is the key determinant of a Connemara *sean-nós* song and is also
an important aspect of local performance aesthetics. Because the story
told by the song is as important as the song itself, ornamentation can be a
connective feature in that it ties the melody to the text by calling attention
to both.

In this section we differentiate between the famous long melismatic
passages of many of the Connemara singers and the equally interesting
performance practices of *sean-nós* singers from other regions within
Ireland. The regions of Donegal, Cúil Aodha, Waterford, Kerry, and elsewhere outside of Connemara have their own standards of appropriate
performance practice. Heaney, however, exemplifies the Connemara style,
which is characterized in particular by the ornaments detailed in the
following.

Many types of melodic ornaments can occur in a single performance of Connemara *sean-nós* singing. Among these are the long, melismatic ornaments for which Connemara songs are justly famous; short grace notes that can precede or follow a held note from a half step above or below; grace notes used as jumping-off points in crossing a large interval; rolls, turns, wavers, and short glottal stops. The technique of deliberate non-ornamentation as a form of embellishment can be yet another effective means of calling attention to the story of the song: "Ornamentation gives the movement between main notes a logicality and inevitability which it would not otherwise have: it smooths the musical texture and, while indispensable, its overall effect should be so subtle as to make the listener barely aware of it" (Ó Canainn 1978:3).

The long, melismatic ornament is probably the most remarkable aspect of Connemara-style *sean-nós* singing. It is a difficult and creative way of getting from one note to another; but more important, it calls attention to the lyrics being sung. Even ornaments that, because of their complexity, obscure the word being sung, are understood and appreciated as the singer's own personal form of expression. The melisma also serves as an important destabilizing element. Ornamenting an unstressed or weak word or syllable throws off the inherent poetic rhythm of the song, and when the next stressed word occurs unornamented on the pulse, the sense of restabilization is quite strong. This stress and release is an important factor in properly ornamenting a song in this tradition. Note that in each case, the melismatic ornament occurs on an unstressed syllable; though this is not a hard-and-fast rule, it occurs often enough to be noteworthy. In the song "An Raibh Tú ar an gCarraig?" (figure 2.1), the melismatic ornament occurs on the syllable *mé* and is used not only to move gracefully from pitch A to D before it climbs back up again to the A,[7] but—more important—to highlight the difference between this word (*mé*, as in "*I* was on the rock") and *tú* in the previous verse ("were *you* on the rock?").

"Going to Mass Last Sunday" (figure 2.2) contains an example of melisma on the word "Amerikay" and is also a demonstration of the use of melisma to highlight the text. In this song, the singer has been spurned by his sweetheart and plans to emigrate. Performing a melisma on "Amerikay" emphasizes the dramatic choice to leave one's homeland.

In every verse of "An Tighearna Randal" (figure 2.3), a long melisma occurs on the word *dhriotháirín* (little brother). As a refrain, the word serves the same function that the *ochón* does in a religious lament like "Caoineadh na dTrí Muire."[8] It is a symbol for the audience, a

Fig. 2.1: Melisma in "An Raibh Tú ar an gCarraig?"

A - me-ri - - kay lies____ far a - way

Fig. 2.2: Melisma in "Going to Mass Last Sunday"

A____ drio-tháir - - ín_____ ó

Fig. 2.3: Melisma in "An Tighearna Randal"

reminder that this is a woman at a dying man's bedside, asking questions about who poisoned him and what he plans to leave the members of his family.

The second type of ornament is a short grace note that precedes or follows a "functional" tone, which would constitute one of the main melody notes of a song. If a melody is created through these building blocks, then that same melody can also be enhanced through the employment of grace notes. In the following examples of grace notes preceding functional tones, grace-note ornamentation of certain structural tones, such as the fifth and the tonic, is more prevalent than that of almost any other tones. In grace notes preceding these two important tones, ornamentation does not seem to vary much between verses. Grace notes are also used as jumping-off points for intervallic leaps. In the following example (figure 2.4), grace notes precede the longer notes of the final phrase of "A Stór mo Chroí."

and the love____ that's nev - - er____ ol - den.

Fig. 2.4: The final phrase of "A Stór mo Chroí"

Irish instrumentalists use terms like "roll" to describe elements of performance practice, but singers usually do not. Ó Canainn describes melodic ornaments as "a group of adjacent auxiliary notes decorating or replacing a main note of the melody" (1978:71) Nonetheless, the terms "roll" and "turn" are used here with the aim of clarifying how particular ornaments appear in singing. Rolls—in which a note is highlighted by notes above and below it in a linear fashion, as in d-e-d-c-d—are distinguished from turns by the fact that a roll returns to the same note that it started on, whereas a turn ends up on a different note. Rolls usually occur one at a time, as in the word *ngrásta* in this line from the song "Anach Cuain"—the roll starts and ends on the D (figure 2.5).

A   Rí   na   nGrás -   ta

Fig. 2.5: Roll in "Anach Cuain"

A turn is defined by its limitation to stepwise motion and to a cluster of five or six notes at a time. It leaves one note and ends up on another nearby note such as from an A to a G, having made a brief circuit of the first note's neighboring tones. A turn may rise or fall. However, a turn normally becomes a melisma when the rule of stepwise motion is broken and when many more notes than the usual five or six are sung. In the following phrase from "Bean a' Leanna" (figure 2.6), the turn occurs on the final word, *leanna*.

Ó__   éir - igh'n____   do shuí__ bhean   a'   lean - na

Fig. 2.6: Turn in "Bean a' Leanna"

The waver is not necessarily characteristic of all *sean-nós* singers but may be specific to certain performers only (Heaney among them). The technique of wavering on a single note involves a slight tonal oscillation or instability of pitch, somewhere between a vibrato and a roll. The waver is slower than a vibrato and actually seems to include microtonal variants on each side of the main pitch, yet these variants are not quite distinguishable enough aurally to pinpoint as an ornamental roll. Transcriptions of wavers do not graphically illustrate what wavers sound like but simply point to their occurrence. Heaney deliberately chose certain pitches on which to waver, particularly the fourth or seventh degree of an upward-moving melody. It is related to a slide because of its position in the melody. The waver occasionally appears in verses in the same place that a more clearly defined turn would occur in another verse, and is a technique of variation.

Some *sean-nós* singers employ the technique known as the glottal stop. This involves stopping the air in the throat between important parts of a line, then continuing almost immediately afterward, with no break for a breath. According to Heaney, the purpose of the glottal stop is to call attention to that particular line. In some cases, the stop occurs where the singer would normally take a breath, but most often it occurs at a non-breathing point. When the singer stops for a fraction of a second, the word immediately preceding the stop can be echoed in the listener's mind, and the words just following the stop can be heard more clearly because of the stop.[9]

Occasionally singers proceed straight through a line with no ornamentation. Although Heaney never specifically discussed contrasting verses by using non-ornamentation, he may have used this technique to outline the words without distraction. It is likely that non-ornamentation may be more deliberate than circumstantial. The preceding examples have demonstrated types of ornaments used in *sean-nós* performance.

In a particularly interesting interview from tape #78–15.9 of the Joe Heaney Collection at the University of Washington Ethnomusicology Archives, Heaney was asked to contrast an unornamented verse of a song with an ornamented one. He chose the song "The Rocks of Bawn," one of his personal favorites (see chapter 5). After puzzling about how to *un*-ornament a song for a minute, he launched into the following first verse (figure 2.7):

Fig. 2.7: Unornamented verse of "The Rocks of Bawn"

Fig. 2.8: Ornamented verse of "The Rocks of Bawn"

Fig. 2.9: Unornamented line from a verse of "The Rocks of Bawn"

Joe Heaney then offered a particularly heavily ornamented version of the same verse (figure 2.8), duplicating some of the ornaments that he could not leave out of the verse, but adding much more to it. In most performances of this song, Heaney generally chooses not to ornament a particular opening phrase to a verse later in the song: "and my curse attend you Sweeney." In the next example (figure 2.9), contrast what Heaney does with this opening line and what he does to open the song in the previous example.

Figure 2.9 highlights the ways in which Heaney—and other singers—could draw attention to a phrase that would normally be ornamented by making it stark; contrast, then, the florid decoration of "come all you loyal heroes" in figure 2.8 with the cursing sensibility of figure 2.9. Now that each ornament type or technique has been illustrated, we may examine how ornaments are used and where they are most likely to appear.

Ornamentation in Irish-Language Songs

Although the idea of the pulse in *sean-nós* singing was briefly discussed earlier, it is fundamental to an understanding of the ornamentation of *sean-nós* songs and therefore warrants more explanation. As mentioned earlier in this chapter, Joe Heaney vaguely referred to ornamentation when he said, "You get away from the melody for a bit, and then come right back to it on the pulse" (see Cowdery 1990:35–36 for more discussion). In other words, ornamentation should *not* occur on the pulse. The pulse in *sean-nós* singing is influenced by poetic rhythm. For example, in the song "Eileanóir a Rún" (see chapter 5), the poetic stress of a line that reads "Eileanóir a rún" ("Eleanor My Treasure") occurs on both the first syllable of the word *Eileanóir* and on the word *rún*. Using the general idea that ornamentation occurs on unstressed syllables in Irish-language songs, it would follow that ornamentation can occur on the third syllable of the name Eileanóir, which indeed it does in figure 2.10.

Ornamentation is also influenced by melodic contour. In the following example (figure 2.11), the word *acu* (from the song "Anach Cuain") includes a melisma on the unstressed syllable but also guides the singer from one note to another so as to reach the tonic. It appears consistent, not just in this example but in many others, that two main criteria for ornamentation are melodic considerations and poetic stress patterns.

Fig. 2.10: Unstressed ornamentation in "Eileanóir a Rún"

lán   an   bháid___   a - cu_____   a   sua-ba   ar   súil.

Fig. 2.11: Ornamentation influenced by melodic contour
in "Anach Cuain"

The phenomenon of melodically ornamenting unstressed syllables has
been observed but not clearly defined as specific to Irish-language songs
by Travis in his *Early Celtic Versecraft* (1973:15). He includes a brief
discussion of the influences between music and words and does mention
that "the influence of Celtic song on associated verse would be to lighten
the intensity of strong vocal stresses, and to lengthen the duration of weak
stresses." By lengthening the duration of weak stresses—in other words,
allowing more time for unstressed syllables to be ornamented—ornamentation is an appropriate fill-in element.

Tomás Ó Canainn also mentions the ornamentation of unstressed
syllables, describing the "main beats" of songs as unornamented. He
does, however, point out that this same main beat is "usually quitted
with a decoration, so that the ear is led smoothly to the next main beat"
(1978:115). Therefore, although he does mention the connection of
ornamentation to pulse, he does not specifically point to where ornamentation occurs. Many examples of this scheme of prescriptive
ornamentational grammar occur throughout Irish-language *sean-nós*
songs.

In the song "Amhrán na Páise" (see chapter 4), the chorus primarily
comprises ornaments on the word *aililiú*. It is appropriate, considering
that this is a lament for Easter Sunday, that the refrain would contain a
word such as *aililiú* to tie the verses together and keep the sacred quality
of the song. The melismatic ornament of this example (figure 2.12) occurs
on the last, unstressed syllable of *aililiú*.

It should be clarified that the tendency toward ornamentation of
unstressed syllables is not always applied. The melody line of the song
is an essential factor in the ornamentation of a song. If the melody calls
for ornamentation of a certain note throughout the course of the song,
then the word that corresponds to that note will be ornamented whether
it is unstressed or stressed. Another reason for a singer to melodically
ornament a stressed syllable is that when the melody line moves only
one or two notes at a time, the singer is likely to add a turn or a roll for
decoration, rather than singing the line plainly. It may therefore be
taken as a general tendency in the development of a grammar for the

ail - li - liú_____

Fig. 2.12: Unstressed ornamentation on *aililiú* in "Amhrán na Páise"

ornamentation of Connemara-style Irish-language songs that a melisma, turn, or roll occurs on unstressed syllables, except when overruled by melodic contour.

Ornamentation in English-Language Songs

In the same way that the pulse or poetic meter of Irish metric structure can be an important determining factor in the ornamentation of Irish-language *sean-nós* songs, the pulse of the English language similarly affects songs in English. Although not nearly as predictable as the Irish language, ornamentation in English-language *sean-nós* songs does depend on poetic meter. "The Nobleman's Wedding" was developed in accordance with Irish syntactical structure; it corresponds to the rules governing ornamentation in Irish-language songs. In examining one line of "The Nobleman's Wedding," it is evident that this song is ornamented in the same way as an Irish-language song. The line, if read normally, emphasizes "I *once* was in*vit*ed to a *noble*man's *wed*ding." The pulse in that line occurs on the words "once," "invited" (second syllable), "nobleman" (first syllable), and "wedding" (first syllable). Accordingly, ornamentation occurs on words outside the pulse, particularly the second and third syllables of "nobleman" (figure 2.13). The nobility of the character is highlighted here through the use of melisma. James Cowdery has also offered the idea that Heaney's ornamentation of the word "nobleman" has a touch of irony to it, considering that the nobleman's behavior in the song is ultimately less than noble (Cowdery, personal communication).

Songs in English can be divided into two categories: those derived from Gaelic melodies, and using Hiberno-English, and those of British origin. Ornamentation on unstressed syllables in English-language songs occurs most often when the songs use Irish-language poetic rhythms or are literal translations from the Irish. Unstressed syllables can be ornamented in a stylistically correct way even in songs using more standard forms of syntax. O'Boyle briefly discusses the differences between songs composed in Hiberno-English and those composed in English that bore no relation to what was commonly being spoken in Ireland (1976:15). He claims that although the latter category of songs are not Irish metrically, they do express a certain Irish character, either through their melodic lines or through what is being spoken textually. Therefore, they ought to be

Fig. 2.13: Unstressed ornamentation on the first line of "The Nobleman's Wedding"

considered as Irish as songs that do conform more to the normal poetic structure of Irish song. It is likely that these songs derive their origins from the large body of Irish song types borrowed or inherited from the English and Scottish songs of the seventeenth and eighteenth centuries.

The real problem in the ornamentation of English-language *sean-nós* songs is that the stress patterns (and, therefore, the ornamentation) can be much less predictable. It is clear that English *sean-nós* songs using Irish syntax and meter follow most of the same rules that govern ornamentation of Irish-language *sean-nós* songs. Other English songs seem to rely more upon following the contours of the melodic line for ornamentation than anything as simple-sounding as ornamenting unstressed syllables. Although influenced by Irish ornamentation, songs in English are primarily ornamented according to the melodic line. Consequently, they tend to utilize fairly simple forms of ornamentation such as rolls, turns, and grace notes, without the very long melismatic ornaments.

One example of a song derived from English tradition in which ornamentation follows the preceding ideas is "The Trees They Grow Tall." Here, notice that the poetic rhythm is basically iambic; in other words, stress occurs on every second word or second syllable:

> As *I* was *walk*ing *down by* the *col*lege *wall*
> I saw *four* and *twen*ty *col*lege *boys* a-*play*ing *with* their *ball*
> *There* I *spied* my *own* true *love*, the *fair*est *of* them *all*
> *For* my *bon*nie *boy* was *young*, and *grow*ing.

In this example the rhythm of the melody in each line seems to clear up any problems in iambic ambiguity, so that even though discrepancies exist, the singer may be able to adjust the melody to rework the poetic stress (figure 2.14). Although ornamentation occurs on unstressed syllables, a large proportion of turns occur on stressed syllables, following the melodic line. This method of ornamentation is stylistically correct because of its emphasis on the importance of the melody, rather than on the grammatical rules.

In the preceding example, the words "by" on the first line, "playing" and "with" on the second line, "of" on the third line, and "boy" on the fourth were all examples of stress-word ornamentation. In each case, however, the ornamentation occurred because Heaney followed the melody line and chose to decorate the otherwise straightforward stepwise movement

Fig. 2.14: Reworking the poetic stress by adjusting the melody of "The Trees They Grow Tall"

with a turn. Otherwise, the fairly meager ornamentation occurs on unstressed syllables as is to be expected.

Any discussion of ornamentation in Irish song should conclude with an emphasis on the importance of ornamentation as an outlet for the singer to put his or her own feelings into the song. Although the implication here is that songs in the English language are always less ornamented than songs sung in Irish, if Joe Heaney felt very strongly about the meaning of a song in either language, he would decorate it more. Heaney may also have ornamented them more because of their personal meaning to him and not necessarily because they were in the Irish language. Therefore, in both Irish and English songs that use Irish syntax or poetic rhythm, ornamentation occurs most often on unstressed syllables, whereas in songs utilizing a non-Irish form of syntax or poetic stress, ornamentation is guided by melodic contour.

James Cowdery's book *The Melodic Tradition of Ireland* (1990) includes interviews with Joe Heaney in which Heaney emphasizes his love for particular airs, his need to hold on to certain melodic lines, and the need to do things his own way in discussing the ornamentation of the song "Going to Mass Last Sunday": "'I don't think I ever heard a more beautiful air than that, you know. I love that song, I love to sing it, and I love it so much that I don't want to leave it. I just want to hold on to it as long as I can when I'm singing it. That's the way to treat a good song'" (Cowdery 1990:31).

In holding on to a song through the judicious but effective use of melismatic ornamentation—together with all the other technical virtuosity that Heaney was able to employ—he felt that he was doing justice not only to the melodic composition but to the content of the lyrics and, by extension, his entire tradition. For Heaney, to highlight something for which his region is justifiably famous was to celebrate Connemara singing as the ultimate in *sean-nós*. His claim that anyone singing *sean-nós* at home sang the way he did was not so much an effort to exclude the Ulster and Munster styles but rather to point out that within his own area, he should not be considered remarkable.

Heaney's university students undoubtedly comprised highly gifted individuals who were accustomed to being proficient on a wide range of instruments. This proficiency included different languages and their disparate forms of vocal production and technique. Such individuals, who hoped to be able to sing competently in Irish with only a small effort, were often brought up short by Heaney's exacting standards. Identifying the source of this seemingly insuperable challenge as Heaney's ornamentation, they were sometimes apt to forget that the ornaments were bound up with the very sounds of the language itself.

The obsession with how to ornament a song properly—comments about which were ubiquitous in questions from students and audience members alike—may not even reflect the impossibility of ornamentation. Rather, the fetishization of ornamentation referred to by Steve Coleman may reflect instead the audience focus on what it was that made these songs so different from the songs with which they were familiar. An audience familiar only with primarily syllabic forms of singing, in which each syllable is performed on a single note, would be unprepared for sixteen or twenty notes in rapid succession on a single syllable, or for the seemingly infinite ability of a singer like Joe Heaney to vary the ornaments from verse to verse. Thus, while the actual technique of ornamentation can be (somewhat) demystified, Heaney's taste and artistry cannot.

Part II

๛◑◐๛

The Iconic Repertoire

This second part has as its focus an array of songs that were considered by many to represent the best of Joe Heaney's repertoire. Any selection that claims to represent iconic items in a singer's repertoire, however, will undoubtedly reflect personal choices. Consequently, it runs the danger of not fulfilling the expectations of those familiar with Heaney's songs. The following three chapters nonetheless attempt to develop a coherent discourse in understanding aspects of Heaney's song repertoire. He had a large storehouse of full and complete texts and airs that he performed regularly in different contexts, and also an extensive repository of fragments and less complete items, from which he drew frequently as he illustrated points in order to drive them home to both students and followers. Nevertheless, it is important to try to accomplish this recognition of a few of the salient items that are more than ordinarily important for an understanding of Heaney the man, as well as Heaney the singer.

We refer to these songs as iconic, a term that deserves some glossing here. It is used in the sense that these texts are icons or images that represent aspects of reality, specifically Heaney's reality or world. In his frequent performances of these items, Heaney unfolded a world in front of itself (Ricoeur 1983:81). Such depictions augment reality by telling a narrative, a story. There is the story of the text itself, the historical circumstances that led to its making; the events that befall its characters and how things turned out in the end. There is also the more immediate story of Heaney's inclusion of these disparate narratives into his regular repertoire, as images that redescribe reality in *his* terms, telling *his* story with meanings that themselves depend upon "the virtues of abbreviation, saturation, and culmination" to form a plot (Ricoeur 1983:80). It is this aspect of the songs that is most interesting, and the reason that they are described as iconic.

The following three chapters, then, ostensibly deal with unrelated aspects of history and memory. However, they emerged from one embodied mind, as parts representing the whole. In performing the Famine, or the faith of his people, or the exploits of the great Cearbhall Ó Dálaigh, Heaney provided an immediate engagement with *his* Ireland.

3

⤳⟲⟲⟲⤶

Singing the Famine

---

 ongs dealing specifically with the Great Famine of 1845–50 are rare in
Irish oral tradition, although some do exist.[1] Joe Heaney came from a
community in which some of these were current in the local repertoire
and, indeed, part of his own family heritage. He was often asked about the
Famine during his years in the United States, where a popular awareness
of the catastrophe has become associated with the narrative of Irish immigration. Heaney consequently had a well-established performance
sequence that dealt with the Famine, including local narratives and, especially, one song in English that he offered as an interpretation of this
seminal event in modern Irish history. His was an alternative history, differing from, but not completely independent of, official academic historiography. It constituted a kind of history telling that placed the events of
the Famine at a microlevel, allowing his audiences to deal with its events
on a personal level. While containing factual errors, his narratives also
contained some factual truth and—more important perhaps for the audiences—emotional truths that could have a powerful cathartic effect
(Beiner 2007:81–85). It is interesting to note, however, that Heaney did not
sing a song called "Johnny Seoighe," which deals with events directly
connected with hunger and want in his own parish of Maigh Ros. This
song remained off limits, and a consideration of the song's life as a
performance item, its relationship to the English song he did choose to
sing, and the reasons he may have had for his avoidance of it in public
form the basis of the current chapter.

In early November 2005, Pól Ó Ceannabháin, a nineteen-year-old of An
Aird Thoir, Ard East, Joe Heaney's own townland, Carna, County Galway,
participated in the adult *sean-nós* competitions at the Oireachtas festival
for the first time. The young man chose "Johnny Seoighe" as one of his
songs, which by then did not stand out in any way except that it was
regarded as a particularly good choice. Ó Ceannabháin perfectly embodied
the vocal style that has made his home region justly famous during his

performance of the three-verse song with an aaba structure and a modal air. Originally first recorded by Séamus Ennis (1961), the song has become widely sung since Seán Mac Donnchadha (Johnny Mháirtín Learaí) and the late Seán 'ac Dhonnchadha (Johnny Joe Pheaitsín) (1919–96), Heaney's boyhood friend, both also from the Carna area, recorded it (see the discography).[2] These recordings made the song a "hit" among singers, and it was subsequently recorded by some (see, for example, recordings by Ó Flathartha and Ó Faracháin).

The interest in and dispersal of "Johnny Seoighe" show the influence of recording on recent Irish transmission patterns. However, the song has only relatively recently come to be considered a suitable item for public performance. Associated with people living in the Iorras Aithneach or Carna region during the Great Famine of 1845–50, it was a song that could and, in the past, did attract controversy. Conflicts alluded to in the song were very much alive in the minds of the twentieth-century descendants of those involved in events that led to its making, regardless of the time that had elapsed. Even now, many local people are shy of discussing the song and its events. Thus, we do not probe deeply into the narrative details surrounding the song in the area, choosing instead to respect the privacy of those who would prefer that these details not be aired, especially in print. The song continues to be a live issue.

Here, instead, we follow some threads pertaining to that conflict, particularly in relation to Joe Heaney's career. As already mentioned, Heaney did *not* sing this powerful song as far as we can discover from a search of the sound archives, though he mentioned its existence multiple times. Given the frequency with which Americans asked Heaney to discuss the Famine, and how he readily responded to such questions by narrating and singing about it, his avoidance of the song is conspicuous. We consider here some plausible interpretations of its absence and go on to discuss examples of what Heaney did choose, in fact, to say and sing as a representation of the Famine. Finally, we explore the relationships between the various texts and tunes discussed here and offer insights into Heaney's American performance contexts and his rapport with American listeners.

Cormac Ó Gráda discusses some ambiguous and contradictory narratives told about "Johnny Seoighe" in his short but groundbreaking work on Famine songs and folklore (1994), republished and developed in his 1999 book (see also Ó Gráda 2001). Ó Gráda's study reveals two distinct and opposing views of the song in its home district of Carna, where Pól Ó Ceannabháin grew up as a member of a musically distinguished family, in a region renowned for its rich oral traditions, including especially song; it was the same region that produced Heaney (for a brief discussion on the richness of the Carna area for folklore, see Alwyn and Rees 1978; uí Ógáin 2009, Partridge [Bourke] 2007).[3]

Ó Gráda reveals that some local people view "Johnny Seoighe" as a panegyric in honor of a charitable distributor of meal during the Famine. Others, however, regard the song as a biting satire on Johnny Seoighe because of his high-handed and unjust treatment of those affected by the calamity.[4] For this reason the song long remained taboo, sung only in restricted gatherings. Indeed, tracing the chain of transmission of "Johnny Seoighe" from a secret song seldom sung in public to one that many of today's singers include in their repertoire shows how slender that chain was and how the project of folklore collection undertaken by the Irish Folklore Commission in 1935 influenced it.

Séamus Ennis, chosen because of his formidable communication skills, as well as his musical abilities as a piper, a singer, and, crucially, someone with a high level of musical literacy, was appointed a collector of music for the Irish Folklore Commission in late May 1942 (uí Ógáin 2007:10–14, 2009; see also Briody 2007: 277–80). His first field trip took him to Carna, where he struck up a friendship with a singer named Colm Ó Caodháin that blossomed into a fruitful singer-collector relationship.[5] This association resulted in the accumulation of more than 200 songs from Ó Caodháin for the Irish Folklore Commission. Ennis recorded "Johnny Seoighe" from Ó Caodháin, subsequently incorporating it into his own repertoire and singing it on a commercial recording (Ennis 2006 [1961]). On this record, he presents the positive view of Johnny Seoighe as a charitable figure. Interestingly, it was from Ennis's singing, and not from neighbors or relatives in Iorras Aithneach, that both Johnny Mháirtín Learaí and Johnny Joe Pheaitsín acquired the song, a fact further emphasizing the secrecy surrounding it (Ó Gráda 1999:239). Indeed, Johnny Joe Pheaitsín (Seán 'Ac Dhonnchadha) remembered being publicly criticized for performing this song in the Damer Hall in Dublin at the *Oícheanta Seanchais* (Folklore Nights) concerts organized by Gael Linn in the late fifties and early sixties (Carolan 2003: 6-31).[6] These renowned entertainments were attended by many Gaeltacht people living and working in Dublin. Heaney was also a featured guest at these nights, returning from Southhampton to participate.

Historiography of the Famine

Clearly, the song "Johnny Seoighe" has come a long way from a rarely performed item, known to few and hidden from outsiders, to one sung openly in a major competitive event, broadcast live nationally on radio. Its status as a piece directly linked to the Great Famine of 1845–50 bears directly upon the secrecy and controversy that for so long surrounded it. The Famine, until the 150-year commemoration in 1997, was not a part of the Irish history or folklore prominent in public discussion in Ireland. Indeed, an air of shame and denial characterized popular memory. Ó Gráda comments that the linking of sympathy expressed in Ireland for recent modern famines elsewhere with Irish Famine memory is largely a modern invention, reflecting the fact that Irish Famine memory has long centered around a number of key words—"Black '47, mass mortality, the potato, emigration, clearances, fever, official neglect" (Ó Gráda 1999:3). Indeed, the popular nationalist interpretation of the Famine, particularly in the Irish American diaspora, has gone so far as to apply the term "geno-cide" to the catastrophe, which most historians, nationalist or otherwise, refuse to accept. Many nationalists, however, have leveled this charge at the British government for its mishandling of the Famine crisis. Ó Gráda rejects this accusation, preferring the term "doctrinaire neglect" (Ó Gráda 1999:10). David Lloyd argues that such rigid British attitudes were shaped by a desire to create a new, modernized, disciplined Irish subject, in which values of patience, prudence, and industry would replace shiftlessness and sentimentality, requiring "the subordination of that most undisciplined of Irish orifices, the mouth," an idea with particular relevance for this discussion of Famine narratives and songs (2003:214).

James S. Donnelly shows how the construction of public memory of the Famine reveals that the terms of debate and the basis for the dominant nationalist narrative were established as soon as the Famine began. Discussing the many critics of the Famine from 1850 to 1900, he finds a nationalist memorial narrative constructed upon a rhetorically cogent repetition of selective and often dubious statistical analysis, much of which can be refuted on factual grounds. He contends that the unremit-tingly bitter allegations of genocide from Irish America in particular stem from a steady stream of writings by John Mitchel and other nationalists. These writings include personal recollections of evictions and large-scale clearances, the callous official attitude to Irish distress and mortality dis-played by some important organs of the British press, and, finally, the sense of moral outrage that such a humanitarian disaster should have happened in the backyard of what was then the world's richest nation. For nationalists, this incontestable disgrace weighs more importantly than any factual evidence that can be amassed to dismantle their arguments on the question of food exports. Donnelly further suggests that accepting the validity of such a sense of grievance is equally as important as maintaining an accurate record of what provoked it (1996:26–61). Beiner's argument for the importance of including vernacular ways of history in official his-toriography claims that "each historical tradition can operate on several levels and carry various meanings in different contexts" (2007:11). Such a claim validates the ways in which Heaney's narratives and songs satisfied his audiences' need to relate to the Famine in ways not readily available from official history books.

The discussion of the memory of the Famine as interpreted and dissemi-nated through written sources prompts questions about oral evidence for Famine experiences. The Irish Folklore Commission issued a questionnaire in 1945, designed to collect accounts of the Famine. Folklore of this kind is often discounted by historians as being "selective, evasive and apologetic," as Ó Gráda has put it (1999:195; see also Póirtéir 1995). There is some jus-tification for the suspicion of folk memory because its facts are often plain wrong, confusing details from different periods and conferring them with the authority of tradition, often adding what Patricia Lysaght refers to as a kind of "schematization," by which she means the incorporation of well-worn narrative motifs into the stories (1999:21–47; 1996–97:63–131).

Henry Glassie, discussing the phenomenon of inaccurate chronology in oral history, has remarked that oral history tends to be "set...primarily in space, only secondarily in time" (1982:633–34). As Ó Gráda further points out, "The reliability of oral tradition hinges ultimately on the reliability of people's memories of things they witnessed and heard," also showing, from his examination of the surviving folk record, that "twentieth-century images of bloated bellies or skeletal emaciation find virtually no echoes in the folklore material collected in Ireland" (1999:197). Nevertheless, the Famine material collected by the Irish Folklore Commission in the 1940s has yielded interesting observations and powerful images of the suffering endured. However, as all commentators on this material indicate, it was gathered mostly from people who were born after the Famine and who did not actually witness events themselves (McHugh 1956 [1995]:391–406). Beiner agrees that "folk histories do not adhere to the criteria of professional historiography [but] this does not mean they are one-dimensional or unsophisticated" (2007:11). If approached with a sympathetic skepticism and with suitable horizons of understanding regarding its opportunities and limitations, however, folk memory in general and of the Famine in particular can reveal much vivid anecdotal detail about the popular attitudes of the time. Such detail can only augment the official record.

"Johnny Seoighe" as Mediator of Folk Memory

The song "Johnny Seoighe" provides an excellent example of how folk memory can add to the picture we have of the Famine by drawing attention to a particular event or sequence of events. As in many other Irish songs, the verses are allusive, evoking a "previously undefined context of intimacy" but providing no direct linear narrative (Shields 1993:74). Songs in this style depend on a separately told story, called *údar*, *brí*, or *scéal*, for their fullest interpretation, consequently leaving them open to multiple and varying readings (Shields 1993:82–83). The conflict about the correct meaning of "Johnny Seoighe" discloses the often irreconcilable oppositions that may coexist in outwardly harmonious communities, testifying to the Famine's "unequal and divisive" impact (Ó Gráda 2001:121). Therefore, because of the contested stories that adhere to it, the song can provide no support for a simplistic binary division of helpless Irish people maltreated at the hands of the hateful English.

In the lyrics, the singer approaches Johnny Seoighe in the first stanza with the traditional high praise that one would find in much older texts (see, for example, praise songs in honor of lords, kings, drink, and swords in Hoagland 1999). A narrative begins in the second stanza, when we learn that the singer has no hope of obtaining relief tickets in spite of having traveled far, that his family is homeless, and that the workhouse, which might have provided some kind of employment for him, is full. In the final stanza the song returns to one of praise, this time in honor of "the queen":

'S a Johnny Seoighe, tuig mo ghlórtha, 'S mé tíocht le dóchas faoi do dhéin
Mar is tú an Réalt Eolais is deise lóchrann, as mo shúil ag Teampall Dé.
Is tú bláth na hóige, is binne glórtha, dhearc mo shúil ó rugadh mé
Agus as ucht Chríost, is tabhair dom relief, nó go gcaitear Oíche Nollag féin.

Ó 'gus lá arna mháireach fuair mé an páipéar, 's nach mé a bhí sásta 's ghabh
*   mé 'un siúil*
Ach ní bhfuair mé freagra ar bith an lá sin, ach mé fhéin 's mo pháistí amuigh
*   faoin drúcht.*
Tá mé tuirseach, sciúrtha, feannta, liobraithe, gearrtha ó neart an tsiúil
Is a Mhister Joyce, tá an workhouse lán, is ní glacfar ann isteach níos mó.

'S nach mór a' cliú do bhaile Chárna, an fhad 's tá an lánúin seo a' goil
*   thríd*
'S gur deise breáichte dreach na mná, ná an "Morning Star" nuair a éiríonn sí
Tá an bhánríon tinn, is í go lag ina luí, 's deir dochtúirí go bhfaighidh sí bás
'S gurb bé fios a húdair léir mar deir siad liomsa, nuair nach bhfuil sí póstaí
*   ag Mister Joyce.*

Oh Johnny Joyce, heed my voice, as I come to you full of hope
For you are the Star of Knowledge, the brightest beacon in the Temple of
   God.
You are the flower of youth, of the finest speech that my eye has seen since
   I was born
And for the love of Christ, grant me relief, or at least until Christmas Eve
   is past.

And on the next day I got the piece of paper, and wasn't I the happy one,
   and I set out
But I got no answer at all that day, but myself and my children left out
   under the dew.
I am tired, bitter, lashed, frozen, upset, and lacerated because of my stren-
   uous journey
And Mister Joyce, the workhouse is full, and they won't accept any more
   people inside.

It is a great source of fame to the town of Carna while this couple is passing
   through
For the woman's appearance is as fine as the Morning Star when it
   shines.
The queen is ill and lying low, the doctors say that she will die
The reason for it all as they say to me, that she is not married to Mister
   Joyce.

Johnny Seoighe, addressed also as "Mr. Joyce" in the song, whether in
praise or in irony, was, according to one view, an Irish opportunist from

the nearby district of Oughterard, who allegedly tried to usurp the position of the local relief distribution officer. Likewise, Peg Barry, the woman named as *an bhanríon*, "the queen," reputedly his mistress in the story that supports a reading of the song as satire, is also clearly no *Gall*, but of Irish descent. Moreover, because of the taint of sexual irregularity, a conventional scenario of "saints and scholars" abused by "heretical foreigners" cannot be adduced from its elements. Therefore, the song introduces inconvenient shadings to a stark black-and-white picture of Irish versus English, exposing the fact that the poor and helpless were sometimes victimized by those who shared their ethnicity.

However, for Pól Ó Ceannabháin's 2005 debut, such considerations seem to have been secondary to the choice of a good song with a grand, sweeping, modal air (figure 3.1) combined with an equally gripping story. Arguably, the song's associations with Famine-era corruption and wrongdoings had been mitigated by its acceptable performance in public in the years since the two Seán Mac Dhonnchadhas had recorded it commercially. In a purely aesthetic sense, the song is no less powerful in some ways, but if it has lost its mordant edge as a direct commentary on community values and mores for some, for others it remains disputatious territory.[7]

This discussion of "Johnny Seoighe" in both its present and its past situations may be further contextualized in light of the career of Joe Heaney. As Fred McCormick has noted, Heaney performed different songs for different audiences with different expectations throughout his life.[8] No recording of Joe Heaney singing "Johnny Seoighe" has, so far, been identified. If he ever sang it, it is not now a song closely associated with him. The standard Gaelic items in Heaney's repertoire that come to mind include the great classic versions of the songs of his native townland and parish—"Eileanóir a Rún," "An Buinneán Buí," "Úna Bhán," "Amhrán na hEascainne," "Bean a' Leanna," "An Droighneán Donn," "Caoineadh na dTrí Muire," "Casadh an tSúgáin," "An Sagairtín," and others (some of

Fig. 3.1: "Johnny Seoighe"

which are treated elsewhere in this book). But it is difficult to think of "Johnny Seoighe" and of Joe Heaney together. In fact, the song was originally more closely associated with Séamus Ennis, with Johnny Mháirtín Learaí, and with Heaney's friend and neighbour Seán 'ac Dhonnchadha (Johnny Joe Pheaitsín), and the chain of transmission that led to that association has also been partly traced.

Heaney's Presentation of the Famine

Heaney was often asked about the Famine during his performances and workshops in America, and he felt obliged to come up with answers to those questions. As discussed earlier, a large element of the popular memory of the Famine was produced by nationalist writers in Ireland and in the United States between 1850 and 1900, which included claims of food leaving the country while the poor starved, bitter testimony about wholesale clearances and of an uncompromising British antipathy to the Irish crisis. Such viewpoints must certainly have informed the understanding of audiences who came to listen to Heaney, as they also would have influenced his own beliefs about the Famine experience.

We contend that in Ireland and Britain, neither Heaney nor his audiences would have prioritized the Famine as a major element in performance. In the United States, though, it was to become one of his performative focal points during concerts and recitals, particularly during the final years of his life, when the political situation of Northern Ireland became front-page news in the United States. The hunger strikers of the H-Block were known by name to many attending Heaney's performances. The irony of hunger loomed large in the minds of some of his audience members, and the hunger of 1845–50 became conflated with the hunger strikes of 1981 in Belfast. Naturally, Heaney's audience members had questions about Irish and British politics, and their curiosity represented a uniquely American way of understanding Irishness through the politics of loss (see, for example, Hayden 1997).

It is significant, then, that Heaney never availed of "Johnny Seoighe" as a way to answer these questions about the Famine in Ireland. Occasionally, in workshops he would allude to an Irish-language song about the Famine but invariably refused to sing it, claiming that "nobody sings it anymore" and, when pressed, that "it belonged to other people." Because of the ambiguity in the narrative or údar of the song, and because of its status during Heaney's youth and early adulthood as a "secret" song, it is highly likely that he was referring directly to "Johnny Seoighe" in his attempts to interpret or explain the Famine to students or others. Such a claim is strengthened by the fact that his brother Seán collected a version from their father, Pádhraic Ó h-Éighnigh[9] in 1932 (Ní Fhlaitheartaigh 1976).

There is also a tradition that Heaney got into trouble for recording another song from his home area that was considered sensitive.[10] The song's association with Séamus Ennis, together with Heaney's rivalry with him, documented by Tom Munnelly, may have also contributed (*Dál gCais* 7, 1984, quoted in Mac Con Iomaire 2000). Additionally, the fact that the song was in Irish, that it had a story with a shameful element, and that he himself agreed with the view that it should not be sung in public are other plausible reasons for his avoidance of "Johnny Seoighe."

Without the song and its narrative to rely upon, how did Heaney perform the Famine for his audiences in the United States? Heaney told stories and sang about the Famine that succeeded in moving his audiences and satisfying their curiosity about the disaster. Such narratives and songs reveal important aspects of Heaney's relationship with his American listeners, and indeed with his own repertoire, particularly when we frame them against a backdrop of the Carna *seanchas*. Heaney tells a short Famine story to a student during an interview:

> That's how they made their living, lobster or any kind of fish at all, any kind of fish they caught, you know, that was there, even during the Famine, when things were getting very bad, people from other parts of Ireland used to come around. And they used to build them a little hut out in the field, they couldn't take them into their house because these people had, were sick, and had the disease, you know. They used to bring plates out, plates of fish, and food, and give it to them outside. Now the people in the village, they were well fed, because this is what they lived off, the sea, you know. And when these people died, they buried them where they died, and digging the ground around that, sowing crops, you can see mounds of earth six feet high, that nobody dare touch it. But anytime we were going to school, we were asked to throw a little stone there, and say a prayer for that particular person; nobody knew who they were. And they left a lot of songs around that area too, and a lot of the songs I think came from people like that. Especially the English ballads.[11]

Here, Heaney indicates the people's wariness of catching fever from the destitute by feeding them outside, a method that was also availed of in other areas (Póirtéir 1996). He ends the anecdote with a reference to English-language songs, in order to refocus on that part of his store of knowledge. His claim that the people of Carna were well fed because of their access to seafood is interesting, in that other accounts from the area corroborate his. It creates an effective counternarrative to the prevailing attitudes toward Gaelic backwardness and poverty. According to his account, it was mainly "people from other parts of Ireland" who were begging alms that were adversely affected. Nevertheless, as Ó Gráda has deduced from a survey of similar stories from other areas in the archives of the Folklore Commission, "perhaps the belief that one's own area was spared occurs too frequently to be plausible" (1999:205).

Statistics show that in the parish of Maigh Ros in West Connemara, the population declined from 11,969 in 1841 to 8,558 in 1851. Although this figure is not directly attributable to famine mortality, it nevertheless indicates that Heaney's narrative is partial at best. Another narrative from Carna reveals that the storyteller Éamonn Liam 'A Búrc kept silent about certain extreme cases, believing that to speak aloud about them was *peacúch*, "sinful" (Ó Gráda 1999:212; for 'A Búrc, see Ó Ceannabháin 1983). Such stories are also confirmed by Heaney.

Heaney's anecdote also refers to, but does not provide significant detail about, survival strategies, confirming to some degree Ó Gráda's claims of evasion, apology, and selectivity. It is difficult to think that for Heaney this could have been otherwise, since he was born more than two generations after the Famine, and also because silence was the preferred response to certain harrowing events and details of the Famine.[12] Heaney does not mention the souphouse remembered in another Famine song from his area, "Souphouse Mhaigh Rois" ("The Souphouse of Maigh Ros"), and we have already speculated about possible reasons that he avoided singing "Johnny Seoighe." For Heaney, though, storytelling and singing were part of an indivisible whole, elements in which he was deeply invested as a performer. It was almost inconceivable that he should recount Famine narratives and have no song to accompany them. In recordings made during his time in Seattle, there is an example of one such song where the palpable bitterness he so often expressed in his discussions about the Famine comes to the fore.

In his approach to the Famine, Heaney's anger was generally directed at those who had the power to do more for victims of the Famine but who did not. In performances, however, he rarely blamed the English government. In keeping with the nature of popular memory as discussed by Donnelly, Joe Heaney laid blame squarely on "local landlords, bailiffs, proselytizers, corn dispensers, clerics, and Poor Law guardians," as Ó hAllmhuráin puts it (1999:104–32). He also told allegorical stories connected to his Famine discussions about the spiritual cost of stinginess or poor hospitality, or what happened when people who could well afford to be generous resorted instead to parsimony. After setting the scene with such narratives, he would sing a song that he called "Come Lay Me Down." The following transcription is typical of his presentation of the Famine to American audiences:

> While we're on the subject of sad songs, I'd like to sing you a few verses of a famine song, the only few verses I know of this song. And I don't know there's many songs about the Famine. You know the Famine of 1845–50, where out of eight million people there was only four and a half million alive, in 1850. Million and a half died on the roadside, and another couple of million emigrated, and the funny part, there was plenty of food in the country, but nobody was—they were all sending it all away. In fact in 1847 a boat came over from America with food, and the bigshots in Queenstown kept the food and sold it, never gave it to the people. Now there was a time when people, they were so weak and feverish, they used to have a can tied around their necks, and they're lying on the side of the road. And anybody passing there, "fill my can." That's put a drop of water or something in

my can so that I can have a drink or something before I die. But whatever you do, treat me decently, because I'm sure you're honest, the same as I am myself. Now I'll sing you a few of the verses I heard of this. Now, I don't know, I heard somebody else singing this in the form of some other song, but this is the way I heard it.

The claim of "this is the way I heard it" was a frequently uttered phrase and armored Heaney against any potential criticism. In particular, his evocation of his grandmother and other community elders as the final authority stilled any questions about the relative degree of authenticity that he might bring to any of his songs, stories, or anecdotes. His lyrics of the song he describes are as follows:

> Chorus:
> Come lay me down, and treat me decent
> Come lay me down, and fill my can
> Come lay me down, love, and treat me decent
> For surely you're an honest man.
>
> As I walked out through Galway City
> As I walked out on a pleasant walk
> As we were walking, I could hear them talking
> Oh surely he's an honest man
> (Chorus)
> The crops are dying, the children crying
> There is widespread hunger all over the land
> But when you return, will you treat me decent?
> For surely you're an honest man.
> (Chorus)
> When I return, I will treat you decent
> When I return, I will fill your can
> When I return, I will bury you decent
> For I know that you're an honest man.[13]

The text, organized as "a string of black letters bounded by white spaces" (Foley 2002:17), looks fairly unprepossessing on the page, but given Heaney's considerable charisma as a performer, it is not surprising to report that his audiences could be profoundly moved by this song. It is essential to note that Heaney's air for this text (figure 3.2), discussed later, was a variant of "The Galway Shawl," also related to the melody that Heaney uses for Raftery's "Máire Ní Eidhin" (see Cowdery 1990:95–109; he calls it "Ballylee"). Sung as a slow air in Heaney's inimitable, distinctive style with the full array of embellishment so characteristic of his singing, the text gathers power and meaning that simply cannot be conveyed on the page. This may well be an instance of what is known as imagining rather than remembering the past, a practice some scholars believe is integral to the construction of history (Beiner 2007:318).

Fig. 3.2: "Come Lay Me Down"

The Constellation of Song Sources

Heaney's lyrics can be directly connected to a complex of texts and related melodies originating in the American music hall or vaudeville tradition and circulating in printed, oral, and recorded sound formats from about the last quarter of the nineteenth century until the present (Meade 2006). One possible ancestor, in terms of the text, seems to be "Muldoon, the Solid Man," a song composed by New York Irish playwright, director, actor, lyricist, and singer Edward Harrigan (1844–1911), famous as one half of the theatrical duo Harrigan and Hart. The "Muldoon" of Harrigan's song is a typical stage Irish caricature, with the redeeming feature that he represents a much more positive portrayal of an Irish American than was generally seen on the stage anywhere at the time (Williams 1996:138). New York politicians on whom Muldoon was modeled loved this portrayal of themselves and flocked to Harrigan's shows. The idea of being "solid," that is, wealthy and respectable, appealed to these upwardly mobile individuals, who had created the political machine of Tammany Hall to help them achieve those ends (Meade 2006). The song was probably first performed in 1874, but it remained popular among the New York Irish so that, into the 1950s, some Irish American politicians were still popularly known as Muldoons (Moloney 2002:25).

> Muldoon, the Solid Man
> I am a man of great influence, and educated to a high degree
> I came when small from Donegal, and my cousin Jimmy
>   came along with me
> On the city road I was situated in a lodging house with
>   me brother Dan
> Till by perseverance I elevated, and I went to the front like
>   a solid man.
> Chorus:
> So come with me, and I will treat you decent
> I'll sit you down and I will fill your can
> And along the street all the friends I meet
> Say "There goes Muldoon, he's a solid man."

At any party or at a raffle, I always go as an invited guest
As conspicuous as the great Lord Mayor, boys, I wear a
	nosegay upon me chest
And when called upon for to address the meeting with
	no regard for clique or clan
I read the constitution with great elocution because you
	see I'm a solid man.
(Chorus)
I control the Tombs, I control the island, my constituents
	they all go there
To enjoy their summer's recreation, and take the enchanting
	East River air
I am known in Harlem, I'm known in Jersey, I am welcomed
	hearty at every hand
And come what may on St. Patrick's Day, I march away
	like a solid man.
(Chorus)

Popular as the song undoubtedly was in New York, it did not remain there. An Irish American performer named William J. Ashcroft (1840–1918) relocated to England after his marriage to the English actress Kitty Brooks and became a star attraction with music hall audiences. This fame later brought him to Belfast and Dublin, where one of his favored items was "Muldoon, the Solid Man." The air specified in the songsters in which "Muldoon" was printed was the "Colleen Rue." Don Meade has been unable to identify the particular air in question (figure 3.3), but the tune in Harrigan's sheet music is closely related to the airs of "Omagh Town," "Youghal Harbour," and "Boolavogue" (Meade 2006). Interestingly, these airs are also recognizable variants of another of Heaney's favorite songs, "The Galway Shawl" (see later discussion).

As the song spread outward from its New York origins, its lyrics were altered to suit the new locations where it took root. The late Frank Harte knew two verses of the song, and Dominic Behan, another Dublin singer, also knew "Muldoon." He published a version of it, titled "Sit Yeh Down and I'll Treat Yeh Decent," adapting the words to make it a workingman's song (Behan 1965). Meade argues that despite the similarities with "Muldoon," Behan's version resembles even more closely a Scottish song,

Fig. 3.3: "Muldoon, the Solid Man"

"I'll Lay Ye Doon," an item originally collected from the Scottish singer Jeannie Robertson in the 1960s and represented here as "For I Will Lay You Doon," as it was titled on one of her recordings. Apart from the chorus, Robertson's version shows no similarity to "Muldoon," having been adapted to a traveler's perspective, but Meade argues for an Irish origin based on the mention of "the banks of the pleasant Bann" in her text. This song was subsequently recorded by both Norman Kennedy (1968) and Jean Redpath (1973).

> "For I Will Lay You Doon"
> I will lay you doon, love, I'll treat you decent
> I will lay you doon, love, I'll fill your can
> I will lay you doon, love, I'll treat you decent
> For Blair (?) he is a solid man.
>
> For as I strode out on a summer's evening
> Doon by the waters of the pleasant strand
> And as I was walking, sure, I could hear them talking
> And saying surely he is a solid man.
>
> I hae traveled far frae Inverney
> Aye, and doon as far as Edinburgh toon
> And it's I maun gae, love, and travel further
> But when I come back, I will lay ye doon
> I maun leave ye noo, love, but I'll return
> Tae ye my love and I'll tak' your hand,
> Then no more I'll roam frae ye my love
> Nae mair tae walk on a foreign strand.

Clearly, since "Muldoon" was known in Ireland and in a more distantly related, and perhaps older, version, in Scotland, Joe Heaney had opportunities to pick it up, either at home in Carna or subsequently at singing sessions in Ireland, Scotland, and England over the course of his life. It could well be that hearing it sung by others reminded him of versions he had heard at home. His air for the piece (figure 3.4), "The Galway Shawl," is clearly related to the one that was printed with the original sheet music, suggesting that the transmission proceeded directly from an Irish music hall source.

Fig. 3.4: "The Galway Shawl"

One of the most interesting aspects of Heaney's text is that the perspective changes from that of the giver of alms to the recipient, thus taking the underdog's perspective and destabilizing a dominant Irish American narrative of material success. The speaker in Heaney's song praises the giver's generosity as an honest man, asking him to put something in his can to help him in his need. Heaney stresses an egalitarian perspective in his accompanying *údar*, implying that, materially, both men in the exchange are fundamentally equal despite economic differences. The melody of "The Galway Shawl" also resonates with the text (figure 3.5). As well as resembling "Muldoon," the stanza beginning "As I walked out through Galway City," echoes the text of "The Galway Shawl." In fact, the specific lines in Heaney's version of "The Galway Shawl" are in the second verse: "As we were walking, we still kept talking, 'til her father's cottage came into view."

Heaney's allusions to other versions and his repeated assertion of his setting's authenticity, "this is the way I heard it," might intimate a concern about the song's status as a legitimate "traditional" item. He used such statements to assert his authority and reinforce his belief that his own version was right. Never one to back down in such situations, nevertheless, his concern may have emanated from his song's similarity to Behan's, or to that of both Norman Kennedy and Jean Redpath, renowned singers in the Scottish folk revival, whom he met on the circuit. In fact, Kennedy was at the Newport Folk Festival in 1965, and Redpath served as artist in residence at Wesleyan between 1972 and 1976. Regardless of this unease, deriving also perhaps from his understanding of what, for purists among his listeners, constituted authentic folk material, his performance of "Come Lay Me Down" is worth considering in detail.

How he came to make the link between "Come Lay Me Down" and the Famine, and where the changes in lyrics emanated from raise interesting questions. Because other singers adapted "Muldoon, the Solid Man" to their own needs, it seems plausible that Heaney did likewise, so that some variations may well be his own. Further evidence of his creation of lines may be found in "The crops are dying, the children crying, there is widespread hunger all over the land," a suggestion strengthened by the rhyming of "dying" and "crying," which approximates Gaelic assonantal patterns. These lines are unique to Heaney and suggest deliberate adaptation to suit his own purpose. The change of perspective from that of the solid man to the insubstantial man is striking and effective. There is a desperate sycophancy in the poor man's request for alms, underscored by Heaney's claims

Fig. 3.5: "For I Will Lay Ye Doon"

for equality; the pathos is heightened by Heaney's description of him lying on the roadside with a can tied around his neck.

Heaney evokes a harrowing picture, using a text sparse in descriptive detail, depending mainly for its deepening of affect upon the music—an air with an old sound lending itself easily to a high degree of musical enhancement by variation and decoration, what Heaney sometimes referred to as the battle dress (Cowdery 1990:38). The phrase is a direct translation of *culaith ghaisce or cóiriú catha*, a term denoting rhetorical runs or flourishes used by storytellers in hero tales (for examples and a discussion, see O'Sullivan 1966).

The battle dress was the way Heaney was able to give conviction and authority to his performances, to bring them fully alive. In the case of Gaelic songs for predominantly English-speaking audiences in America, he was dependent on the music alone, and he usually kept those items to a minimum in concerts, often shortening them accordingly. In this song, however, already short, but in English, he used the chorus to draw in each audience member and create a feeling of belonging and solidarity among them, which only increased his ability to move them emotionally. Heaney was known for his dislike of the American sing-along, but he must also have been keenly aware of the power of a chorus to animate an audience.

Arguably, then, the choice of this song was a pragmatic one, made by a seasoned performer acutely aware of the needs of his audience and of his own task of delivering the required affective impact. Had he stuck purely to Gaelic items alone, even perhaps using a song like "Johnny Seoighe," it is unlikely that he could have brought the listeners to where he wanted them to be and where they wanted to go. It is worth remembering, however, that Heaney bluntly refused to be told what to sing and when to sing. This song made a clear statement to his audience that discussions of the Famine were not to be silenced by one's relative degree of wealth or by the use of the English language, suggesting that the colonial "subordination of the Irish mouth," as Lloyd has termed it, had had only limited success in Heaney's case.

A thematic comparison of "Come Lay Me Down" with "Johnny Seoighe" reveals an approximate correspondence. In "Johnny Seoighe" the potential giver of alms is praised in a somewhat obsequious way, in order to remind him of his obligation as a generous "solid" man. This idea also runs through "Come Lay Me Down" so that, on this important point, the two songs closely parallel one another. The elaborate Gaelic metrical pattern, with its long line and verbal embellishment, and wrenching details such as "mé fhéin is mo pháistí amuigh faoin drúcht" (myself and my children out under the dew) would, of course, have been difficult to replicate beyond "the crops are dying, the children crying." In the matter of music, however, the similarity between the songs is greater. The airs of "Johnny Seoighe" and "Come Lay Me Down," both old-sounding and amenable to vocal elaboration, may be favorably compared, allowing the two songs to stand on a par with each other. In a sense, then, what Heaney achieved with his adaptation of "Come Lay Me Down," to illustrate and heighten his narratives of the Famine, was a rough but serviceable English-language equivalent to material he almost certainly knew but avoided performing for his own reasons. As oral poetry it "does not divorce entertainment from instruction, artistic craft from cultural work" (Foley 2002:28). By performing an English-language song to enhance his narratives, Heaney created a spontaneous community of understanding and, through his history telling, imbued his listeners with some of his own interpretations of the Famine's events. Because of his authenticity as a representative of Irish vernacular tradition, these could be received as virtual testimony.

Julia Kristeva has referred to the phenomenon of intertextuality, where individual written works show the clear influence of others, as a "crossing of texts" (2004:24). In the crossings from "Johnny Seoighe" to "Come Lay Me Down," other links emerge. "Johnny Seoighe" came out of Famine conflicts spurred by extreme want, and "Muldoon, the Solid Man" from the experience of the members of the Irish diaspora who had escaped its ravages by going to America and forging a new existence in a difficult, often hostile environment. "Come Lay Me Down" references both experiences and additionally reflects the crossings of Heaney's own life journey, from mostly Gaelic-speaking to mostly English-speaking surroundings, from the local, intimate gatherings at the firesides of his youth, to his experience as an Irish immigrant and stage performer in Scotland, England, and finally America, never relinquishing an intractable struggle to reconcile tradition and its defining opposite, modernity, on his own terms (see Ó Giolláin 2002 for a discussion of issues involved in such a transition). Such crossings entailed tremendous gains but also, inevitably, some disillusioning losses. The twining strands of personal, ethnic, and cultural histories are intriguing and poignant (Coleman 1996, 1997; Mac Con Iomaire 2007 also sheds fascinating light on this subject).

Joe Heaney was often faced in America with audiences who wanted, even needed, to be able to connect with an imagined Irish past. Despite his seeming lack of Famine songs from Carna, as a resourceful performer, Heaney was able to enlist his power as an icon of unassailable cultural authenticity to reconfigure a text with no direct references to the Great Famine, investing it with meaning and significance for listeners. That he chose to avoid a controversial local song that gives a less-than-flattering portrayal of relationships within his own community suggests that he understood that such uncomfortable truths were not what his American audiences wanted to be presented with, as little as he wanted to present those truths to them. It seems likely that his long experience as a performer provided him with an understanding of his audiences' requirements, and that by choosing a relatively simple ballad with a chorus, repeating a plea for dignity and respect as well as for charity in the face of dire want, he answered their need to make sense of a trauma dimly remembered but always lurking in the background. Through the assertive conviction of his performances, he mediated for his audiences a cultural experience for which they fervently longed.

We do not claim that he created a travestied false consciousness. Through the illusion of his art, Heaney, for all the mistakes in his facts, channeled his justified anger about the events of the Famine and provided his listeners with a conduit through which they could access and relate to a partial truth on a human scale and achieve a small measure of meaningful engagement with this vast tragedy. As Donnelly has commented, Heaney's active sense of outrage validated an understanding that the Famine could have been prevented, and his performances bore witness to that belief. That his listeners' perceptions created in him an incontrovertible symbol of an idealized, unruptured haven that was Ireland only enhanced his ability literally to enchant them. The ghosts of the dead appeared as they were conjured to do.

4

e⌒⊙⌒⊙⌒s

The Religious Laments

When one considers the potential themes to explore from Joe Heaney's *sean-nós* repertoire, the array of options is rich: the Famine, love, relationships, alcohol, masculinity, and emigration all form essential parts of this critical analysis. Before the ideas are developed further, however, it is important first to note that Heaney had a rich and thorny relationship with religion, both individual and organized; his deep sense of spirituality belied his near-continuous quarrel with the institutional clergy. For that reason, his religious repertoire looms large in potential topics that analysis can illuminate. Heaney sang several religious laments, none of which have been studied in relation to himself in any great depth, although surely Angela Bourke's classic book-length study of "Caoineadh na dTrí Muire" ("The Lament of the Three Marys") provides a beacon in this regard (Partridge [Bourke] 1983).

Religious song was mainly a women's repertoire, and Heaney's adaptation of it to his own needs was a reflection of how (in many cultures, not just Ireland) when certain activities such as weaving, singing, and other tasks were carried out at home it was the women who performed them. When those skills became professionalized, it was often men who stepped into the public arena, essentially performing in public what had hitherto been a private act. When Heaney began to sing these religious laments in a public context, he brought the integrity and righteousness of the women of his family to the stage with a dispassionate dignity. Nóirín Ní Riain points out the centrality of Mary among the religious songs, and indeed, the three songs examined here are focused on Mary (1993:203). These emotional songs are self-contained portrayals of three important episodes from the life of Christ: the times of his birth, harrowing death and crucifixion, and resurrection.

In order for Heaney to perform any of these religious laments, he had to first set the stage as for a religious ritual. The only props were his voice, his demeanor, his face, his accent, and his absolute power to enchant (as discussed in chapter 3). He was well known for drawing an audience of any size into the quiet interior of the context he presented, and the audiences marveled at it every time. We have already discussed his consummate and highly effective performance of the Famine in detail. This performance of the Famine was but an element in his larger framework, an equally convincing and flexible context for the situating of the other items that he presented, from religious laments to fighting songs to love songs. At the Sydney Opera House in 1981, Heaney managed to successfully take an enormous audience into the intimacy of his grandmother's home: "'This is a huge shiny place and ye are all out there sitting all over the place. What I'd like to do is to bring ye all into an Irish setting, a kitchen in a country cottage, and we'll have a céilidh, and listen to the songs and stories of Ireland and its people; songs and stories that come from mother earth and our Gaelic language and nowhere else'" (Mac Con Iomaire 2007:352).[1]

When Heaney encouraged the audience to join him in a journey back—and it certainly *was* a journey back, as far as he was concerned—to an imagined country cottage in the rural Ireland of his youth, he was deliberately laying out the precincts of performance. He opened the imagination for the suspension of disbelief, for a retreat from the everyday into the imagined world of preindustrial, premodern Ireland. For those who did not live in Ireland—as in the members of his audience at the Sydney Opera House—it carried them across oceans into the Ireland of their imagination, which is, for many non-Irish people, perpetually in the past. Although Heaney's directions were precise, each member of the audience had to imagine that place for him- or herself, since no two people would imagine it alike. By doing this, Heaney allowed people to live for a short while in a better, more ideal world, bringing them out of their mundane, everyday, and quite pressured lives in modern America (or England, or Canada, or Australia), to a time when people were masters of their own time and not enslaved to it (Freeman 1920).

Mick Moloney has pointed out that Heaney was easily able to hold the attention of his audiences, no matter what language he sang in:

> There was a dignity about him. I think it was his carriage, his deportment, his appearance, plus the way he represented himself. And people saw him almost in a priestly way. I would always call what he was doing a vocation, because it was almost a priestly function. He saw the sacred—priestly is probably not the word—sacred would definitely be the word. I never saw anything like it. (Mac Con Iomaire 2007:364–65).

While Heaney's own spiritual beliefs were complex, not to say contradictory, simultaneously encompassing a devout faith and a strong anticlerical bent, he stressed the close integration of church and community to his audiences, asserting in effect that the church *was* the community. Religious rituals marked the life cycle events of community members, such as weddings, christenings, confirmations, funerals, and weekly Mass on Sunday was important as a social gathering as much as it was a religious observance. But official Catholic practices existed alongside—and sometimes in opposition to—a vernacular spiritual tradition that had formerly sustained communities across Ireland during times of religious suppression. Joe Heaney prefaced any discussion of the religious laments by telling his audiences and especially his students about one such lay tradition: the Irish women's custom of keening, both in public and in private.

Keening or lamenting the dead is a ritual common across many cultures. In Ireland keening has deep roots and was primarily a women's form of public, ritualized discourse that existed to manage the private and collective grief of the family and the community. From early times in Ireland, it faced opposition from religious officials, and directives were issued proscribing the practice (Ó Súilleabháin 1980). Additionally, as Britain modernized and abandoned such practices, keening came to be regarded as backward, an activity that no civilized person would have anything to do with, and additionally a salient mark of the primitive and 'maladapted' Irish other (Lloyd 2003:205–28; Cleary 2005:3; Whelan 2005:142). Because keening persisted strongly in Ireland, it came to be seen by dominant colonial culture as a symbol of the incorrigibility of the Irish, representing their recalcitrant resistance to civilization and domestication. In short, it was seen as a prominent sign of Irish wildness and savagery. Indeed, it was regarded as one of the "must-sees" for foreign travelers, whose writing provides many vivid accounts of the practice (Ó Muirithe 1978:20–29). Religious songs cast in the form of laments on the death of Christ were likewise once widespread (Partridge 1983:15–16). Although these were closely associated with keening at death rituals, and were also the special preserve of women, it is necessary to view them as separate from the lament over the corpse. Their singers regarded these items as sacred, their performance thereby connecting them directly to the events surrounding the passion and the crucifixion of Christ. Mary is seen as a mother, and many of these women identified their own sorrows strongly with Mary's maternal grief for her son (Partridge 1983:68–81, 167–69).

The religious lament "Caoineadh na dTrí Muire"[2] (one of the three dealt with here) and Heaney's other religious songs were central to his performance repertoire, and he invested them with a calm, grave dignity that many found deeply moving. This gravity on the part of a male singer may be contrasted with a female performance of the same lament by Máire an Ghabha Uí Cheannabháin recorded in 1975 by Angela Bourke, during which the performer was so affected by the lyrics of the song that she broke down in tears as she sang it. Unable to continue singing, she explained to Bourke that every mother who had sons identified strongly with Mary's loss as portrayed in the lament (Partridge 1983:167–69).

In Heaney's performances of the religious laments, then, he offers a counter-narrative to the stereotyped images of wild, uncontrollable grief characteristic of the keening women, which nonetheless authorizes that emotion (Coleman 1997:46). The change in performance style is marked by a change of gender, context, and intention, enabling a more controlled, formal, and less obviously emotional presentation than the fireside context in which Máire an Ghabha sang it for Bourke. Heaney's engagement with the text may have been as strong as Máire an Ghabha's, but his intensity was expressed more obliquely, in a modality culturally consistent with male performance of emotionally charged texts. Moreover, the contexts in which Heaney performed were public professional spaces, worlds away from those of Máire an Ghabha (Bourke 2007:15–42). His intentions were also, particularly in the United States, to use the performance to teach lessons about the Gaelic culture of Ireland, so that the text had a didactic function beyond a strictly religious or spiritual one.

The backdrop of nineteenth- and twentieth-century individualized, vernacular approaches to Catholicism is the Penal times in Ireland. The Penal times lasted from the end of the seventeenth century through most of the eighteenth century and are represented by a series of laws that discriminated against both Catholics and Protestant Dissenters in favor of the Church of Ireland. Among these laws were Catholics and Presbyterians being banned from holding public office; voting; carrying weapons; inheriting land owned by Protestants; owning a horse worth more than five pounds; teaching school; and building Catholic churches out of anything but wood (which was difficult to come by). While Heaney's grandmother would have had to have lived many decades earlier than the mid-nineteenth century to have actually experienced Penal Laws, Heaney imaginatively situates her in their aftermath to illustrate the immediacy of oppression in the collective memory:

Now in my grandmother's time, it was a crime to speak Gaelic. Because when she was going to school, and not alone her, but her mother before her, when she was going to school, at that time they weren't allowed to be taught at all. So they used to hire what they call Seán na Scoile [John of the School], John-Behind-the-Wall they used to call him. He had to bring the kids behind the wall and teach them. Because if anybody saw him going into the house and teaching they'd be persecuted for the rest of their lives. So the more they could afford to give him, the more food they could afford to give him, that the more education their children got. Then when my grandmother was going to school they had the stick tied on their back, her and all the other children. And for every word of Irish they spoke, anybody who heard them was supposed to put a notch in that stick, and the following morning at school they got ten slaps on each hand for every notch in that stick. Of course a lot of people wouldn't notch the stick unless they met a peeler [policeman], or a local politician or something, he'd put a *couple* of notches in the stick. (interview, February 24, 1978)

It is unlikely that Heaney is referring to the Penal Laws in this piece, but the fact that Irish was ridiculed by the children themselves, as part of a punishment regime instituted by the cultural climate of the school itself.

His discussion here, although chronologically diffuse in its conflation of different periods, is only to be expected in an oral discussion. This retelling in an oral mode does not privilege exact chronology. It is quite understandable that Heaney might mention the prohibition of Irish and the Penal Laws in (literally) the same breath.

English efforts to turn Connemara into a tourist destination were thwarted by what they perceived as the poverty—moral and material—of the people who lived there. William H. A. Williams describes the sudden encroachment of the Protestant missionaries during the Famine years: "[In 1845, Rev. Alexander Dallas] moved to Castlekerke on the western shores of Lough Corrib, where he set up a school, organized Irish-speaking Gospel readers, and worked for the anticipated destruction of Romanism in Ireland.... To the imperial imagination, godliness, as well as sublimity, was inseparable from productivity" (Williams 2008:172).

Official hostility to Gaelic Catholicism, together with a consequent scarcity of clergy, allowed a rich tradition of vernacular religious song to develop. Such songs spoke to the heart of local spiritualities, persisting through the twentieth century, despite continued hostility from the reorganized Catholic Church after 1850. In his performances of "Caoineadh na dTrí Muire" ("The Lament of the Three Marys"), Joe Heaney engaged a vernacular spiritual tradition reaching back to medieval times (Partridge 1983). It had survived in the face of a complete reorganization of religious practice in Ireland that began in the late eighteenth century and culminated in Cardinal Paul Cullen's rigorous Romanization and, indeed, Anglicization of the Irish Catholic Church from 1850. This suppression of popular religious practices, while not entirely successful, nonetheless brought Irish Catholic religious life more closely in line with Rome; prior to Cullen's work, it had operated largely on its own since the twelfth century. Emmet Larkin has famously called this reorganization the "devotional revolution" (Rafferty 2003:169). During the eighteenth century and for much of the nineteenth, it was the pilgrimage to the holy well dedicated to a local patron saint, rather than regular attendance at Sunday Mass, that was the focus of Irish vernacular religious activity (Ó Cadhla 2002:5–60; Ó Giolláin 1998:201–21; 2005b:11–41).

During Penal times priests were scarce, and communities developed local religious resources in ways that afforded them a certain autonomy of practice (see, for example, Gillespie 1999:30–49). Such independence was frowned upon by many in positions of authority, not least because secular amusements, such as drinking, music, dancing, courting, matchmaking, and occasionally fighting, frequently accompanied sincere religious devotions at the site of the holy well. Despite the nineteenth-century decline of these traditions, they continued in Irish-speaking areas, although even here they became increasingly marginalized as the official Catholic Church continued to consolidate its liturgical innovations. Heaney's performance of popular religious material is therefore more than the sum of its parts. It represents a direct continuity with pre-Famine practice and a site of contest, where a counterargument against the devotional revolution and its deleterious effects on native tradition is presented. In addition, Irish Singers' tendency to apply religious texts to popular tunes (Ní Riain 1993:191) dates from at least the fourteenth century, which makes the melodies of these religious laments immediately familiar from their earliest performances. The fact that this argument emerged from his own personal experience and family history only served to enhance its appeal for his listeners.

These three laments, then, were used by Heaney as symbols of older and more egalitarian modes of spirituality, traditions regarded as belonging to women, more than men, as important custodians of the repertoire of sacred song and devotional lore. In performing the religious laments, Heaney is simultaneously supporting the continuance of the older, pre-Famine religious songs and the vernacular folk religious tradition in the face of church revisionism. Heaney used those songs to bridge the gap, reinforcing his claim that he was in a direct line to the pre-Famine Gaelic past. He had the authority in his repertoire, and he used it to assert the primacy of his belief system over the authority of the reorganized system. Since the reorganization of the Catholic Church, these songs had been labeled as ignorant and superstitious, inaccurate and wrong, evidence of how far the Irish Church had fallen in the absence of guidance from a literate, theologically minded clergy. The Gaelic League's prestige and its interest in vernacular traditions, coupled with notions about the deep spirituality of Gaelic speakers, helped to rehabilitate these songs to some extent. For Gaelic cultural enthusiasts, as well as for their singers, these sacred songs could simultaneously represent a point of resistance and confirmation of a unique, localized, independent Catholicism.

Religious laments are among Heaney's oldest songs; many of the other, more recent, songs belong to the aristocratic, literate Gaelic culture that persisted in folk culture. In celebrating the development of vernacular religious expression, the Gaelic League attempted to add legitimacy to the folk culture. It celebrated links between folklore and medieval aristocratic culture, imagining a direct continuity that could serve as the basis for the resurrection of the Gaelic nation. This interpretation of history gained acceptance among some in Gaelic communities, and folklore collection became a popular project. Heaney's older brother Seán (1914–80), for example, collected both stories and songs from their father, Pádhraic, which are now a part of the National Folklore Collection, stored at the Delargy Centre for Folklore at University College Dublin. Consequently, among families of tradition bearers, a certain pride becomes evident in their presentation of their family heritage. Much of Heaney's pride in the exclusivity of Gaelic folk material in a largely English-speaking milieu arguably stemmed from such understandings of his material. In a description of why English speakers would never be able to learn the laments, Heaney said the following: "No, they're so hard, they're hard you know, the lament is hard to sing you know. To do, you've got to put yourself in the place of the person on the cross, both the nails, driving the nails, born in the stable" (interview, February 28, 1978). Heaney framed his own religious beliefs around the performance of three different religious laments from the Gaelic tradition. These laments—"Caoineadh na dTrí Muire," "Dán Oíche Nollag," and "Amhrán na Páise" ("The Lament of the Three Marys," "The Poem of Christmas Eve," and "The Song of the Passion," respectively)—gave Heaney the opportunity to present to his Irish and other audiences a markedly different view of Irish engagement with spirituality than the ones they knew from their own backgrounds. In the following interview from 1978, Heaney first discusses laments in general:

> Well, a lament is always sad, and the setting of course has to be sad, too. Because most laments were sung during funerals; people crying out for the dead one. There used to be what you called keening women in Ireland; years and years ago, they used to cry at every wake. They were specialized in crying over the dead person, and telling about his good points—never his bad ones—and even at the graveyard they used to cry till the last sod was put over the person.... They left nothing out, everything, and the sadness and sorrow of their own life, helped to make it even better.... They'd cry, because this is something they could see, as the person carried on, they could see what was happening, the event taking place, which is the real meaning of the song anyway, to follow the story, follow a path, until they come to the turn. (interview, March 3, 1978)

Lest the impression be given that all of Heaney's songs were steeped in the depth of historical pain, it must be clarified that Heaney had a wicked sense of humor and took plenty of pleasure in (Irish- and English-language) comic songs, bawdy songs, wordplay, macaronic songs, and upbeat syllabic songs like "Casadh an tSúgáin" ("Twisting the Rope"). In general, Heaney's strict approach to his music and the seriousness with which he imbued each lesson and performance were steeped in gravitas. However, he sought balance in his personal and professional life, leading easily from lighthearted story to religious lament; from English-language ballad to love songs. The religious laments discussed in this chapter are among his most profound expressions of his spiritual self, his region, and, by extension, his nation. They also reveal his relationship to the older women in his community: to his grandmother, whom he credits with teaching him many of his most important songs, to the women who once keened publicly at wakes, and to the family members who would mourn privately in their own homes. As nonlexical mourning belonged in the realm of female activity, men such as Heaney were responsible for the lyric—sung—performance of grief.

"The Lament of the Three Marys"

Each of the laments here includes some type of refrain. In the case of "Caoineadh na dTrí Muire," the refrain is *ochón*, a word associated with keening as discussed briefly by Heaney in the preceding quote. Breandán Ó Madagáin further describes the tradition of keening by professional mourners as the use of a single line or even just the name of the deceased, followed by a nonlexical refrain. He further points out, "No words were used, only vocables such as 'och ochone' or 'ululoo,' so that the community gave poignant expression to their emotion in purely musical terms, using their voices as a musical instrument, just as in the instrumental lament played on the pipes or the harp" (2005:84). In "Caoineadh na dTrí Muire," the keen-like refrain uses the word *ochón* to build the image of keening women in the mind of the listener.

This song had multiple functions for Heaney in both Ireland and abroad. It allowed him to indicate that the suffering in the song was not that of Jesus but of the women mourning him. It became a central part of his pedagogy in the States, and a way for his American audiences to know and understand not just Heaney himself but the long line of powerful women from whom he drew much of his spiritual authority. In much the same way that Irish mythology acknowledges women as the teachers of its male warriors, Heaney gleaned his spiritual and musical authority from that most formidable of Irish women: the grandmother.

> Well, Good Friday you see was, a time, when I was growing up a little boy, our grandmother, who had a fantastic way of singing, of doing the lament, and she used to really do the lament, would gather us around her. And not a murmur would be out of us till she finished the Passion of Christ right from the cross, when Peter was standing there, and the Blessed Virgin came up to Peter, and she said, "Who is that man on the cross of Passion?" And Peter said, "Don't you recognize your own son, mother?" And then she said, "Is that the son I carried for nine months, is that the son that was born in the stable, is that the son I reared on my knees? Oh, child," she said, "your face and mouth is bleeding." And then they go on to the streets of Jerusalem. And they lifted her up to get her out of the way, and they threw her down on the bare stones. And she said—"Beat me," he said, "beat me, but don't touch my mother." And the answer he got back, "We'll crucify you, and beat your mother." And then it goes on to tell how Simon, who was such a man that he used to, he was laughing at him when he started out first, and he took pity on him when he fell with the cross three times, you know. And Simon helped him with the cross, you know, up to Calvary. And of course, on Calvary, while—when he was dying—the fourth king, the man who set out on Christmas Eve, gave him a drop of the bottle of water he was carrying. He was the fourth king; that's all he could give him. And he kept the bottle of water for thirty-three years, till that day, and he gave it to him. And this is how my grandmother used to do it. [sings "Caoineadh na dTrí Muire"] (interview, March 2, 1978)

When Joe Heaney passed away in Seattle on May 1, 1984, his students, friends, and colleagues discussed how to honor him at the funeral. Because of its prominence in his lessons, and its appeal to his students, "Caoineadh na dTrí Muire" stood out clearly over other songs. Despite the brevity of his tenure in Seattle, Heaney had succeeded in inculcating his spiritual views and repertoire into a largely female cadre of students and other listeners, so that in choosing this lament to express their grief at his loss, they also joined the generations of women who had mourned their dead by keening and singing Marian laments about the passion of Christ on Good Friday. Arguably, a circle had been completed, where the old transformed into the new and subsequently took up its place in the United States, a modern, urban, supposedly nontraditional settler society. Strikingly, the Caoineadh also formed a part of his requiem Mass in his native Carna, although there, an argument erupted about the appropriateness of such a performance, almost exemplifying the historical tensions between differing modalities of Christian spirituality. That this argument took place along gender lines with a priest arguing against and a woman arguing for the performance further reveals cultural differences between the two societies in which each one took place.

The lyrics to "Caoineadh na dTrí Muire" are presented here, followed by English translations; the lament *ochón, is ochón ó*, though not notated here, follows each phrase. Verses are grouped into related phrasal pairs. The dramatic question-and-answer format of the first part of the song echoes a tradition rooted in early Irish tradition, in which stories could be begun through a series of questions and answers.

"Caoineadh na dTrí Muire"
A Pheadair a aspail, an bhfaca thú mo ghrá bán? (Ochón, is ochón ó)
Chonaic mé ar ball é dhá chéasadh ag an ngarda (Ochón, is ochón ó)
Cé hé an fear breá sin ar Chrann na Páise?
An é nach n-aithníonn tú do Mhac, a Mháithrín?
An é sin an Maicín a d'iompair mé trí ráithe?
An é sin an Maicín a rugadh in sa stábla?
An é sin an Maicín a hoileadh in ucht Mháire?
A mhicín mhuirneach, tá do bhéal 's do shróinín gearrtha.
Is cuireadh calla rúin ar le spídiúlacht óna námhaid
Is cuireadh an choróin spíonta ar a mhullach álainn
Crochadh suas é ar ghuaillí arda
Is buaileadh anuas é faoi leacrachaí na sráide
Cuireadh go Cnoc Chailbhearaí é ag méadú ar a Pháise
Bhí sé ag iompar na Croiche agus Simon lena shála
Buailigí mé féin ach ná bainidh le mo mháithrín
Marómuid thú féin agus buailfimid do mháithrín
Cuireadh tairní maola thrí throithe a chosa agus a lámha
Cuireadh an tsleá trí na bhrollach álainn.
Éist a mháthair, is ná bí cráite
Tá mná mo chaointe le breith fós a mháithrín.

Oh Peter, apostle, did you see my loved one?
I saw him some time ago, tormented by his enemies
Who is that fine man on the Cross of Passion?

Don't you recognize your own son, mother?
Is that the son I carried for three seasons?
Is that the son that was born in the stable?
Is that the son that was nursed at Mary's breast?
My dearest little son, your mouth and nose are bleeding.
They dressed him in purple and spat on him with scorn
They put a crown of thorns on his beautiful forehead.
They lifted his mother up high on their shoulders
And threw her down on the flagstones of the street.
He was taken to Calvary Hill to hasten his Passion
He carried the cross and Simon helping him
Beat myself, but do not harm my mother
We'll kill yourself and we'll beat your mother
There were blunt nails put through his hands and feet
There was a lance put through his beautiful chest.
Listen, Mother, and don't be grieving
The women who'll weep for me have yet to be born

Musically, the song includes four complete phrases, with the two *ochón*
passages serving as refrains (figure 4.1). The first and third phrases are
melodically quite different in the first few words but follow a nearly identical pattern between *an bhfaca tú mo ghrá bán* and *dhá cheasadh ag an
ngarda*. Irish lament verse is characterized by stanzas with irregular lines.
The structure of the song differs from that of an actual keen in its use of
four phrases, immediately identifying it as more like song than like a keen.
While the preceding transcription—from one performance early on in
Heaney's career—is not particularly rich in ornamentation, the transcription of a different (later) performance (figure 4.2) reveals much more
musical detail.

It is this high level of ornamentation that sets Heaney's performance
apart—not only from singers elsewhere in Ireland but particularly from
those who would perform it purely as a lament rather than as a song.[3]

The lone keener (more usually a woman) sang her verse to old *reacai-
reacht* music, chant-like, many syllables on the same note, with little
ornamentation and ending in a falling cadence....The keener com-
menced it [*ochón*] at the end of the verse, and was joined by the entire

Fig. 4.1: Early performance of "Caoineadh na dTrí Muire"

Fig. 4.2: Later performance of "Caoineadh na dTrí Muire"

company singing it as their "Amen" to the sentiments expressed in the verse, and significantly extending the social function of the keen. (Ó Madagáin 2005: 83–84)

In performing "Caoineadh na dTrí Muire" as a four-line song, Heaney produced a more formal, songlike structure than was usual in ritual lament performance. It is tempting to see a gender division in the treatment Heaney gives this now-renowned and much-performed piece. In contrast with the intimacy of Máire an Ghabha's highly emotional performance for Bourke in her own kitchen, Heaney produces a grave, male, professionalized version of a ritualized form of community- and female-based grief. It is also striking, as Bourke notes (Partridge 1983:32), that Heaney omits the lines in which Mary is portrayed as jumping and leaping, and that her hair is loose and disheveled. Máire an Ghabha's version includes these details, which are clearly similar to keening practices. It may be that Heaney deliberately omitted these details from his performances, considering them unsuitable—even though his audience in the United States would be almost exclusively English-speaking. Whatever his reasons, his texts may be regarded as gendered in this respect; solemn, decorous male grief replaced wild, uncontrollable female lamentation.

"The Poem of Christmas Eve"

Heaney recorded this Christmas song, "Dán Oíche Nollag" ("The Poem of Christmas Eve"), in 1978, a recording posthumously released in 1996 on the CD *Say a Song: Joe Heaney in the Pacific Northwest*, consisting of selections from the Joe Heaney Collection at the University of Washington, Seattle. Heaney seldom sang it and rarely taught it. The first few verses, transcribed here, focus on the events of Christmas Eve (Mary and Joseph walking from place to place, having the doors shut against them, delivering the baby among the animals in the stable). Immediately following, however, the entire content of the song shifts over to the time of Lent, thirty-three years later. Jesus tells his mother what will happen shortly (his being sold and tormented). When Heaney used to tell the background story of this song, he would often bring in the addition of a fourth Wise Man who got lost on the way (for thirty-three years), whose gift—a simple drink of water—was offered to Jesus at the time of the crucifixion.

In an especially detailed recorded interview, Heaney discusses "Dán Oíche Nollag" ("The Poem of Christmas Eve"). As he describes his learning process, he clearly indicates that his grandmother expected nothing less than perfection before he performed it. Heaney himself was quite a stickler, suggesting that this teaching method was one acquired early in life from his own experience.

In the interview, Heaney also stresses Christ's spirituality, hinting at his disapproval of worldly acquisition among the clergy. Twice he points out that Jesus said he "came to save, not to be bought," followed directly by a discussion of priests and official Catholic dogma. The alleged avarice of priests is a standard motif in Irish folklore. Heaney told several stories illustrating the idea, which appears in popular expressions such as the saying that "four priests without greed" are a thing never to be found in Ireland.[4] He further locates the song in place and time by saying that it was appropriate only for a domestic performance on Christmas Eve, citing again his grandmother's authority. Heaney's mischievous sense of humor also emerges here. Despite his seriousness, it is noteworthy that he jokingly (and invariably) refers to frankincense as "Frankenstein." The absurdity here disguises a clever mnemonic technique. Because students insisted on correcting him about Frankenstein as much as he insisted he was right, he ensured that the lesson was remembered. The interview is reproduced verbatim here, with a lowercase *f* for frankenstein!

> I picked it off her [my grandmother]. But she wouldn't let me sing it until I could do it justice....I sang it for my grandmother before she died, and she liked what I did and she said, "Keep at it, you'll be able to do it yet." And the story is of how they were going around; they were refused permission to go into the hotel and they came into the stable. And Jesus was born, and the three kings came. And they were all looking out the door at the fourth king that was following them, who got lost—as the other lament tells—appeared in Calvary, on Good Friday. They brought frankenstein [*sic*], gold and myrrh. And the song says he refused them all, because he came to save people, not to be bought by them. But they [the gifts] were still held on and used as an example afterward, even in the Mass, on what the kings brought him. And then, as he grew up a little bit he was walking with his mother, and she asked him, "Is this the way you'll always be?" And he said, "No, I'll be sold on the Wednesday for thirty pieces of silver. I'll be hunted on the Thursday, and I'll be crucified on the Friday. And the drop of blood that's in my head will be down to my toes before they've finished with me...."
>
> That is the basic story of the song. And as I said before, these songs have no English translations. Unless you told the story in English I

don't think you could ever do justice to the song the way they do in the old Gaelic, the way the people sang it. That song is directly dedicated to Christmas, and it's better to leave it like that because then it will never get abused by thrashing it out at the wrong time and the wrong place. So it's just kept strictly, preserved for that occasion alone.... My grandmother, she wanted us to have it, and she used to sing for us; any time we asked her she did it for us. But publicly, no. I mean with the gathering in the house she'd only do it on Christmas Eve....

Ailliliú, this is the mournful word. They had in the old Gaelic language, *Ailliliú leá*. That's you're crying over something. You're saying goodbye to the bad and welcoming the good. That's in each one of them three, there's *ailliliú*. Praise, praise to the time, that this'll do good, know what I mean? You're praising, you're welcoming the sign that something wonderful is going to happen, you know. And that's the meaning of the whole *ailliliú*, in the old Gaelic....But they used it in a lot of Latin songs too; it came from the East, anyway. And the meaning, my grandmother went *ailliliú leá, ailliliú leá*, that means, glory, glory be to God, for what he's doing, but I'm sad because he's doing it. It's a very, very sad occasion, because she knows, the mother knows, because he told her what was going to happen to him. And she was saying the *ailliliú*, you know....It's sung at home.

Now, I'm not sure if it's sung today, but I know there's a recording in the church of this on Christmas Eve and it's played over the radio on Christmas Eve. But no other time. This is the only one that explained the whole part of what the kings did and all that came to see him at Christmas. This was the only one that explained properly what occurred, when they offered him the gold, frankenstein [*sic*] and myrrh. He refused it, because he said "I didn't come to be bought, I came to save." But it's still used in the Mass, especially at Benediction, you know the frankenstein [*sic*] is burned during the Benediction. Of course the gold is in the chalice. The myrrh is what the, they burn it....

[The priests] never heard it, especially our parish priest, you know. Not one of them. It was only in the one little house. That's it. One little village, one little house, that was all.[5] And that took the courage to do them, you know, publicly, in Dublin you know. [The response was] very good; very, very, very, very good. That's a Gaelic concert I was doing. So the next night I had to do it, and the next night I had to do it, and the next night. Every night I had to do it. It was something unique, you know, somebody had to do it and I was the only one available to do it at the time. I hope they're all singing it now, because the record, so many people bought the record, you know. (interview, March 2, 1978)

"Dán Oiche Nollag"
Chuadar siar is aniar na sráideannaí
Ní bhfuaireadar aon dídean ann
Go dtáinigeadar don stábla naofa
Dhá uairín roimh lá.

Dhiúltaigh an teach ósta,
Muire a thabhairt as an sneachta
Agus rugadh an leanbh naofa
Idir bulláin is asail.

Chorus:

Aililiu-leá, is aililiu-leá; á-bhó bhó is óch óch ó, is aililiu-leá.

Tháinig na trí rí
Le bronntanaisí ag an leanbh
Mar thugadar
Úllaí ór buí is aiteas

Dhíultaigh tú 'lig an méid sin
A' sábháil gach peacach
Dá dtiocfa' is dá ndeacha'
Is dá mbeidh againn feasta.

(Chorus)

Lá dhá raibh an cúpla
Ag siúl lena chéile
D'fhiafraigh an Mhaighdean Ghlórmhar
"An mar seo bheas muid feasta?"

Díolfar mé Dé Céadaoin
Ar leath chróinín airgead bán
Agus beidh mé ar an Déardaoin,
Do mo ruaigeadh ag mo námhaid

Tiocfar anuas orm
Le chúig mhíle buille
Is an braon uasal a stór atá in uachtar
Beidh sé síos le mo shála.

Chorus
They went back and forth in the streets
No place was open to them
Until finally they came to the holy stable
Two hours before daybreak.
The inn refused
To take Mary out of the snow
And the blessed child was born
Among cattle and asses.

(Chorus)

The three kings came
With presents for the baby
For they brought
Yellow-golden apples and joy

You refused all that
To save all sinners
To save all creatures
That went and are yet to come.

(Chorus)
One day as the couple
Were walking together
The Blessed Virgin asked him,
"Is this the way we'll be from now on?"

I'll be sold Wednesday
For a half crown of silver
And on Thursday
I will be driven out by my enemy

I will be struck
With five thousand blows
And the blood coming from my head
Will be streaming down my body.
(Chorus)

The refrain of this song is a variant on the word "alleluia" ("praise ye the Lord"): *ailliliú leá*. It was used frequently as an expression of surprise or dismay, perhaps akin to "alas." Heaney correctly associates this word with the keening tradition, and he might well have mentioned that the

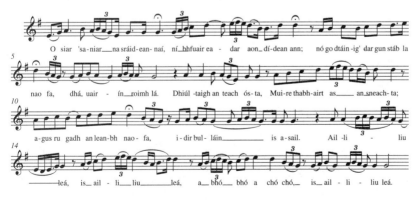

Fig. 4.3: "Dán Oíche Nollag"

two other vocables in the chorus (*a bhó* and *ochó*) are also consistent with keening vocables. In his interview discussing the song, Heaney describes *ailliliú* as a "mournful word," thereby classifying it as appropriate for a lament. The form of the song, as he improvised it, includes repeating patterns of two verses and a chorus. The chorus uses the exact same melody as the verses (figure 4.3), which—unlike songs with a classic *ochón* phrase in them—has only a partially descending vocal line. This is not necessarily a hallmark, then, of a classic keen performed by a professional mourner; instead, each of these religious laments is far closer in style to that of a *song*, performed by a male singer. His counterbalancing of those features with the relative syllabic density of the verse and the use of *ailliliú* as a refrain are the elements that bring it back into the realm of a lament.

"The Song of the Passion of Christ"

"Amhrán na Páise" ("The Song of the Passion of Christ"), also known as "An tAiséirí" ("The Resurrection"), was one that Heaney performed, but, like "Dán Oíche Nollag," he seldom taught it. In addition to having asserted that only a native speaker of Irish could do justice to it, he repeatedly expressed concern that its sheer beauty, as a song, might attract a guitar player, who would destroy it. This discourse of purity versus contamination reveals how Heaney had made the discourse of purity, dominant in Gaelic folklore at the time, part of his own outlook. In a 1978 interview, he again drew attention to the Catholic clergy's unsympathetic attitudes to his spiritual songs. He also, however, claimed that things had changed directly as a result of the recordings he had made of this material, claiming a victory over entrenched antivernacular bias by the Catholic establishment. Heaney discussed one of the ways in which his recording of the song was by this time being used in Carna:

> I had more faith myself than they [the priests] had. They didn't know [the song], but now they're doing that in the church now in Good Friday, they're doing the lament I sang. They're doing the one I did a recording of, they're playing it in the church every Good Friday and around the Stations of the Cross. And they play the Easter Sunday one on Easter Sunday. It's something you see, that must be handled with care. It could be easily ruined you see, if you don't do justice to a lament you may as well leave it alone. I mean, you couldn't get somebody up with a guitar singing it. That would destroy it. (interview, February 28, 1978)

The song is described as one of Heaney's favorites for its uniqueness to the Carna area. In a newspaper article from July 15, 1976, writer Dónal Foley discusses Heaney's *Ó Mo Dhúchas* recording (rereleased by Shanachie Records as *From My Tradition*):

"Seosamh now lives in America, but comes home for three weeks every year, and for the last number of visits Gael Linn have been kidnapping him and shutting him into a recording studio. . . . they have just released the second of these, *Ó Mo Dhúchas*, and the songs on it are all fine examples of the Connemara style of sean-nós singing. . . . His own favourite on the record is 'Amhrán na Páise,' the song about the Passion, because 'it is completely unique, a song you wouldn't find anywhere in the world outside Carna.'" (Mac Con Iomaire 2007:305)

Joe Heaney was honored to hear that people in Carna had used his recording of "Amhrán na Páise" to relearn the song—which, according to him, had been lost—and that it was being sung on Easter Sunday in the local church:

They had to [learn this song from my recording] because I was the only one who had it. Now my grandmother was the only woman who had that in the whole of Ireland. And the other two I sang for you, the other two, the Christmas one and the lament, now she got them from her mother. But they were noted for this folklore, and nobody else had it. I'm glad they're singing it now. . . . These things are not meant for [guitarists]; they're meant for solitude and nice company, and at the right time and the right place and the right moment, you know what I mean? . . . There's a lot of songs in books I suppose about Easter, but that's the one we always did. And that's as good as them all put together I think. (interview, March 3, 1978)

The "right time and the right place and the right moment" all characterize Heaney's engagement with his entire repertoire as a deeply personal quest that came through his ancestral lineages. "Dán Oíche Nollag"—the poem of Christmas Eve—could be performed only at home, only on Christmas Eve. "Amhrán na Paise" ("The Song of the Passion") could be performed only at Easter. Songs that were not a part of that constellation of values ("right time, right place, right moment"), including any song that might be accompanied by a guitar, were beneath contempt. Whereas "Caoineadh na dTrí Muire" could be (and was) sung and taught at any time of the year, the other two songs were reserved for more deeply intimate contexts for those connected to the tradition and cognizant of the songs' deeper meanings. Heaney's insistence on ritual correctness reveals the spiritual sustenance he derived from these items, marking them off as especially sacred and, accordingly, requiring special treatment.

"Amhrán na Páise"
Is é Íosa an fíréan, Dia dílis don athair
Is é a rinne ár gceannach ón daoirse;
Nuair a d'fhulaing sé an pháis, agus bás ar an gcroich
Ag tabhairt sásaimh sna peacaí seo níonns muid.

Chorus:

> Is aililiú leá is aililiú ailiú;
> is aililiú;
> Má maslaítear ár gcolainn ní baolach dár n-anam
> Ná séanaigí m'ainmse choíche.

Siúiligí amach sa ngairdín, a Pheadair
Tá uaigneas mór ar mo chroí-se;
Is é meáchan na bpeacaí is ciontach le m'uaigneas
Is fairigí uair liom an oíche seo.
Tá an t-arán seo déanta in d'fhianaise, a Pheadair
A Pheadair, caithidh an t-arán seo;
An té chaithfeas an t-arán seo caithfidh sé mise
Idir fheoil, anam is diachta.
Tá an fíon seo déanta in d'fhianaise, a Pheadair
A Pheadair, caithidh an fíon seo;
An té chaithfidh an fíon seo caithfidh sé an fhuil
A bhí ag tíocht ina braonta as mo thaobhsa.

(Chorus)
Chuaigh na trí Muire ar maidin Dé Domhnaigh
Go leigheasfaidis cneácha Iosa;
Chuartaíodor an tuamba thart timpeall le mearbhall
Ach ní bhfuaireadar amharc ar Iosa.
Tháinig an t-aingeal anuas as na Flaithis
Is d'ardaigh sé an leac ina bhfianais';
Bhí leac ar an tuamba—ní thógfadh céad pearsa í
Ach thóg an t-aingeal a bhí naofa í.
Tá sé ráite i dtairngreacht Mhaitiú
Leis an magadh a fuair Íosa;
D'éirigh an coileach a bhí ag fiuchadh sa bpota
Chuaigh ar an mbord is lig glao as.

Chorus

Jesus is the true one, the God beloved of the father
He lifted us from oppression;
When he endured the Passion, and died on the cross
Bringing salvation from these sins that we had committed.

Chorus:

> Alleluia;
> If our bodies should be abused, it is no danger to our souls
> Do not deny my name ever.

Let us go out walking in the garden, Peter
There is a great loneliness on my heart;
It is the weight of the sins and guilt that causes my loneliness
And watch the hours with me this night.

This bread bears witness, Peter
Peter, take this bread;
He who eats of this bread will eat of me
Between flesh, soul and divinity.
This wine bears witness, Peter
Peter, take this wine;
He who takes of this wine takes the blood
That comes in drops from my side.

(Chorus)
The three Marys came on the morning of Sunday
To heal the wounds of Jesus;
They gathered at the tomb
But they didn't get sight of Jesus.
The angel came down from Heaven
And raised him up high;
There was ice on the tomb; a hundred people couldn't move it
But the holy angel moved it easily.
Matthew had said in prophecy
About the mockery that was put on Jesus;
That the cock that was boiling in the pot rose up
Went up on the table and let out a cry.

(Chorus)

The melodic content of the verses represents a constellation of varying phrases that coalesce around four core notes (figure 4.4). Clearly, in performance, the melody is secondary to the lyrics (cf. Ní Riain 1993:203), and in the traditional context for these songs, attempting to impress an audience with melodic virtuosity as a part of any of these songs would be

Fig. 4.4: "Amhrán na Páise"

inappropriate. All three airs have musical features in common. The triple repetition of the tonic at the end of the song is a salient feature of many traditional melodies. Each one uses a refrain—either *ochón* or *ailliliú*, vocables closely associated with keening. This link emphasizes the elegiac tenor of these items and also a connection between keening and Christianity. This is striking in view of the usual construction of keening as the very opposite of Christian doctrines of salvation and resurrection.

The most important pitches for "Caoineadh na dTrí Muire" (1, 2, 4, 5, and 6) are echoed by the importance of the same pitches in "Dán Oíche Nollag" and "Amhrán na Páise." The third degree of the scale—which at a very basic level determines whether a melody is in major or minor—appears consistently in many instrumental tunes. In fact, all three of these laments use the major third, but very often as a passing tone to the more frequently used fourth degree. As for the seventh degree of the scale, only "Dán Oíche Nollag" includes its use, and just barely: it appears in a few melismas, but never in its customary usage as a leading tone up to the tonic. The most important musical element joining these three religious laments is their similarity of melody; they are *three* sides of the same musical structure.

In his examination of *sean-nós* singing and music theory, Seán Ó Riada discusses the song "An Raibh Tú ar an gCarraig?" ("Were You on the Rock?"), another song Heaney used to teach his students about vernacular religious practices and metaphor during the Penal times. Ó Riada pointed out the example of "An Raibh Tú ar an gCarraig?" to demonstrate the ways in which a melody can be built upon the manipulation of a particular motif (a short melodic phrase, for example) and suggested that this may have been a compositional technique employed in oral tradition (1982:35). Motifs of this sort may be reversed, doubled, shifted in register, altered in terms of rhythmic focus, and otherwise utilized for the expansion of a tune, variation of a melody, and aesthetic interest.

The variations in melodic contour of these songs display exactly the kind of motivic transformation characterized by Ó Riada. The music is old, and it draws from a common well: the authority and source of Heaney's oft-repeated authenticity. Ó Riada implied a link between songs like "An Raibh Tú ar an gCarraig?" and the aristocratic tradition. Simple though these melodies may first appear, they connect with a primeval stream of European music inaccessible to most modern Americans and disdained by many Irish people. The endless variations possible on these fundamental melodic contours, as expressed in Heaney's performances, represent a musical assertion of continuity and authenticity.

As unsympathetic an observer of Irish culture as the twelfth-century Welsh writer Giraldus Cambrensis—the first ethnomusicologist, perhaps, to describe Irish music—remarked on this point of the subtle development of fundamental motivic ideas, using the example of harping as a feature that was both salient and redeeming of an otherwise uncivilized people:

> They introduce and leave rhythmic motifs so subtly, they play the tin-
> kling sounds on the thinner strings above the sustained sound of the

thicker string so freely, they take such secret delight and caress [the strings] so sensuously, that the greatest part of their art seems to lie in veiling it, as if "That which is concealed is bettered—art revealed is art shamed." (Giraldus Cambrensis, cited in Rimmer 1977:29)

The word *fonn* in Irish—to describe a sung melody—is borrowed from the Latin *fundus*, the base or fundament. *Fonnadóir* and *fonnadóireacht*—terms for singer and singing, respectively, in the Irish of the Carna area—were, until recently, used only locally (Mac Con Iomaire 2007:51). The *fonnadóir* proceeds from the basic theme of a song and works with it in myriad subtle ways, not just through melismatic ornamentation but through variation, transference, and reversal of melodic motifs and a type of gentle play between poetics and sound. Ó Riada's term for what Cambrensis described is the "variation principle" (1982:24). Although Ó Riada's strident rhetoric has been justifiably criticized, his insight here seems sound, in that similarities and differences of the melodies are far from random but follow a systematic pattern, however difficult to comprehend. Tensions between the individual and the collective, between the official and the vernacular, between the modern and the traditional are reflected in Heaney's passionate commitment to these items in his repertoire. His pride in achieving recognition and acceptance for these items, long excluded from official religious expression, represents a sophisticated, formalized contestation between (private) spiritual and (public) formal authority.

5

The Medieval Transformed

$\mathcal{T}$his chapter focuses on several songs for which Heaney was well known; it amplifies and continues the previous discussion of his songs. The chapter includes three songs connected with the seventeenth-century poet Cearbhall Ó Dálaigh, followed by the well-known English-language song titled "The Rocks of Bawn," and concludes with "A Stór mo Chroí," a song about emigration. Heaney performed these songs both at home and abroad—unlike some of his other songs—and they reveal something of the core of his presentation of the Irish past, of himself as a connecting figure, and of the cultural legacy that he wished to engage in his audiences and among his students. His encyclopedic memory—which enabled him to perform hundreds of songs in both Irish and English—gave him the (somewhat dubious) freedom of choosing songs gauged to the comprehension and readiness of a particular student or audience member, whether it was a drinking song in English or a richly metaphoric song in Irish outlining layers of history and spirituality. Viewing him as an icon, Heaney's audiences might project onto him their own wants and desires (see chapters 8 and 9), often to construct him as the antithesis of the drab modernity they inhabited; in essence, he represented a living embodiment of earlier, simpler, and more colorful times. How Heaney understood and responded to those needs is an additionally fascinating element in the equation.

Two short examples from Heaney's time in Seattle serve to set this stage. As is often the case, the efforts of the students often fail to meet the expectations of the teacher. Heaney was a stern taskmaster, and his students did not always come to their regular lessons with their new songs memorized. If they had not prepared the songs perfectly, Heaney invoked a hierarchy of value when reprimanding wayward individuals, by making some of them memorize very simple songs in English as punishment for their transgressions. The Irish-language songs—which Heaney referred to as the "big songs"—were the special, reserved material. Only those whom

Heaney considered to have the requisite combination of determination, grit, and talent had earned the right to learn them. He had no qualms about excluding those whom he felt did not live up to this standard. In the time that Heaney was teaching in Seattle, his students shared tales of their punishments with each other and knew when one or another of them had broken the rules. The Irish-language material was at the top for Heaney.

Another example dates to the period shortly after Heaney's death in 1984, at a gathering of his friends in Seattle. An Irish-born musician living in Seattle saw a typewritten collection of Heaney's songs that a student had transcribed and compiled, took it in his hands, and paged through it. "He never sang this," he said, referring to "Dark Is the Color of My True Love's Hair."[1] "Nor this one. Nor this one." One by one, he went through the book and vehemently denied that Heaney ever sang most of the English-language songs. Every song in the book had been among the repertoire of Heaney's performances and lessons, but when the student tried to explain that to the musician, his response was an accusation of fabricating the connection between Heaney and the songs that he, the musician, refused to accept as Heaney's.

These two examples show that both Heaney and the musician at the gathering were heavily invested in the celebration and perpetuation of the Irish-language aspect of the song repertoire. By using English-language songs as a way for students to "do penance" for the sin of not learning their songs properly, Heaney placed himself in the role of both priest and gatekeeper of that which he held to be most sacred. He simultaneously set up a tiered system in which the English-language comic songs were at the bottom and the historical, many-versed, heavily ornamented songs in Irish reigned supreme. As the gatekeeper, he refused to listen to his students sing any Irish songs that he himself had not passed on to them, nor was he interested, necessarily, in any other songs they knew. It was Heaney's hierarchical repertoire, or no songs at all.

In denying that Heaney ever sang most of the English-language songs (except the venerable "Rocks of Bawn" and a few others of its kind), the Irish musician in Seattle refused to allow the possibility that Heaney could be anything other than his own preformed image of a utopian nineteenth-century Irish-language singer who used English only to make his way in the world. Similar sentiments characterize both journalistic and social commentary in Ireland about Heaney's work in America—that it was dumbed down to meet the leprechauns-and-shamrocks needs of the Yanks, and therefore unworthy of consideration. Instead of this binary view of Heaney as the epitome of the Gael, or Heaney as someone who sang only in English to satisfy his ignorant American audiences, it may be more fruitful to consider Heaney as a master mediator with the full range and repertoire of social skills and songs necessary to connect effectively with a constantly shifting audience. He was intensively observant, was sensitive to a variety of situations, and was at all times the "man for the job" without compromising his art or his sense of self.

How do these two sets of values work together without canceling each other out? First, the hierarchical nature of Irish song was well formed in Heaney's mind not just from his own early exposure to the values of the Gaelic League and his older family members and neighbors but also from his own mature grasp of the repertoire as a professional. Second, he had come to know that specific audiences had specific needs, from Carna to Galway to Dublin, all the way to Philadelphia, Seattle, and Sydney. As a professional, he put together programs that included stories, English-language songs, anecdotes, and Irish-language songs, varying the proportion and selection according to his understanding of the context. He managed to work his rare "failures" at reading his audience into further stories, which not only revealed his human side but also publicly and repeatedly emphasized that those audiences who failed to appreciate him in the past were anomalies.

In the mid-1960s Heaney was famously booed at Dublin's Grafton Cinema the first time he performed there with the Dubliners for a drinking crowd who had been expecting English-language ballads with popular sing-along choruses. He said, "Joe Kennedy, who used to write for the *Evening Herald*, was in the Grafton the night I tried to sing an Irish song and I was booed. And I said to Joe it wasn't me they were booing but what I stood for. But I never blamed anybody. I'm not saying now a Dublin man did it; it could be anybody who was drunk. But it wasn't nice. I don't think it would happen today" (Mac Con Iomaire 2007:220). Heaney was brought back to the Grafton later to perform with Seamus Ennis, and the singer Liam Clancy introduced him as "one of the greatest singers of Ireland that I have ever heard." In response to the enthusiastic applause of the audience after his performance, Heaney said, "You listened to me tonight because Liam Clancy told you to listen to me. But ye booed me before! Ye booed me before!" (Mac Con Iomaire 2007:219). In a 1978 interview, he said, "At that particular time there was places in Ireland you couldn't sing a Gaelic song. They'd call you a 'boggee' or a countryman or something. I was booed in Dublin for singing a Gaelic song. It was in 1962. They weren't booing *me*; they didn't want the Gaelic, but I kept on doing it, and I did another one too."

It is unlikely that a single member of the first audience was present at the latter performance; the second performance was also in a different time in terms of the audience's ability to receive traditional music and song with respect and enthusiasm. But Heaney's bitterness over the early reception of his singing never abated. For him, the moment symbolized the difficulty of his struggle for acknowledgment and led him to effectively punish Dublin audiences forever after. He repeated the story ("I was booed in Dublin, you know") all across the United States as a preface to his lengthy discourses on the shortcomings of the guitar and his anger at what he believed were the profitable and popular groups (the Bothy Band and others). He used this story, again and again, as a way to *teach* something of his culture, of himself—to join two metaphors—as an almost Sisyphean figure swimming against Yeats's "filthy modern tide." He claimed these as reasons he felt that he had to leave Ireland and succinctly expressed his own reaction to how a rapidly changing nation was discarding what he felt it should cherish most: himself, his language, and his *dúchas* (traditional heritage), each of which was quintessentially Irish.

It is interesting to compare this story of being booed in Dublin with another incident in which Heaney became controversial. Heaney did not include this story in his American performances. Accounts of it were gathered after his death by Liam Mac Con Iomaire from those who had witnessed it. The incident took place at a festival in the Aran Islands, a small group of islands just off the south coast of Connemara and within sight of land. Heaney was annoyed that the audience was not listening to him and called out to them in Irish at one point, "Can you hear me?" After the affirmative reply came, he retorted, "Well, I'm afraid that *I* can hear *you*!" This retort had the effect of irritating the audience, who only talked and whistled all the louder. In contrast, another singer, Tomás Mac Eoin from Carraroe, County Galway, got up and sang some lighthearted songs that got a great reception (Mac Con Iomaire 2007:279–80). This episode reveals that there was always a point to be made by the stories that Heaney told—or did not tell—that he was the outsider seeking recognition and that that recognition was hard-won and only grudgingly bestowed.

It is in the context of Heaney the professional singer, then, that we offer an examination of some of the other iconic songs in his repertoire, which he carefully selected for performance in Ireland and abroad. As with all study of performance, context is crucial. The surroundings in which Heaney performed and recorded these items reveal his ability to read his audiences and to adjust his material accordingly. In this way, though he may have had to simplify and to translate for those unversed in Gaelic tradition, he managed equally to transmit the core of his ideas.

Cearbhall Ó Dálaigh and Eileanóir a Rún

Three related songs stand out among the hundreds from which Joe Heaney drew in performances. "Seachrán Chearbhaill," "Eileanóir a Rún," and "Eileen Aroon" ("Wanderings of Cearbhall," "Eleanor My Treasure," and "Eileen My Treasure," respectively) trace back to the seventeenth century through the figure of Cearbhall Ó Dálaigh, both a historical figure and a character in folklore. All three songs are attributed to this poet, a scion of the Gaelic aristocracy, and in Heaney's performance an embodiment of the living continuity of the medieval Gaelic tradition into the modern era of political independence and cultural resurgence. An examination of these items, and Heaney's performances of them, reveals much about contemporary cultural attitudes in Ireland and in America.

The figure of the poet Cearbhall Ó Dálaigh is prominent in Irish learned tradition and folklore. Although he is regarded as a seventeenth century figure, there were in fact a number of poets named Cearbhall Ó Dálaigh from earlier times. The name itself may be regarded as a symbolic representation of the whole Gaelic literary tradition, and of the poet's central role within it. This is especially true of Cearbhall in oral tradition (Doan 1980–81, 1–24). He may, in fact, be mixed up with Carolan (d. 1738) and other figures who carried similar names;[2] like many of the poets in the folk tradition, he is portrayed as a trickster figure: a dealer in words, seductions and musical enchantments. He is often associated with an older family lineage of Ó Dálaigh,[3] who were hereditary bards associated with the Ó Lochlainn family of Corcomroe in Clare (Doan 1985:37) among other noble Gaelic families. An Ó Dálaigh bardic school had existed in the Burren – also in Clare – in the Middle Ages (Doan 1985:38), and the fame of the name Ó Dálaigh subsequently led several later historians to assume that the bard-poet Cearbhall Ó Dálaigh of the Middle Ages was the same as the Cearbhall Ó Dálaigh of the seventeenth century (and of these songs). Indeed, one renowned poet of the name, Muireadhach Albanach Ó Dálaigh, established a new poetic dynasty in Gaelic Scotland, which continued to practice its hereditary craft into the eighteenth century. Regarding Cearbhall, the editor Kathleen Hoaglund, for example, lists the song "Eileen Aroon" as a composition of "Carrol O'Daly, 14th Century" (Hoaglund 1999:117), although James Doan more plausibly suggests that the songs emanated from a later vibrant tradition of Gaelic vernacular composition that had grown up around the figure of Cearbhall (Doan 1985:67–86). This suggestion indicates that the song was not composed by any of the Cearbhall figures in literary tradition.

Little is known for certain about the identity of Cearbhall Ó Dálaigh. Manuscript traditions mention more than one individual of this name. The most likely candidate is the man who lived at the beginning of the seventeenth century, who is addressed by another poet in verse and whose own poems also survive. In folklore Ó Dálaigh is considered an archetypal lover because the songs that survive are mostly love songs. As with many famous folkloric figures, things that he never did were attributed to him (Doan 1980-81, Harrison 1979:86). Yet, his historicity is important because when Heaney sang items composed by Ó Dálaigh, he conformed to an idea prominent in folklore of *gesunkenes kulturgut* (high culture that has come downward) (Bohlman 1988:11). This German phrase is used to categorize items originating in high culture and ending in folk culture: folksongs by destination rather than by origin.

Séamus Ó Duilearga's (a.k.a. James H. Delargy) ideas, expounded with conviction in his lecture "The Gaelic Storyteller," testify to the dominance of such ideas in folklore studies in mid-twentieth-century Ireland. In this famous lecture (Delargy 1945:9), he enlarged upon the thought that medieval aristocratic Gaelic culture survived among the Gaelic-speaking inhabitants of the western people. This lecture undoubtedly reinforced views already well established by Gaelic cultural nationalism. The three items, then, from Cearbhall Ó Dálaigh's repertoire, easily traced as they are in folk and in manuscript traditions to the seventeenth century and earlier, provide hard evidence of such concepts. The symbolism of a subculture carrying the fact of a cultural continuity from the seventeenth century is certainly interesting, and in a decolonizing context, its symbolism is more than ordinarily powerful.

"Seachrán Chearbhaill" – The Wandering of Cearbhall

"Seachrán Chearbhaill," arguably the oldest song in Heaney's repertoire, is an example of *crosántacht*, a combination of alliterative sung poetry and spoken rhythmic prose with roots in medieval performance practice. Because of its associations with élite literary forms, it represented a symbolic continuity between Heaney as a modern Irishman and the pre-conquest Gaelic polity that supposedly had been swept away after the wars of the seventeenth century. It also gave Heaney authority as the direct heir to that tradition, and additionally was not commonly known outside of Connemara. It was certainly rare to find a young man in the nineteen forties who could deliver as convincing a rendition as Heaney did. Thus, as a performance work, it became an icon that was much sought after.

The idea that aristocratic items of medieval culture continue in an unbroken line among ordinary or materially poor farmers and fisherfolk in remote areas contained tremendous power for those who received it. As a *crosántacht*, "Seachrán Chearbhaill" is a specific genre of a Gaelic subliterary tradition. To the melody enthusiasts of the nineteenth century, such a genre might not have held much interest. But to twentieth-century folklorists and others more aware of the diversity of Gaelic literature, such an item was striking in its rarity.

The term *crosántacht* comes from the word *crosán*. *Crosáin* (plural) were professional fools in Gaelic medieval courts; entertainers, they were part of the poet's retinue, or *dámh* (Harrison 1979). That Heaney had this item in his active repertoire gave him a tremendous advantage in the authenticity stakes. This item alone, because of its comparative antiquity and rarity, its identification with an aristocratic seventeenth-century poetic figure, and its status as a medieval literary genre, had an important impact that was difficult, perhaps, for non–Irish speakers to appreciate. However, a song that goes some way toward an understanding of what *crosántacht* might mean to an Irish speaker is "As I Roved Out," a rollicking dialogue ballad with two different melodies and two different choruses.[4] The musical and textual complexity of form and the length of the song loosely parallel similar characteristics in the *crosántacht*. Heaney frequently performed "As I Roved Out," often opening his concerts with it.

All these factors together could be read in the view of the time as a representation of the direct continuity from the medieval to the modern era. "Seachrán Chearbhaill" was further seen as concrete evidence of the survival of the old Gaelic nation, and to find it in one so young in the 1940s, when the abandonment of the language and tradition seemed unstoppable, must have seemed like a miracle. Whereas "Caoineadh na dTrí Muire" ("The Lament of the Three Marys" [chapter 4]) was easy to

Step it out! Mrs. Annie O'Brien (a.k.a. Annie Devaney) dances in *sean-nós*
style at the 2004 Joe Heaney Festival in Carna, Connemara. All the
Devaney family are noted performers of *sean-nós* dance. Photo courtesy
of Cary Black, 2004.

A locally made wooden *currach* on a sandy beach at Bertraboy Bay, near where Heaney was born and raised, with the Twelve Pins of Connemara in the background. Photo courtesy of Cary Black, 2004.

Singing session at Leavy's pub in Ard Mór (An Aird Mhór) during the Joe Heaney Festival. The late *sean-nós* singer Dara Bán Mac Donnchadha (1939–2008, right) with poet, singer, and festival organizer Mícheál Ó Cuaig. Photo courtesy of Cary Black, 2004.

"A face as strong and craggy as his own native Connemara, and a voice to match" (Donal Foley, *Irish Times*, cited in Mac Con Iomaire 2007: 305). Heaney in classic performance posture; note the V-neck sweater and the open-neck shirt underneath, rather than the cream-colored *báinín* sweater of his days with the Clancy Brothers. Photo courtesy of Mark Mamalakis.

Joe Heaney's gravestone in Maigh Ros cemetery near Carna. Note the contrast between the items placed on the grave and the imposing nature of the incised stone. Photo courtesy of Lillis Ó Laoire, 2009.

The view from Inish Nee (Inis Ní): a small house on a promontory with the Twelve Pins in the background. This image gives a sense of the bleak landscape of Heaney's upbringing. Photo courtesy of Lillis Ó Laoire, 2009.

"The Rocks of Bawn": these rocks—the result of Ice Age glaciation—are stacked in walls all over the west of Ireland, revealing the intensive labor invested in domesticating the Irish landscape over time. Photo courtesy of Lillis Ó Laoire, 2009.

Misty autumn morning near Maam, County Galway. Photo courtesy of Lillis Ó Laoire, 2009.

The pier at Ard East/Ard Castle (An Aird Thoir/Aird an Chaisleáin). Note the lobster pots, familiar items to Heaney in his daily work as a young man. Photo courtesy of Lillis Ó Laoire, 2009.

Scoil na hAirde (School of the Ard) outside of Carna, where Heaney was a student. Photo courtesy of Sean Williams, 1998.

The old Heaney dwelling; the family later moved from this house to another, more modern building. Photo courtesy of Sean Williams, 1998.

Teach na Scléipe (house of gaiety), the house of Seán Choilm Mac Donnchadha (father of Dara Bán Mac Donnchadha), next-door neighbors of the Heaneys. They were another family of experts in oral traditions of song and story. Photo courtesy of Lillis Ó Laoire, 2009.

The new house of Seán Choilm Mac Donnchadha, built in 1956. The hip-gabled roof is characteristic of the kind favored by government agencies of that era. Photo courtesy of Lillis Ó Laoire, 2009.

The holy island of St. MacDara from Más pier, a familiar sight for Heaney; the restored oratory can be seen on the shore to the left. The pilgrimage takes place annually on July 16. Photo courtesy of Lillis Ó Laoire, 2009.

The two winners of the Oireachtas *sean-nós* competition—Joe Heaney and Cáit Ní Mhuimhneacháin, a singer for whom Heaney expressed lifelong admiration. Photo courtesy of An tOireachtas, 1942.

Fig. 5.1: "Seachrán Chearbhaill"

teach to students with its relatively simple melodic line and repetitive, nonlexical chorus, "Seachrán Chearbhaill" could have been taught to the mostly non-Gaelic-speaking American students only with great difficulty. Even though the melody (figure 5.1) is less challenging than many of his Irish-language love songs, the text of "Seachrán Chearbhaill" is its greatest test. While "Caoineadh na dTrí Muire" persisted in America, then, "Seachrán Chearbhaill" seems never to have been taught there. In selecting "Caoineadh na dTrí Muire" as a way to build cultural knowledge around a particular text, it is clear that Heaney wisely regarded the form of "Caoineadh" as accessible, and the form of "Seachrán Chearbhaill" as beyond the capability of his students—and his audiences—to grasp. This was a clever and effective pedagogical strategy. Like any responsive teacher, Heaney had to simplify and gauge the material in order to teach it to the level of his audience, no matter how much they clamored for ever more authentic performances.

In the following lyrics, the young lady in question is the very same Eileanóir of the song "Eileanóir a Rún," discussed later. Ó Dálaigh meets and woos her on the eve of her wedding to another man.

Sung:
Is lá breá a ndeachaigh mé ag breathnú ar an spéirbhean bhreá
Ó b'iúd í ainnirín na malaí is na ngealchrobh lámh
Bhí a grua mar na ballaí le go mbreactar ar an aol mar bhláth
Is a seang-mhalaí searca le go nglaoitear air an aol-tsúil bhreá.
Ó bhí siúd aici deir Peadar más fíor le rá;
Ó rósbhéilín tanaí le caiseal agus taoimbhéal tláth
Bhí pingin ins an maide aici 'gus leithphingin eile anuas ar an gclár
Is ní raibh fáil aici ar an gcluiche údan ó mhaidin nó go n-éireodh lá.

Muise an gcluineann sibhse mise libh a chailíní na háite údan thiar,
Le a bhfuil mé i ngean oraibh le fad is mé faoi ghrásta Dé.

Tabhair scéala uaim chuici agus aithris di nach taobh léi atáim
Mar go bhfuil ansin bean eile údan le fada do mo chloí le grá

Ó lán doirne díomhaine ins gach buine dá dlaoifholt bhreá
Ná a' bhfuilSibh ina gcodladh mar is mithid dibh m'úrscéal fháil.

Spoken:

Air seo agus air siúd, 'sé an túrscéal a bhí ansiúd:
Triúr bodachaí i dtús earraigh a chuaigh ar thóir móna iad fhéin agus an
    dá mhada con a bhí acub.
Chuadar ag iarraidh cead coille ar an gCoirbíneach agus thug
    sé sin dóibh.
Chrochadar a bpéire tuannaí cúl ramhra béal tanaí
Dhearmadar an tapa, thugadar an míthapa leo.
Bhriseadar na giarsaí ach ligeadar na maidí rámha leis an sruth.

Sung:

Muise ar arraingeachaí agallta dhomh nó pianta báis
Mar tá mé dho mo stancadh ag an arraing atá dul thrí mo lár
Ó b'fhearr liom seal fada bheith ag breathnú ar a mínchnis bhreá
Nó dá bréagadh go maidin cé go mb'aoirsiúil dom a leithéid a rá.

Spoken:
Air seo agus air siúd, sé an t-úrscéal a bhí ansiúd:
Ná Cormac Mac Airt Mac Chuinn Mac Thréanmhóir Uí Bhaoiscne.
Chuaig ag tois na léime binne brice bua a bhí ar an mBinn Éadair Mhic
    Céadta Mhic Amhlaí
San áit a dtáinig an chéad loing agus an chéad laoch go hÉirinn ariamh.

Sung:

Muise dheamhan sin gort socair nach bhogas chugat a' nóinín fraoigh
Is dheamhan sin loch ar bith gan abhainn a bheith ag dul uaithi síos.
Tá an rotha seo sna sodair agus níl aon chónaí faoi
Is ní minic a tháinig sonas gan an donas a bheith ina orlaí thríd.

Spoken:

Air seo agus air siúd, sé an t-úrscéal a bhí ansiúd:
Rotha mór mo mháthar mór a chuaigh isteach sa teampall mór ag réabadh
    amach deskannaí
Mara dtaga siad roimhe rotha mór mo mháthar mór
Déanfaidh sé an diabhal sa teampall mór.

Sung to a different air:

Is má théann tú thart siar ansin ag seanbheainín bhéasach
Bhfuil aici scata do pháistí bréagach

Cuimil do bhosa go sleamhain dá n-éadan
Is fainic an lochtófá tada dá dtréithre
San wagero eró, sí an chraoibhín gheal donn

Má théann tú thart siar in easc údan tomáin
Fainic thú féin ar easc údan Shiobháin
Báitheadh dhá chaora inti, minseach is mionnán
Capall Uí Dhomhnaill, a chú 'gus a ghearrán
San wagero eró 'sí an chraoibhín gheal donn.

And one day as I went to see the beautiful fine woman
She was the maiden with the brows and the white hands
Her cheek was as pale as the wall washed with enhancing lime
And her slender love inspiring brows which are called the fine lime
    bright eye.
She had, according to Peter, if it is true to say it;
A little honey rose mouth with a set of teeth and thyme scented gentle
    mouth
She had a penny in the staff and another penny laid down on the board
And she couldn't find that game from morning until daybreak again.

Now, do you hear me talking to you, girls of that place yonder
And how much I love you for so long and I under the grace of God.

Bring her a message and tell her I am not depending upon her
Because there is yet another woman who has overcome me with love this
    long time.

There is a generous handful in every hank of her luxuriant
    beautiful hair
Or are you all asleep for it's time for you to hear my fable.

Spoken:
By this and by that the fable that was there:
Three churls at the start of spring who went to cut turf, they and the two
    hound dogs they had.
They asked Corbett for permission to roam the woods and he gave it to
    them.
They brought along their pair of thin-bladed, thick-butted axes.
They forgot readiness and brought misfortune along with them.
They broke the joists but let the oars away with the stream.

Sung:
Indeed, now by screaming stabbing pains or the pains of death
I am being weakened by the pain that is going through my center.
Oh, I would prefer a long spell looking at her fine delicate skin
Or coaxing her until morning although it is mockery for me to say that.

Spoken:

By this and by that, the fable that was there:
Cormac son of Art, son of Conn, son of Tréanmhór descendant of
    Baoiscne
Who measured the speckled cliff leap which was in the Ben of Éadar son
of Céadta son of Amhlaí [Binn Éadair = Howth, County Dublin]
Where the first ship and the first warrior ever came to Ireland.

Sung:

Now indeed there is not a settled field that does not provide the heather
    daisy
And no lake without a river that flows down out of it
This wheel is galloping and there is no sign of it stopping
And it's rare that fortune struck without a streak of misfortune too.

Spoken:
By this and by that the fable that was there:
My grandmother's big wheel that went into the big chapel tearing out
    desks
If they don't intercept my grandmother's big wheel
It will do the devil in the big chapel.

Sung to a different air:[5]

And if you go back there to the courteous old lady
Who has a crowd of untruthful children
Rub your palms sleekly against their faces
And be careful not to fault any of their characteristics.
And *wagero aero*, she is the bright dark little branch.

If you go around into yonder bushy cleft
Be careful around yonder waterfall of Siobhán
Two sheep were drowned there, a nanny goat and a kid
O'Donnell's horse, his hound and his gelding,
And *wagero aero*, she is the bright dark little branch.

"Eileanóir a Rún"

Despite the fact that the complexities of "Seachrán Chearbhaill" would
have been too much for the average Anglophone American, Heaney was
still able to avail of other strategies to invoke the authority that association
with Ó Dálaigh conferred upon him. He knew another love song attributed
to Cearbhall Ó Dálaigh. Variants of this song have been recovered from
oral tradition all over Ireland, and the Carna version as Heaney sang it vies
with the best, from the musical point of view. Like the melodies of "Johnny

Fig. 5.2: "Eileanóir a Rún"

Seoighe" and "Come Lay Me Down" (see chapter 3), the melody of "Eileanóir a Rún" (figure 5.2) contains the qualities that have made Gaelic melody so appealing to listeners as far back as the eighteenth century.[6] Its modality, its soaring melodic line, the capacity for ornamentation and variation all make it a classically appealing piece to insiders and students of folk music alike.

Additionally, as in "Caoineadh na dTrí Muire," a certain amount of repetition characterizes the verses, of which Heaney sang three. Here, then, for Heaney, was an item that could be taught to non–Irish speakers with greater success because of these very characteristics. Associations with a seventeenth-century aristocratic poet, and narratives to accompany the song, lent it added appeal. Heaney's narrative introduction to "Eileanóir a Rún" exemplifies a common strategy in Gaelic song, in which the story is told separately, adding extra elements and explaining often enigmatic lyrics (Shields 1993). Here follows one rich, complex, oral telling of Ó Dálaigh's story by Heaney:

Now, I suppose, this is the song, the air, that Handel set, in Dublin; he'd give his right arm if he'd composed it. And the story goes that Cearbhall Ó Dálaigh was gifted in a way that, whatever he did, that he did well. And he was a Jack of all Trades, and a master of all of them. Even in love he was good; so they say, any woman who looked at him: that's it. But anyway, he was a poor man; he was working for people here and there, and this day he came to a farmer's house, and the farmer told him to look after three cows he had. "That's all I want you to do," he said. "Two black cows, and a white cow. Well, whatever you do," he said, "keep a good eye on the white cow. Because the white cow is supposed to give birth to a calf. And whoever tastes the milk of the cow first will have the gift of all knowledge." And Cearbhall took the three cows out and he started looking after them every day, until this day.

He was watching the cows beside a huge, big, rock. And the cows are grazing away, and suddenly the rock started shaking. And it opened up. And out came the most beautiful, the most ferocious-looking bull—black bull—he ever saw in his life. He had three horns and two tails. And he walked straight up to the white cow and gave her a swish of his tail. And himself and the white cow went to the far end of the field, and they stayed there all day, whatever they were doing, nobody knows, but when the sun was setting they ambled back, tired and weary-looking, and up back to the place where Cearbhall was looking after the other two cows. And the bull gave the white cow a little lump of a kiss on the side of the head, and the rock opened up and the bull went into the rock. The rock closed up and that was it; Cearbhall took the cows home, and he told the farmer what he had seen. "Now," said the farmer, "watch the cow," he said. "Because that cow will give birth to the calf," he said. "And when she—call me, wherever I am, when you see the cow in pain, with the calf."

But when the cow was having the calf, Cearbhall was too busy doing something else. But when he saw the calf going to suck the—his mother, he ran up and he threw the calf's mouth off the cow's udder. And some of the milk touched his lips. And that's what the voice said to him: "Now you've tasted the milk of the white cow first. You have the gift of all knowledge, but whatever you do, run away from the farmer because he'll kill you if he finds out."

So Cearbhall went away and he was traveling and traveling for weeks and then, until one day he came to a shoemaker's shop. And he went in, and he bid the shoemaker the time of the day, and the shoemaker said "Wait. Sit down a minute," he said, "I can't talk to you now. I have two shoes to finish for the lady in the big house. And the minute I finish them, I'll talk to you." And Cearbhall said to him, "I can do one of the shoes for you," and then the cobbler or the shoemaker said, "No, you can't. I must do these myself, they're a special job. They're for the lady who lives up there what's called Eleanor Kavanagh."

So whatever the shoemaker was doing, he was tired and he fell asleep. And Cearbhall took the shoes, and he finished the shoes. And when the shoemaker woke up, "Oh my God," he said, "what happened?" And he said, "Well, you fell asleep and I finished the shoes." "Well, if you did," he said, "you take them up now. I wouldn't take them up," he said, "because she wouldn't like anybody else to do the shoes."

So he went up to the house to give her the shoes. He knocked on the door, she opened the door, and that's what he said the minute she opened the door, he said, "*Mo ghrá thú den chéad fhéachaint, Eileanóir a rún.*" Eleanor was amazed. "My love to you at first sight, Eleanor *a rún*." And then he gave her the shoes. She tried on the shoes. One of the shoes fitted her, and the other didn't. The shoe the shoemaker had done didn't fit her; the shoe that Cearbhall [made] did fit her. And she said, "Whoever knitted—made this shoe, I'll follow him to the ends of the world." And that's when they eloped. And they—then he composed this song then:

Mo ghrá thú den chéad fhéachaint, Eileanóir a rún. My love to you at first sight, Eleanor. *Is ort a bhím ag smaoineamh.* I'm thinking of you even when I'm asleep. *A ghrá den tsaol, is í chéad searc, is tú is deise....*Oh, my love, you're fairer than any woman in Ireland, he said. *A bhruinnilín deas óg, is tú is deise milse póg.* You're the sweetest thing that ever lived, and your kiss must be sweeter than yourself. And I'll love you as long as I live. *Is deas mar sheolfainn gamhna,* oh, I'd love to drive the cattle with you, Eleanor a rún.

And then he started praising what a sight she is. She'd take the birds off the trees, with her beauty. She'd even the corpse lying dead would get up when she passed with her beauty. And anyway, this is the song, in Irish, the way it was.

"Eileanóir a Rún"
Mo ghrá thú, den chéad fhéachaint, Eileanóir a Rúin
Is ort a bhím ag smaoineamh, tráth a mbím i mo shuan
A ghrá den tsaol, is a chéad searc, is tú is deise ná ban Éireann.

Chorus:
    A bhruinnilín deas óg, is tú is deise milse póig
    Chúns a mhairfead beo beidh gean agam ort
    Mar is deas mar a sheolfainn gamhna leat, Eileanóir a Rúin.
Bhí bua aici go dtóigfeadh sí an corp fuar ón mbás
Ba milse blas a póigín ná an chuachín roimh an lá[7]
Bhí bua eile aici nach ndéarfad, 'sí grá mo chroí, mo chéad searc.
(Chorus)
An dtiocfaidh tú nó an bhfanfaidh tú, Eileanóir a Rún?
Nó an aithneofá an té nach gcáinfeadh thú, a chuid den tsaol is a stór
Tiocfaidh mé is ní fhanfaidh mé, is maith a d'aithneoinn an té nach gcáin-feadh mé
(Chorus)

From the moment I saw you I loved you, Eileanóir my love
It is of you I think when I'm resting
O love of life and my first love, you are fairer than all the women of
    Ireland.
Chorus:
    O young fair maiden you have the nicest and sweetest kiss
    As long as I live my affection will be for you
    For I'd gladly drive the calves with you, Eileanóir my love.
She had a gift that she could revive the cold corpse from death
The taste of her little kiss was sweeter than the cuckoo at dawn
She had another gift I'll not mention, she is the love of my heart, my first
    love.
(Chorus)

Will you come or will you remain Eileanóir my love?
Or would you know the one who would criticize you my darling and heart's delight?
I will come and I won't remain, well I know the one who would criticize me:
(Chorus)

"Eileen Aroon"

In the same vein as composer-arranger Thomas Moore's work with traditional songs (see chapter 6), it was a frequent occurrence that nineteenth- and twentieth-century composers and singers tried to rework materials that had originally been sung in Irish. By changing (and sometimes cleaning up or editing) the lyrics to fit a then-contemporary set of sensibilities, Irish-language material could be made safe for consumption by the English-speaking parlor set and also made appropriate for singing by, for example, an Irish tenor (see chapter 7). Variants on the courtship theme of "Eileen Aroon" were popular in England and Anglophone Ireland in the eighteenth century, and it is Limerick-born playwright and essayist Gerald Griffin's (1803–40) "Eileen Aroon" (composed in the early nineteenth century) that has become fairly standardized as the English-language version of the song, especially in America. His lyrics include the words "Eileen Aroon" sung at the end of lines 1, 2, and 4 as a refrain; they make a series of statements praising the young woman's beauty and demeanor or ask questions (as in "Who in the song so sweet?") to be answered with her name.

> "Eileen Aroon"
> I know a valley fair, Eileen Aroon
> I knew a cottage there, Eileen Aroon
> Far in that valley's shade, I knew a gentle maid
> Flower of a hazel glade, Eileen Aroon.
>
> Who in the song so sweet? Eileen Aroon
> Who in the dance so fleet? Eileen Aroon
> Dear were her charms to me, dearer her laughter free
> Dearest her constancy, Eileen Aroon.
>
> Who like the rising day? Eileen Aroon
> Love sends its early ray? Eileen Aroon
> What makes his dawning glow changeless through joy or woe?
> Only the constant know, Eileen Aroon.
>
> Is it the laughing eye? Eileen Aroon
> Is it the timid sigh? Eileen Aroon
> Is it the tender tone, soft as the stringed harp's moan?
> Oh, it is truth alone, Eileen Aroon.

Youth must with time decay, Eileen Aroon
Beauty must fade away, Eileen Aroon
Castles are sacked in war, chieftains are scattered far
Truth is a fixed star, Eileen Aroon.

Joe Heaney recorded this song for Lucy Simpson when he lived in Brooklyn and visited her house regularly. He told her during that session that he was fifty years old before he learned this song, and that he had learned it from a printed source. When Simpson expressed surprise at this admission, since he rarely owned up to using printed materials for songs, he said he had not known that there was a translation of Eileanóir a Rún. He added that he himself had adapted his own tune to suit the English lyrics and that, despite its printed origin, the style in which he sang it was not based on printed music and could not be acquired in that way.[8] He used it as a way to introduce "Eileanóir a Rún." Consequently, the context is again important. Heaney sang this English-language version of the song in performances where large numbers of Irish Americans[9] might be present; he also taught it in lessons to his students in Seattle when he was not going to teach them to sing "Eileanóir a Rún." The melody of "Eileen Aroon" (figure 5.3) is far less challenging, with far fewer ornaments, than that of "Eileanóir a Rún." Rather like the way that "Come Lay Me Down" acted as "Johnny Seoighe" in disguise (see chapter 3), this song served, in essence, as a stand-in for the Irish-language version, except that the correspondence was instantly recognizable. Heaney did not shy away from relying on English-language versions of songs when he felt they were appropriate for Americans. Since this song was sung by other folk performers, Bob Dylan, Jean Redpath and his friends the Clancys among them, and popular with folk audiences, Heaney could not afford to ignore it. For example, he readily sang the English translation of the east Galway *sean-nós* song "Anach Cuain" (which he called "Annydown" when he sang it in English) because he felt that although a song is always better in its original language, if a pedagogical point were to be made, and the translation was excellent, then the audience could learn from it. In such a circumstance, a larger purpose—such as teaching something of Irish culture

Fig. 5.3: "Eileen Aroon"

to those whose eyes otherwise might simply glaze over at the first phrases of a song in Irish—would be served.

Séamus Ó Duilearga (James Delargy) points out that "a story consists of three parts: the story, the narrator, and the audience" and warns us to "never forget the existence of the audience when studying folk-tradition—these invisible literary critics are there all the time. The story-teller reacted to their presence, to their attentive interest and their occasional plaudits and conventional phrases of approval" (1999:160). That the "final" incarnation of this song type should have become so popular (including its recording by John McCormack, using lyrics by Thomas Davis set to a melody by Dermot MacMurrough) is an indication that multiple performing artists, writers, and—by extension—politicians were engaged in a continual process of translation for their constituencies. Heaney's work as a cultural translator of the medieval ethos of "Seachrán Chearbhaill" across several centuries places him in excellent company.

In each of these three songs, several pitches stand out as essential to the overall melodic shape. All three center around the tonic, the sixth degree of the scale, and the fifth. It is clear that they are variations on the same melody, from the much older style of "Seachrán Chearbhaill" through "Eileanóir a Rún" to the song at its most modern, "Eileen Aroon." Further, Heaney's performance of "Eileen Aroon" brings a potentially maudlin romanticized adaptation closer to *sean-nós* performance practice, emphasizing its connection and descent from "Eileanóir a Rún"—and, by extension, the medieval context of "Seachrán Chearbhaill." Heaney had all three at his disposal to use as the context dictated.

Heaney engaged in a similar mediation with the song "Roisín Dubh." Like his Ó Dálaigh material, he could access three versions of this iconic song. He knew one from his own family background in Carna and would have learned another at school. The school version, deriving from Munster, was taught widely in the 1920s and 1930s from Father Pádraig Breathnach's seven-part collection *Ceol Ár Sinsear* (Breathnach 1920:28). The school version gained tremendously in performance in the sixties when Ó Riada used it as a major theme in his renowned score for George Morrison's *Mise Éire* (1960), a film about the 1916 Uprising and the War of Independence. Heaney also knew James Clarence Mangan's famous translation "Dark Rosaleen," again probably learned at school, and quoted liberally from it to introduce the song. He sang the "school" version frequently in the States but chose to record the version from his native Carna for the Gael Linn recording sessions, marking it as especially authentic. In this way, the living folk tradition, its educational equivalent, and the impulse to translate Ireland for beginners met again in the variants of one song, in which the themes of love and nation are inextricably mingled. As he did with Cearbhall Ó Dálaigh's poems and Griffin's translation, "Eileen Aroon," Heaney drew upon every manifestation available to him, uniting them to develop and deliver a powerful and moving performance.

The ability to reinvigorate old traditions in the present (as well as to reconnect a more modern text to its past) is revealed with great eloquence in the following poem in honor of Heaney by Mary O'Malley. She highlights his work not only as a translator and mediator in the broadest sense but also as someone who listened, in essence, to the voices of those who could no longer speak. In the final few lines, her direct reference to Ó Dálaigh, and to Heaney's connection with him, makes the revelation of the connection between these three songs all the more powerful.

> He soaked it all in—
> The generations of dead and banished
> Had left words after them, chain-linked
> From Ros Muc to Barna.
> They waited to be voiced,
> Shivering in the folds of hills,
> Leaning against gables
> Like old men, or drowned
> At the mouth of every bay
> From Bertraboy to Carna:
> Famine grass, American wake, coffin-ship.
> He said them among half-sets and jigs
> And set Cearbhall's love-song
> Wandering down the centuries.
> —Mary O'Malley

The Wandering Laborer in Exile

Joe Heaney performed primarily in English during his long sojourns in Britain and North America. Most members of his audiences were unfamiliar with the Irish language, and some learned only from him that such a language even existed. He claimed that he had learned all of his English-language songs from his father, even though he picked up many more in Scotland and England. Heaney also claimed that during the Famine, many English speakers in the interior of Ireland migrated to the Irish-speaking west coast, bringing English-language songs with them, and that these songs joined the existing Irish-language tradition. This explanation is partial, but it is the one Heaney frequently gave. The performance of English-language songs by people whose ordinary vernacular was Irish shows the growing availability of Anglophone culture during the nineteenth century. Performance in English also points to a long tradition of bilingualism among Irish speakers and to a lively interest in English-language ballads. Referring to a gathering of Irish-speaking women from Carna— some of whom were relatives of Heaney—who sang in English for her, Angela Bourke suggests that "English-language songs [in Connemara] appealed to a sense of poetry, or of music, and may have offered an extra dimension in singing sessions: they had gone to considerable effort to learn them, and in some cases had remembered them for a very long time.

It may be that these songs were especially enjoyed when women gathered to sing" (Bourke 2007:48).

Clearly, the mere fact of being a native speaker of Irish—both today and during Heaney's time—never did restrict the speaker to using only Irish in either speech or song. No matter how Heaney created the most remote and romantic vision of an isolated hamlet for his audiences, Carna was well traveled by outsiders, and most people were able to speak English well, however hesitantly. The language in the area immediately north and west of Carna began to shift in the nineteenth century, and by the 1930s, Irish was spoken only by a quickly dwindling number of older people there. Heaney mentioned that his own father had lived in England and was fluent in English. Given the prickly politicized landscape of language in Gaeltacht Ireland, however, it was expeditious for Heaney to create the powerful image of an inflexible song hierarchy (Irish-language songs *always* being better than English-language songs) in the context of an entirely monolingual, communal, rural community. He would then quickly break that image by choosing a couple of English-language songs as being among the most important and central pieces in his repertoire. These two songs, "The Rocks of Bawn" and "A Stór mo Chroí" (which, despite its title, is in English), were a crucial part of Heaney's must-sing repertoire, among the hundreds of songs from which he could draw.

"The Rocks of Bawn"

Of all his English-language material, "The Rocks of Bawn" is among Heaney's signature songs. It resounds in the compelling film *The Irishman* (Philip Donnellan, 1965) like a refrain, linking tune and text to proletarian images of ordinary Irish workers earning their way as immigrants in England. It was already well known prior to the release of the film and to Heaney's frequent performances of it, but it is probably Heaney who popularized the hexatonic tune most commonly associated with it today. The song is supposed to have been a press gang song in origin, but in the mouths of Irish singers, it became an anthem for the hardship of the small holding and the statement of an honorable intention to fight for Ireland's glory albeit in the service of the English crown or sometimes of Patrick Sarsfield.[10]

Much frequently heated debate centers on the location of the place-name Bawn, and such argument can distract from the powerful text. Paradoxically, the text's power may derive from its vagueness, the uncertainty of the place-name, and the lack of any coherent story. Although this song is in English, its sensibility bears strong Gaelic influence in that it demands exegesis; it invites narrative as an additional accompaniment to the scanty detail of its text. All texts are open to some extent, and "The Rocks of Bawn" is more open than most. It may be significant that the word "Bawn" (*bán*) in Irish may mean empty, unwritten, or fallow in addition to its common translation of "white." It can also mean a castle with its courtyard (*bádhún*). The following is Heaney's own spoken introduction to the song:

> Now, coming out of Connemara, you see, there's a song that's known as the daddy of all Irish folk songs sung in the English language. And I think you know which song I'm going to sing for you now [interviewer says "The Rocks of Bawn"]—that's the one. *Bán* means white. Sweeney was the name of the man who was tormented by having to work for this particular landlord, and because Sweeney had the audacity to sit down and light his pipe, the landlord told him, "my curse attend you Sweeney, you have me nearly robbed. Sitting by the fireside with your *dúidín* in your gob." Now a *dúidín* is a short clay pipe, what's left of it, but the old people believed that if you cut off the stem of a clay pipe, that the smoke would be much better that came out of the pipe after the stem was cut off. And then he said, things were getting so bad at the rocks of bawn, that he said, "I wish the Queen of England would send for me in time, and place me in a regiment all in my youth and prime. I'd fight for Ireland's glory from the clear daylight till dawn, but I never would return again to plow the rocks of bawn." (interview, June 8, 1983)

Heaney treated this song, in a typically Irish fashion, as a dialogue and filled in the gaps in the dialogue as a narrator, saying who, what, and why, giving added determinacy to a rather unstable text. The song also belongs to the genre of the Irish street ballad; its conventional "come all ye" opening is essentially a byword for the genre (Shields 1993:vii). "The Rocks of Bawn," with its first words, leads straight into the evocation of the audience—all of them, men and women—as heroes. The juxtaposition in the second line with the image of the heroes hiring with a master reveals the colonized Irish to be under the yoke of the English, heroes or not. The hero of the story is a worker known in Irish as a *spailpín*.

A *spailpín* is a landless itinerant worker who hired out his services to more prosperous farmers. Joe Heaney described such a laborer as the kind of person "that everyone takes his own bite out of you." Ó Dónaill's dictionary includes two meanings for this word: the first is "seasonal hired labourer or migratory farm labourer"; the second meaning is "person of low degree; rude person; scamp" (1138). The experience outlined in "The Rocks of Bawn" has similarities to that expressed in another Heaney song, "An Spailpín Fánach" ("The Wandering Labourer"). This seemingly light-hearted rhythmical song on one hand describes the airy freedom of the footloose migrant. On the other hand, it reveals the lack of security and stability that was an integral part of the laborer's experience. These same factors underpin the text in "The Rocks of Bawn":

> Come all you loyal heroes, wherever you may be
> Don't hire with any master, till you know what your work will be

For you must rise up early from the clear daylight till dawn
I'm afraid you'll ne'er be able to plow the rocks of Bawn.

And arise up gallant Sweeney, and give your horse some hay
And give him a good feed of oats, before you go away
Don't feed him on soft turnip, put him out on your green lawn
Or I'm afraid he'll ne'er be able to plow the rocks of Bawn.

And oh Sweeney, lovely Sweeney, you have me in great dismay
Your walking among the stones and rocks, your hair is turning gray
Your walking among the stones and rocks, your step is like a fawn
I'm afraid you'll ne'er be able to plow the rocks of Bawn.

And my curse attend you Sweeney, you have me nearly robbed
Your sitting by the fireside, with your *dúidín* in your *gob*
Your sitting by the fireside, from the clear daylight till dawn
I'm afraid you'll ne'er be able to plow the rocks of Bawn.

My hands they are well worn now, my stockings they are thin
My heart is always trembling, I'm afraid I might give in
My heart is always trembling, from the clear daylight till dawn
I'm afraid I'll ne'er be able to plow the rocks of Bawn.

And I wish the Queen of England would send for me in time
And place me in a regiment, all in my youth and prime
I would fight for Ireland's glory from the clear daylight till the dawn
But I never would return again to plough the rocks of Bawn.

The bitter paradox of this song becomes starkly obvious as Sweeney's fighting spirit emerges in the last verse. He would gladly "fight for Ireland's glory" as his chosen *gaisce*[11] rather than face another day of plowing. The queen of England—Victoria, at the time of the song's development—would have engaged Sweeney in fighting against other colonial subjects in India and elsewhere. For Irish colonial subjects who fought the Queen's wars (and, later, the King's), one of the advantages of being in the colonial army (besides the steady paycheck and food) was being able to be a white man above the racialized other of India or in other colonies. In reestablishing whiteness in a colonial situation, Irish soldiers reclaimed aspects of lost masculinity and reestablished their maleness over a similarly feminized populace (soldiers or not).[12]

Heaney sang "The Rocks of Bawn" at nearly every American performance. It was easily his favorite English-language song, and he is frequently quoted in newspaper articles as "singing and teaching traditional Irish songs like 'The Rocks of Bawn.'" Certainly his American students were expected to know it by heart or be subject to his stern disapproval. The melody (figure 5.4) is in a relatively simple abba form, and Heaney often used it as a template in his private lessons to illustrate how one could

Come all you loy - al her- oes, wher - e- ver you may be, don't

hire with a- ny mas - ter 'til you know what your work will be; for

you may rise up ear - ly from the clear. day - light 'til the dawn; I'm a-

fraid you'll ne'er be ab - le to plough the rocks of bawn.

Fig. 5.4: "The Rocks of Bawn"

choose to place ornaments in the song. As one of his main English-language songs, "The Rocks of Bawn" served many purposes.

Filmmaker Philip Donnellan, in shooting his documentary *The Irishman*, chose to feature Joe Heaney singing "The Rocks of Bawn." In an unpublished memoir, he discusses the song's use to convey the frustration of Irishmen working in England, whose lives and works, he believed, were never taken seriously:

Alongside Ewan's [Ewan MacColl's] specially written music we had the famous song from the grey and granite west—"The Rocks of Bawn" which marvelously embodies the contradictions in the Anglo-Irish relationship—and that became a linking motif.

"Oh I wish the Queen o' England," sings the superb Joe Heaney against images of an armoured division of earthmoving caterpillars rolling across the Middlesex fields:

"...would send for me in time
An' put me in some regiment, all in my youth and prime
I would fight for Ireland's glory from clear daylight till dawn
But I think I'll ne'er be able to plough the Rocks o' Bawn."

Nor could we ourselves plough them.... The reception of the film by my superiors justified the suspicions of our Irish contacts. They did not believe that I would make or the BBC transmit, a programme which treated them with seriousness or recognised the work they did in Britain. (Donnellan 1988:153)

Donnellan's film, a work of "dissident documentary," criticized both Irish and English governments for their treatment of this generation of Irish workingmen. It was withdrawn by Donnellan's BBC controller on aesthetic grounds and never shown. Donnellan was convinced that the offense taken was because of the film's harsh criticism of political elites and class-ridden attitudes (Pettit 2000:358). A point of bitterness regarding "The Rocks of Bawn" and its potential application to Heaney's own experience is that the life of the wandering laborer reflects local customs relating to the equal inheritance of land. In pre-Famine Ireland, poorer tenants had divided their land to the point where the holdings became so small as to be economically unviable. In its wake, even the poor began to conform to a pattern already established among the stronger tenants— that of allowing one male child to inherit. If others wanted to stay, they must usually remain unmarried. This resulted in households containing numerous siblings in nineteenth- and twentieth-century Ireland.

It is worth noting that Heaney came from an area designated as congested forty years after the Famine. The land in Connemara was poor, and a holding could support only one family, and that with difficulty. Others had to find different means to make a living, and that meant they had to leave. Heaney's path had been marked by an opportunity to be educated, but when that abruptly ended, it curtailed his prospects severely. He was not to inherit the holding, and consequently he would have to leave. Without an education, one of the few other opportunities he had was to work as a manual laborer or perform other unskilled work. Clearly, then, "The Rocks of Bawn" had particular meaning for Heaney's own biography as well as for thousands of others, a point effectively made by Donnellan's film. Though Heaney would never return again permanently, nevertheless the ties to his home place remained strong.

"A Stór mo Chroí"

Another English-language song that evokes the ties between Heaney and his home place, in combination with the experience of emigration, is "A Stór mo Chroí" ("Treasure of My Heart"). Composed by the nationalist and sentimental writer Brian O'Higgins (1882–1963), to the prescribed traditional air, "Bruach na Carraige Báine" and published in his 1918 collection of verse *Glen na Mona, Stories and Sketches*, its emigration theme has made it a firm favorite of traditional singers in Ireland.[13] The majority of Heaney's audiences in North America consisted of the descendants of immigrant populations; depending on where the performance took place, some audience members were only one or two generations from Ireland or from other countries, or had vivid family memories of coming to America during the Famine. For those who were not of Irish ancestry, their own family histories came into play while listening to Heaney discuss the harsh conditions at home, the arduous sea voyage, and the often-unhappy fate that awaited many Irish immigrants upon arrival in the United States or Canada. As part of a larger impetus to encourage his audiences to understand his sense of the real Ireland, he would tell the story of the "American wake," the custom of sending off young emigrants to America by holding a living wake for them. Heaney describes such an event as follows, during his "Afternoon Tea with Joe Heaney" performance in April 1983:

I know some of you already have heard this. And maybe those who *have* heard it will put up with it, another little bit. Now, some of you might have connections or something, and they say the people who don't look for their roots should never—not fit to be born. And I'm sure this country is made up of immigrants from all over; I think maybe some of you people here would someday come to somebody and say 'Why did you leave?' 'What county were you born in?' 'When did you come out to America?' because I'm starting to—now—there's a thing called the American Wake. Ever hear of that?

Now, it's nothing to do with this country, except I'll tell you now, my grandmother, when I was growing up, as I told you before she was strict, she was fair, and she was everything; she had to be cruel to be kind as she said herself. Well every night when she was saying the rosary, and believe me you had to be there to say it, or else! There was no else, you were *there*. She always said a prayer for America, for looking after her four daughters. Now I never met them, but who knows, maybe I met somebody belonging to them; I don't know. But anyway, the American Wake was called, because long ago, when there was no roads, and it took a boat about three or four weeks to get to America. When somebody young was leaving, and they all left when they were young that time, they were lucky to—some of them left when they were seventeen. They came out of this country, and some of them never had anybody to meet them. Nowadays somebody comes on an aeroplane, and you think they're doing a favor to everybody by going into a taxi at Kennedy or whatever they're going to.

Anyway, before they left, there was what you'd call a living wake. And talking about wakes, if anybody tells you Irish wakes are roundabout randies, don't believe it. They're very solemn occasions. But now some people think it's fashionable to put a joke in a book about how the Irish go crackers at a wake. I never saw it. There's a solemn occasion, and they treated the man who was dead, or the woman who was dead, with great respect. *Believe me*, that is true. Well anyway, the person who was going away, whether a man or a woman, they went out and they kissed all the old people good-bye, they invited the young people in, to have a time or a *céilí* in the house, for—before they left. Now, at the time, see, I'm not going into the time where there were musical instruments was barred and all that, but the mouth music used by the people kept the dancing going all night.

Now there's such a thing in every Irish door at that time, as a half door. The half door was hung up after the big door was open. One reason was to keep the chickens out and the children inside, which always seemed to work the opposite way. And on the concrete floors of the country houses you can't have a wooden floor, because the heat of the fire would burn it. They took off the half door and they danced on top of the half door. Now I'll take you to one of these wakes. And this is what went on, and of course at the end, there's a song. But it came to the lilting, and this is two of the most famous tunes they used to lilt were the reel, "My Love, She's in America," and a hornpipe, "Off to California." Now a reel is much slower than a hornpipe, at least it *should* be, and this is the way they used to do it: "My Love, She's in America" first. [lilts the reel, then the hornpipe]

And that's the tuning, all night, somebody would take over when somebody else would stop. The women were the best at this, and that reminds me of an old man, and it's the worst thing he ever did in his life, he said. Two old women was wanting which of them was the best at lilting. And he had the misfortune to be chosen as the referee. And he gave it to one of them over the other, and the one that had lost, she hit him with the stick on top of the head. And when he came to, half an hour afterwards, she asked him, "Why did you give Mary the prize?" "She put more doodlies into the tune," he said, "than you did."

Well, now, at the end, in the morning, when this somebody was leaving home, the mother usually was in a bad way, you know, because they knew they wouldn't see this person anymore. And she, "a stór mo chroí" means "dearest of my heart." And this song is in English, but it's the song, telling the one who is going away, "when you're going, remember: you'll get nothing for nothing on the other side. If you see somebody rich, remember behind that person there can be very poor people. And whenever you're walking the streets, stop, think, look and listen. Because the one you're going to hear in the distance is *my* voice, calling you back. And this is the song."

> *A stór mo chroí*, when you're far away
> From the home you'll soon be leaving
> And it's many a time by night and day
> That your heart will be sorely grieving.
> Though the stranger's land might be rich and fair
> With riches and treasure golden
> You'll pine, I know, for the long long ago
> And the love that's never olden.
>
> *A stór mo chroí*, in the stranger's land
> There is plenty of wealth and wearing
> Whilst gems adorn the rich and the grand
> There are faces with hunger tearing.
> Though the road is dreary and hard to tread
> And the lights of their cities may blind you
> You'll turn, *a stór*, to Erin's shore
> And the ones you left behind you.
>
> *A stór mo chroí*, when the evening sun
> Over mountain and meadow is falling
> Won't you turn away from the throng and listen
> And maybe you'll hear me calling.
> The voice that you'll hear will be surely mine
> For somebody's speedy returning
> *A rúin, a rúin*, will you come back soon
> To the one who will always love you.

"A Stór mo Chroí" is so deeply resonant for local communities in the west of Ireland that it has been translated into the Irish language by Jackie Mac Donncha, a noted poet from Heaney's area. The translation has been taken up by a number of *sean-nós* singers, and it now coexists alongside its English-language parent.

In sharing both the story and the song with his audiences, Heaney reflected upon the trajectory of his own life: the fact that he had to leave home to find work, to leave his rural upbringing to make his way among the people in New York, to confront the appalling disparity of extreme wealth and extreme poverty, and to try—through his performances—to celebrate where he came from. In examining the musical transcription (figure 5.5), the abundant use of melisma reveals a deeper expressiveness in his production of the song than he would apply to most English-language songs. He often reserved the richest ornaments for the songs that he felt reflected some aspect of his own philosophy or experience.

As Munnelly (1994:83–86) has remarked about another such song, it may seem maudlin to the point of oversentimentality. However, as he also points out, songs such as this are inexplicably bound to the context from which they emerge. Heaney's performance emphasized the music to the point where the oversentimental lyrics recede and the expressive power of the Gaelic air acts as a counterbalance. The response of his audience was palpable; people were sometimes reduced to tears as their imaginations rushed past the specific circumstances of the story and song, either merging with, or creating anew, memories of their own forebears' experiences.

"The Rocks of Bawn" and "A Stór mo Chroí" are only two of his hundreds of English-language songs; he could spend several hours singing song after closely related song from a single category like *revenant* (dead lover) songs, broken token songs, ballads, dialogue songs, children's songs, praise songs, and other categories.[14] Other times he could draw one song from each category to build a rich and varied performance. Because his store of English-language songs was so large, and his audiences in the

Fig. 5.5: "A Stór mo Chroí"

final decades of his life were almost entirely English-speaking, he did not have the opportunity to follow the same broad-based selection process from among his Irish-language songs. Instead, Heaney used a smaller selection of Irish-language songs over and over; they were ones he knew well (and were indeed among his favorites), ones that served a first-rate pedagogical purpose, and ones that would appeal melodically or thematically to his mostly monoglot audience members. It is possible that—had he found a similar job in Ireland, where the opportunities to work in Irish might have presented themselves—he might have had an audience ready to receive his Irish-language repertoire. If such a situation had come about, it is possible that the top songs of his English-language repertoire, like "The Rocks of Bawn" and "A Stór mo Chroí," together with "Morrissey and the Russian Sailor" (see chapter 7), might have consequently receded in importance. In each of his performances, however, Heaney chose the right song for the right time.

Part III

❧⊙⊙☙

Masculinity in a Musical Context

Any book with the subtitle *Irish Song-Man* ought to give some weight to the third element in that sobriquet. The third part of this book emphasizes Joe Heaney as male performer. Masculinity provides a useful frame for examining Heaney's musical life because, implicitly, it was a primary driving force of his performances. Because of Heaney's experiences, which were bound up with the circumstances and events of a decolonizing Ireland throughout his life, he knew what it was like to be marginalized and rendered powerless. His image as a man who performed hard labor or low-level clerical work in England and who also performed as a full-time artist in residence in the United States was developed, at least in part, though his deliberate efforts to transform his earlier experiences in the newly created Irish Free State. His association with singers and instrumentalists who understood his genre, his adherence to ideals about what he represented, and his repeated refusal to represent other kinds of a more palatable Irishness all helped him achieve this goal.

In the following two chapters, the contrast between the media-friendly Irish tenor—as exemplified first by Thomas Moore and continued by John McCormack and others—and the *sean-nós* singer as represented by Heaney is an example of a dichotomy in masculinity that has existed in Irish and Irish American society right up to the present. In chapter 6 Heaney is revealed to be a focus of attention for his audiences not only for the way he represented a kind of authentic Irish masculinity to his audiences but also for the way his audiences connected him to the land through repeated descriptions of his facial features, demeanor, and general appearance as akin or even identical to the Connemara landscape. In chapter 7 several songs—"Morrissey and the Russian Sailor," "Bean a' Leanna," and "I Wish I Had Someone to Love Me"—focus attention on how Heaney relied on specific songs to reinforce his own engagement with the Gaelic concept of *gaisce*: the warrior deed. In Heaney's focus on the warrior deeds of others, he himself joined the ranks of warriors of the past (and future) against foes real and imagined. However, other aspects of a more variegated masculinity lurk beneath the bravado. Therefore, this part is also an exploration of chinks in the heroic armor to discover a more complex identity, one more easily understood as an Irishman on the stage than any reductive caricature of a stage Irishman.

6

e✿✿✿✿✿✿✿

Irish Masculinities

The Irish Tenor and the Sean-nós Singer

Singing in Ireland is by no means confined to rural Gaelic-speaking individuals with an ancestral repertoire of song. In fact, despite the esteem in which they are held in some circles, *sean-nós* singers are a distinct minority. Ireland abounds in diverse musical styles both vocal and instrumental, often clearly influenced by American popular culture. For example, rock, rhythm and blues, jazz, and most popularly country and western include similarities to traditional song. Despite the approval it officially receives (see, for example, Ó Riada 1982; Ó Canainn 1978, where *sean-nós* is given pride of place over all other forms of musical expression), many Irish consumers of music in fact dislike traditional song, finding its plaintive airs too doleful and its symbolism perhaps too redolent of past hardship and poverty; it is imbued with collective memories that were better discarded. The "white savage" image that William H. A. Williams describes—in which British travel writers avidly and exaggeratedly described the poverty-stricken, scarcely human Irish with apparent relish—has set up a constellation of images for many contemporary Irish (and Irish Americans) that stands in the way of a compassionate understanding of traditional ways of being and knowing. Indeed, such comparisons threatened to make the Irish peasant into an anomaly: a *white, European Christian savage*—emphasis in the original (Williams 2008:107).

It is in the financial and moral interest of the colonizer to render the colonized as more of an object than a human being. As history is written by the victors, so postcolonial life is colored, inevitably, by shadows of the victors' tastes and standards. In a climate of antitraditional, anti-Gaelic, antilocal, and anticultural expression—against all things that *sean-nós* has come to represent—the modern, English-speaking, international literary world that William Butler Yeats and others developed so effectively at the turn of the nineteenth century led to the adoption of Irish authors who wrote in English as "British" or "English" writers in bookstores and university English departments the world over. Readily claimed by the English literary world in the twentieth and twenty-first centuries, the Irish National Literary Movement produced a kind of value-added English literature. The inherent irony is that even as the members of the National Literary Movement sought through their work to strengthen Irish cultural nationalism and identity politics, many in the English literary community regarded their work as simply more English. David Patrick Moran's well-known piece, "The Battle of Two Civilizations" (written in 1899 and published in 1901), outlines the late nineteenth-century struggle of the Irish to become something other than a direct imitation of the English (Moran 2000:31–43).

In this context it is interesting, then, to compare traditional singers to another kind of male singer with some claim to represent Irish vocal music. That male singer is the Irish tenor, who continues to enjoy popular acclaim in Ireland to some degree, but also especially in North America. The Irish tenor, as both man and image, enjoyed considerable popularity in literary works, media, and professional work as a performer, all of which represent commercial success through the twentieth century and into the twenty-first. The traditional rural singer, on the other hand, has been much less visible in literature, the international media industry, or on the professional stage. This chapter explores the reasons both figures contribute to a sense of what it means to be Irish in Ireland and abroad, and how Joe Heaney simultaneously fit into, and broke out of, narrow definitions of Irish maleness.

The two images—the traditional rural singer and the bow-tied dress-suited tenor—represent social divisions and expectations within Ireland. The *sean-nós* singer—rural, Irish-speaking, oral, communal, focused on the past, frequently with a rugged demeanor, wearing clothing designed for hard outdoor labor—may for some be a harsh symbol of an Ireland that many try hard to forget or to downplay, despite his high symbolic capital among cultural nationalists. The Irish tenor—urban, English-speaking, literate, individual, focused on the future, with refined looks and clothing designed for the salon—is, for many, far more representative of the Ireland of the future. He dates from the dawn of modernity (the late nineteenth century), and the popular imagery surrounding him has remained constant for more than a hundred years. In a sense, he stands for the acceptable modern equivalent of the *sean-nós* singer.

In this exploration of what it means to be masculine, musically, the images of *sean-nós* singer and Irish tenor are juxtaposed as representatives of competing visions of the Ireland in which Heaney came to maturity. Although examples exist that fail to conform to such a binary division, this dichotomy provides a useful framework with which to interpret Heaney's cultural principles. Joe Heaney's identity as a *sean-nós* singer is complicated; this chapter suggests that such an identity represents more than simply a performative position, but instead a symbolic icon onto which audiences—both Irish and foreign—projected their own longing and desire. One manifestation of this desire was the wish to connect with a more robust, authentic reality than they encountered in their everyday lives. Heaney's persona could be a powerful conductor of such emotional needs.

One of Heaney's most appealing traits for many of his listeners was his particular representation of a rural, untamed masculinity: earthy, proletarian, and untainted by the corrupting and Anglicizing influence of the city. At the same time, this robust figure could stand for the present embodiment of the former glory of Gaelic civilization before its disastrous downfall during the seventeenth century. In this context, his persona is emblematic of his supposed polar opposite, the tenor. Therefore, in briefly considering the history of the Irish tenor and his antecedents in a colonial context, this chapter also explores the background from which a singer such as Heaney could emerge to become a major public figure.

Masculinity in Theory and Practice

So far in this book, the representation of Joe Heaney and the world he built around himself has emerged as one kind of truth about Ireland and the presentation of its past through oral performance. It is important to remember that Heaney was not the first Irishman to engage in such presentation. In fact, performance is arguably tied to perceptions of Ireland and Irishness that resonate significantly throughout Irish history. From an early date, Irishness and music have been closely linked. Importantly, such links were observed from a conqueror's viewpoint. Giraldus Cambrensis (Gerald of Wales), a descendant of Norman-French colonists, writing in the twelfth century, praised music as the only redeeming trait of an otherwise barbarous people. This claim of an affinity between Irish people and music was frequently repeated in later times, especially from the eighteenth century on.

Arguments about the gendering of music and musicians, and by extension of Irish people, may likewise have started with Giraldus. He described the male harpers in the courts of Gaelic chieftains in terms of their artistry and craft, suggesting that they were sensitive individuals, almost contradicting himself in regard to his other assertions of Irish barbarism. It is possible that he regarded skills in musical performance as an essential civilizing element within Irish culture. Such attributes were subsequently interpreted as an assertion of the femininity of the Irish and particularly of those Irish who were musicians.

Gendered representations of Irish musicians, then, have been articulated throughout Ireland's colonial history and are linked to strategies of domination, accommodation, and resistance. Leith Davis (2006) argues in an extended study not only that gender has played an important role in colonial representations of music in Ireland but also that the politics of masculinity and femininity surrounding music have deeply affected Irish reactions to colonialism, leading to multiple, sometimes contradictory and often conflicted responses. Davis's seminal work concentrates for the most part on the written record and stops just before the heyday of the Gaelic revival at the end of the nineteenth century. However, she shows how a focus on gender holds considerable power for understanding cultural poetics and politics in Ireland especially during the eighteenth and nineteenth centuries. For the purposes of this work, that focus has continued into the twentieth and twenty-first centuries, in which popular memory and media continue to link certain aspects of gender to music.

Similar attention to concepts of gender during and after the Gaelic revival and continuing well into the twentieth century has the potential to help clarify the period and its characters. Consequently, an interpretation of Joe Heaney's life and work as a performer of Irish songs is enriched by an interrogation of gender in relation to his persona as a male performer and public figure from a rural Irish-speaking background. Joe Heaney represented the ultimate in masculine authenticity to the cultural nationalist ideal that emerged leading up to, and in the aftermath of, the foundation of the Irish Free State.

In the same way that the iconic autobiographies first written in Irish by Blasket Islanders of extreme west Kerry represented a deep Ireland in literary mode,[1] Heaney, in his appearance, his bearing, his speech, and his sound, represented a deep Ireland for his contemporary admirers (Ó Giolláin 2000:148). His unquestioned authenticity stood for an aspect of Irish identity that many felt they had lost, or that had been denied them because of the process of Anglicization that they regarded as a function of colonization. Heaney could be and was regarded as the literal embodiment of such a past mythic wholeness, the representation of an ideal of what once held true and that Irish people might benefit from contact with once again. This sentiment was felt even more strongly in the years following Heaney's passing, when what he represented was believed to be gone forever.

The power of such a view was widespread. Mícheál Ó Cearna, a Blasket Islander but long since having become a resident of the United States, recalled a stint working in Dublin's Davey Byrne's pub in the 1940s. Ó Cearna remembers how customers used to come to marvel at him, precisely because he was an authentic Blasket Islander: "To say you were from the Great Blasket uplifted you, if I may say so. People were glad to meet you. Their eyes used to pop out. People used to come into the bar to meet Mícheál Ó Cearna and listen to him speak Irish" (Moreton 2001:218). The mystique of the West current in cultural circles in Ireland during the early years of the state was undoubtedly the cause of much of this curiosity, leading to Ó Cearna's achievement of minor celebrity status. However, Blasket Islanders and other Irish speakers could be idealized because they came from a region far from Dublin. Physical distance served conveniently to downplay social and class divisions prevalent elsewhere but not so starkly drawn in this atypical part of Ireland (Ó Giolláin 2000:148). Like Heaney, Ó Cearna's capital in Ireland remained symbolic and was not easily translated into economic gain, eventually leading him to follow the well-worn path of the emigrant to Springfield, Massachusetts.

Introducing masculinity as a framework to discuss Joe Heaney's life begs questions because such characteristics are frequently taken for granted in discussions of Heaney's life. This perspective, however, takes gender as a culturally constructed idea and views these essential characteristics of Heaney as informed by "unspoken, unrepresented pasts" (Bhabha 1994:12). The cultural gaze that predominated during his lifetime first arose in resistance against earlier configurations of Irish masculinity, configurations that were rejected in favor of new interpretations at the end of the nineteenth century and for much of the century that followed.

A central trope in any discussion of colonial relations is the gendering of the participants, "a homology between sexual and political dominance" (Nandy 1983:4). Broadly speaking, dominant states, or, in nineteenth-century terms, nations, were regarded as masculine, while those peoples or nations that had been conquered were feminized, regarded as playing a submissive, supporting role to their rightfully ordained masters, an image that was also replicated in gendered ideals of the domestic sphere (Nandy 1983). The male was synonymous with rationality, industry, objectivity, whereas women were thought to be emotional, frail, and sensual. In naturalized correspondences from the domestic to the colonial, the colonists' power was male and superior (and often preordained or at least sanctioned by the colonists' God), with the colonized occupying the inferior and subordinate female role.

These ideologies were efficiently disseminated by bureaucratic machines and were absorbed and reflected by the colonized, turning masculinity into a site of contestation for nationalists opposed to the colonial project. In an ideology that gendered rationality and objectivity as male, expressive and performance aspects of culture came to be viewed as predominantly female. Female performing artists of the colonies were nearly always automatically eroticized as well, as the rigid conservatism of the colonial forces came into contact with differing attitudes toward women in the performing arts. By extension, any male engaged in performance was open to allegations of effeminacy, and men belonging to a colonized group doubly so.

Thomas Moore and His Musical Descendants

Such a complex paradigm pertains easily to Thomas Moore (1779–1852), a musician, singer, and writer, still popularly considered Ireland's national poet. Moore was the son of a shopkeeper and a graduate of Trinity College, Dublin, where he has been duly memorialized in a larger-than-life statue outside Trinity's gates. He was a small man and possessed of cherubic good looks in his youth, a fact that his detractors did not fail to notice. Consequently, he was, tellingly, rather sensitive about his honor, fighting two duels early in his career to defend it. Although a prolific writer, his popular fame rests on his *Irish Melodies* (1808–34), a commercial publishing venture that became a best seller; it comprises romantic nationalistic verses penned by him and set to Gaelic melodies, many taken from the Bunting Collection. Charles Hamm notes that the *Irish Melodies* "share the distinction with the songs of Stephen Foster of being the most popular, widely sung, best-loved, and most durable songs in the English language of the entire nineteenth century" (Hamm 1983:44).

Moore's contract with the publisher stipulated that he perform the melodies in English parlors (Davis 1993:14). He harbored nationalist sympathies, having been a friend of the executed Robert Emmet in Trinity College, but eschewed gratuitous violence himself. He was faced with a dilemma in that he had to represent Ireland both to Irish people and also, crucially, to English and American audiences (England being a more lucrative market than Ireland). Because of this tension, his verse equivocates between calling courteously for justice for Ireland and "flattering the mighty" (de Paor 1994:6), to earn a living, so that he "both paved and blocked the way to the decolonization which is still in process in Ireland" (Davis 1993:23).

Bunting criticized Moore's treatment of the music, and although some defend him against this charge, arguing that the music has an integrity not so easily breached, other modern critics have accused Moore of emasculating the music (Campbell 1999:89–92). The fact that some of his lyrics have female speakers arguably further inscribes the interpretation of the feminized male. William Hazlitt, a contemporary of Moore's, dismissed his verses as "prettinesses," while Charles Gavan Duffy called him the "pet of petticoats" (Davis 2006:162–63), both charges that were augmented and confirmed by the fact that many of Moore's fans were upper-class women.

That Moore should be consigned by contract to contextualize his performances in a crucially feminized location—the parlor—glosses the nomenclature of upward mobility among the Irish in the United States. One of the standard tropes of linear Irish development in the nineteenth and twentieth centuries is that the Irish—paralleling American images of self-reliance and inevitable emergence from poverty—brought themselves up from the shantytown to the lace-curtain townhouse. Part of the achievement of a certain respectably genteel standard of living included the use of lace curtains on the windows (in both Ireland and Irish America) and in many cases the acquisition of a small spinet or upright piano, symbols of modernity, literacy, and civility.

Indeed, the expression "lace-curtain Irish" implies much more than window treatments; it carries a constellation of images that include upward mobility, steady employment for the adult male (and there is one) of the household, respectability, sophistication, and a certain level of education (see discussions in, for example, White 1998; O'Brien 2004). Irishness was a variegated concept, so that it became important to achieve the *right kind* of Irishness, one tied to "ideologies of Anglo-Saxonism,

Teutonism, social Darwinism and Americanism," constituting a "virulent middle-class morality" (Stivers 2000:160). Conversely, it was essential to dissociate oneself from the other (wrong) kind of Irish, associated with drunkenness, violence, laziness, and similar negative stereotypes, considered part and parcel of the identity of the post-Famine influx of Irish immigrants.

Moore's *Irish Melodies* provided a musical dimension to the trappings of respectability, creating, through the combination of tunes and lyrics, a newly authentic sense of English-speaking Irishness while also retaining a sense of national pride consistent with the norms of a civilized people. Moore may also have set the standard for future manifestations of this new English-speaking Irishness in the works of Yeats, Lady Gregory, and others of the fin de siècle Celtic Twilight. Theirs was surely a celebration of the right kind of Irish in terms of the National Literary Movement, in which the only Irish were those of the lace curtain, and those who belonged to the shantytowns and rural countryside would surely have lace curtains if they could only have afforded them. It was a compelling hybrid that retained its appeal for several generations as a way of establishing and maintaining a sense of sophistication specific to urban Ireland or East Coast Irish America (O'Brien 2004:93).

Moore, then, presents a problematic and a controversial image in Irish letters and music, his career symbolizing many of the cultural conflicts of nineteenth-century colonial Ireland. For some he personified the most slavish kind of pandering to the colonial elite, leading one irascible commentator to dub him "a half-fledged pervert" at the end of the nineteenth century (Pryor 1886, quoted in Ryan 1993:65). The "puritanically earnest" (de Paor 1994:7) rancor evident in such a statement accurately captures the mood and anxieties of many later nineteenth-century cultural nationalists. Having absorbed the hegemonic idea of feminization, they were quick to condemn it as perverse and immature where they found it. As Ireland's "national bard," Moore represented a particularly prominent embodiment of nationalist fears and also a foil with which to direct their own cultural program, toward the "real thing—the Irish language, the Aran Islands, the music, songs and poetry of 'the people'" (de Paor 1994:7).

Moore's performance style also deserves mention. According to a contemporary eyewitness account, it was profoundly emotional, suffused "with a pathos that beggars description," eliciting tears from all and in one case, it was said, causing a woman to faint (Parker Willis 1835:109, quoted in Campbell 2001:100). Such weepy feelings, however effective in performance, could also lead to insinuations of sentimentalism, further augmenting charges of emasculation.[2] Moore's great popularity among many nineteenth-century Irish consumers blossomed because he represented their aspirations toward upward mobility, readily allowing them to throw out the Gaelic bathwater, as it were, but retain much of the nationalist baby.

Although national realization remained a goal, according to Moore's view, this would come only in the fullness of time, with the blessing of the dominant partner in the relationship. Moore, then, could be seen at least partly to confirm the colonial stereotype of the subordinate, inferior feminized male in his performing persona. Clearly, the traces of Moore's great success as a writer and performer retained a powerful impetus long after his own demise, sustaining an apprehension that helped determine the politics and aesthetics of cultural nationalism in the twentieth century. What was seen, rightly or wrongly, as his effeminate weakness, paradoxically proved a powerful influence in forming a new mode of expressive presentation, formed in direct reaction to Victorian parlor style, perhaps most particularly for singers. This is the mode that was to become known as *sean-nós*.

The Irish Tenor and the *Sean-nós* Singer

Before looking at that new mode, however, it is important to have a look at Moore's musical and performing heirs. While Thomas Moore may be credited with the establishment of the initial image of the Irish tenor—and one that may be seen as rather dramatically in contrast with the *sean-nós* singer, whether the contrast is explicitly intentional or not—that image has continued unabated to the present. Furthermore, the internationalization of the Irish through emigration from home has perpetuated an enormous array of Irish ideas, ideals, performative genres, and, of course, stereotypes. New York reviewer Will Crutchfield (1987) effectively sums up for his readers what he believes Irish tenors sound like:

> If you don't especially like the sound of an Irish tenor—clear, reedy, sweet, penetrating and somewhat nasal—you surely wouldn't have liked Frank Patterson's recital Friday night in Carnegie Hall, because all the traditional characteristics are quite marked in his singing. If, like this listener, you have an affection for the style and the songs that go with it, a visit to his next local appearance is warmly recommended.[3]

Several aspects of this opening set of two sentences are noteworthy; the first is that "clear, reedy, sweet, penetrating and somewhat nasal" should be considered a traditional characteristic of the Irish tenor sound; the second is that Frank Patterson should stand in for every Irish tenor who has graced American soil; and the third is that the characteristics of the sound, initially presented as negatives, end up as positives for that particular critic. While it is difficult to reconcile the adjectives "clear" and "nasal" in describing the same musical event, "sweet," "reedy," and "penetrating" are simpler to parse. An Irish tenor, regardless of his identity, is expected to employ a standard, trained vibrato, thereby sweetening the tone by making it sound more in tune.[4] Reediness is a quality caused by slightly constricting the throat in such a way that limits the upper range (and in this case the overall tone of Patterson would sound markedly different from that of, for example, the open-throated Luciano Pavarotti). While Crutchfield the critic refrains from openly comparing Patterson with Pavarotti, he effectively consigns Patterson to the nostalgia circuit of a nonetheless "large and appreciative audience" in New York City.

That the Irish tenor should be dismissed as belonging exclusively to the nostalgia circuit was a concept already well in place by the turn of the twentieth century, thanks in part to the success of Thomas Moore's *Irish Melodies* and the development of salon culture in Dublin and other Irish cities. One of the essential features of the salon by the late nineteenth century was the performance of songs, poems, piano pieces, and other events of the kind after a meal or refreshment. Upright pianos had become affordable for the emerging middle and upper classes, and the combination of the new acquisition (the piano, a symbol of modernity) with the English-language golden oldies of the past century (Moore's *Melodies*) both affirmed the salon-goer's distance from the past and simultaneously confirmed his or her connection to it through the repertoire. Moore himself enabled the members of the upper classes to gain access to the music through piano arrangements: several steps removed, the music became safe for urban consumption. To offer up the Irish tenor as the symbol of this already symbolic site of presentation placed the burden of modernity, nostalgia, and reworked, domesticated masculinity squarely on his shoulders.

Part of the rise of the Irish tenor in popularity may well have been tied to the rise of the recording industry in Ireland. In order to be properly recorded, a male singer had to have a piercing voice that could imprint onto wax cylinders. George J. Gaskin (1850s–1920), "The Silver Voiced Irish Tenor" from Belfast and an important early recording artist, was described as being effective at recording because of his tinny voice: "Edward B. Marks recollected that 'Few voices reproduced well, and these, for some reason, were not always voices one should have wished to reproduce.... George had one of the best reproducing voices in the old phonograph days—one of the tiniest voices in the world.'"[5]

Bel canto—"beautiful song" in Italian—is stylistically familiar to anyone who has heard popular song since the mid-1900s. It is characterized by a stable, pronounced vibrato and the primacy of melody over lyrics. Sean Ó Riada asserted firmly that vibrato (and, therefore, the entire Irish tenor repertoire) was not a part of *sean-nós* performance practice (Ó Riada 1982). Yet many *sean-nós* singers have, in fact, sung with quite a pronounced vibrato, including Joe Heaney.[6] Popular culture, including bel canto—in contrast to what has come to be thought of as folk culture—is deliberately stylized and mannered. Folksingers do not necessarily alter their style by trying to sing higher, as in the Irish tenor sound; however, they may add or delete vibrato – as in the case of Kentucky folksinger Jean Ritchie – if their style appears to please their audience (or their personal ethnomusicologist or folklorist). High-pitched voices, such as that of the renowned singer John McCormack, in fact, attract attention and record better. Many Irish and Irish-American tenors of the 20th century and beyond invoke the name of John McCormack (1894–1945), either as a source of grand repertoire or as the great master to emulate.[7]

McCormack, who spoke no Irish, was the most famous Irish tenor of the twentieth century; a newspaper describes his singing as follows: "His voice is one of great resonance, as well as of high range, and his powerful notes were heard in a varied selection of Irish melodies. The audience seemed as if it would never see enough of him, and twice he had to respond to triple encores, while he was recalled times almost without number" (Ledbetter 2006:30). By the time he was in his thirties, McCormack was a wealthy man with a family, and—even as microphones came into popular use, and the big-band era had begun—he still drew the crowds.

Although he was not a lyricist, in the way that Moore was, clearly, McCormack's great popular acclaim parallels Moore's earlier fame. Through his performances of Moore's songs, McCormack makes the link between the two explicit, thereby establishing a particular genealogy of Irish performance style and repertoire, a point that is highlighted, for example, in James Joyce's work. McCormack definitively created a reputable, admirable persona for the Irish stage singer, which before him had been dominated by vaudeville buffoonery and blackface minstrelsy. In fact, he rejected a request to act the stage Irishman in an American performance, furiously handing in his resignation—which was accepted with alacrity (Ledbetter 2006:32). Such representations reinforced already ingrained images of the stage Irishman, red rags to nationalist aspirations of respectability.

A number of films in the twenty-year period between 1930 and 1950 helped to cement the image of the Irish tenor in the popular imagination both in Ireland and in the diaspora. In *Song of My Heart* (1930), John McCormack plays a schoolteacher with an astounding singing voice. The film includes a long concert sequence that introduced McCormack to hundreds of thousands of moviegoers, particularly in the United States. It also revealed him—in Irish tenor mode—to be precisely the romantic, selfless, educated person that conforms to the popular image. Paradoxically, unlike the highly successful McCormack, the character gives up his singing career.

In John Ford's film *The Informer* (1935), an Irish tenor (Denis O'Dea) sings a lament, Orpheus-like, in the misty twilight outside the home of the wake for character Frankie McPhilip; the viewer sees only his round, cherubic face and cannot help but note that–standing–he is almost as short as the seated fiddler next to him. In the same decade, *Wings of the Morning* (1937) was released, not just showcasing the talents of John McCormack but also hammering home the archetype. In the film (otherwise concerned with a horse race—one of McCormack's favorite events) he plays himself, reading lyrics from a notebook and looking portly and uncomfortable. Finally, *My Wild Irish Rose* (1947) chronicled the life of Irish tenor Chauncey Olcott, played by "Irish tenor" Dennis Morgan (who was actually of Swedish descent). Hollywood had ample material on which to build its image of feminized colonial singers.

James Joyce was a lifelong fan of McCormack: he himself aspired to be a tenor and competed successfully (winning the bronze medal in 1904, one year after McCormack had won the gold medal at the same competition). He used the figure of the Irish tenor as a catalyst in his short story "The Dead."[8] In the story, which was made into a film in 1987, the tenor D'Arcy charms everyone, is knowledgeable and well-spoken about Continental opera, flirts with several of the women at the party, and sings a fragment of the British ballad "The Lass of Aughrim" to cause Gretta's abrupt transformation into a tragic romantic figure.

Although Thomas Moore lost his appeal as a representative of Irish nationalist aspirations (and was, in fact, rejected by them), the representation of Irish performance in the body of the tenor, as configured by Moore, permeates popular culture to this day. Through film and other popular media, the Irish tenor continues to appear as a standard icon of Irish performance culture. One century after Joyce and considerably further beyond Thomas Moore's *Irish Melodies*, the image of the Irish tenor is simultaneously affirmed and contested on the Internet through blogs, film reviews, and Web sites of tenors themselves.

The tenor Josef Locke (born Joseph McLaughlin in 1917) was convinced by none other than John McCormack that his voice was better suited to the lighter Irish tenor repertoire than it was to Continental opera.[9] Tenor Ronan Tynan's Web site includes a quote that reveals much about popular concepts of the type of music sung by Irish tenors: "For the first time," the Irish tenor explains, "I'm singing material that has tremendous depth and weight...a greater variety of music [beyond] the classic 'Irish tenor' vein."[10] Tynan focuses attention in this statement on the idea that the standard repertoire of the Irish tenor appears to lack "tremendous depth and weight." The link between the Irish tenor, the immigrant, and Saint Patrick's Day was cemented further with the inaugural concert of Tynan's U.S. tour in 2005 on Saint Patrick's Day at the University of Notre Dame's new theater.

All these characterizations point to an archetype of the Irish tenor as urbanized, English-speaking, finely dressed, educated, romantic, desexualized, sophisticated, polite, and performing not particularly difficult material. As a physical figure the Irish tenor is often portrayed as shorter than average and slightly rotund, from *Wings of the Morning* to *Hear My Song* to Frank Patterson portraying an Irish tenor in a celebratory scene from *Michael Collins* (1996). The Irish tenor is far more romanticized and appealing than physically sexualized.

The persistence of the Irish tenor as an image of Irish success engages an identity that has been successfully modified to encompass the requirements of Irishness in a modern context. It privileges a particular view of the present and the future and gives an acknowledging nod in the direction of the past. Its continuity is not acknowledged, so it continues to be excluded and denied. It is almost too easy, then, to characterize men of Joe

Heaney's era and style as the polar opposite of the Irish tenor. Rural, Irish-speaking, lean, typically dressed in cloth cap and working clothes, and performing challenging material, singers such as Heaney embodied the fears and temptations of the exotic Other.

For many, because of his achievement and hard-won popular acclaim, Heaney embodied a kind of archetype of the rural Irish-language singer. His gravelly, low-pitched voice easily surpassed in depth that of most of his male contemporaries (including his students); his language skills as a native speaker of Irish were beyond the ken of all but a few members of his audiences (in the United States, England, Scotland, and even Ireland outside his native region and a small circle of aficionados); and his claims of authenticity and authority went largely uncontested (for to contest them was to risk his wrath). The way he presented himself—as easily capable of beating or singing anyone else into the ground by sheer power of personality, vast repertoire of songs and stories, and skill—was intimidating, to say the least. Ironically, he became a star, in some ways, because of his antistar attitude.

So far in this narrative, attention has focused on Heaney's unique inimitable sound, but another aspect of Heaney also deserves attention, because as well as coming to hear him, people were coming to *see* him. What seemed to impress and even render his audiences awestruck at least as much as his fine, deep singing voice was his face. He was tall by most standards, relatively fit, and his hair made him seem even taller. In this context, Heaney's physical appearance emerges as an important factor. However, the most remarkable feature that stood out, again and again, was Heaney's face. It is striking how frequently different writers identify Heaney's visual aspect with the landscape of his native region. Such a homology was an important layer in constructions of masculinity, and what those who observed him wrote about it deserves commentary.

Because his face was described variously as Mount Rushmore, the Connemara landscape, made from granite, and other metaphors, his appearance drew attention, again and again, to his performance of physiognomy. Often these metaphors identify his face with imposing topographical features, suggesting a close identification between Heaney and the very landscape itself. The following selection of quotes from Liam Mac Con Iomaire's wonderful and detailed biography (2007), which brings together a myriad of observations from contemporary sources, amply demonstrates the continuous emphasis on his face against the backdrop of the rural past, specifically against the backdrop of the Connemara landscape. The authenticity of the repertoire is expressed in the contours of the face. Note that out of seven comments about his face reproduced here, four of them use the word "craggy," two refer explicitly to granite, and one describes his face as stony. No other descriptions of his face describe anything beyond a litho-landscape. Among those whose comments are reproduced in the following list are people who were good friends with him; linking him with the landscape of Connemara served to connect him to a place he loved:

1. "Seosamh Ó hÉanaí is a great singer, with a face as strong and craggy as his own native Connemara, and a voice to match." (Dónall Foley of the *Irish Times*, p. 305)
2. "His weathered face looks like a craggy stretch of shore along the Ireland coastline: his hair is the damp cold grey wind, the furrows of the brow the waves of the dark ominous ocean, his wrinkles the jagged wrecks of the shore against which the crest breaks." (Dan Nierling of the *Northern Iowan*, p. 349)
3. "Joe had a face carved in granite and I never heard anyone singing like that." (Belgian photographer Nutan, p. 256)
4. "As I watched him I couldn't help feeling that even his physical appearance, particularly his gaunt, craggy facial features symbolised the rugged, dignified grandeur of the Connemara landscape when he came." (Mick Moloney, p. 454)
5. "Joe would fix his eyes somewhere in the far distance and his face would go almost stony, his hands on his knees and his mouth set, like a singing statue." (Peggy Seeger, p. 190)
6. "His face was extraordinary, as if it had been hewn of granite." (Peggy Seeger, p. 195)
7. "He walked like an old man and he looked ten years older than he was. And of course he had that craggy face." (Laurel Sercombe, p. 391)

Audiences in the United States sometimes commented on Heaney's commanding physical presence, noting that Heaney would "look right through you" when he sang, or that it seemed as if he "could see his ancestors sitting in the room with him." In many cases, the audience's gaze constructed the image of Heaney's face as a romanticized gaze of the Irish landscape, with its implications of stony, fierce ruggedness and, more important, a kind of difficult beauty that was not easily accessed or understood. Studies of physiognomy were already out of fashion in scientific circles well before Heaney's heyday, yet they appear to have continued in a near-unbroken line throughout (and beyond) his lifetime in popular memory (see, for example, L. Perry Curtis Jr.'s *Apes and Angels: The Irishman in Victorian Caricature*). In some ways, the craggy landscape and jagged coastline of Connemara were imagined as a gendered landscape, an incontrovertibly masculine symbol. Comparisons between Heaney's face and that landscape, then, also reinforced a particular kind of masculinity, possessing a wild, indomitable grandeur that suggested an essential, fundamental authenticity.

Tomás Ó Canainn has claimed that "no aspect of Irish music can be fully understood without a deep appreciation of *sean-nós* ('old style') singing" (Ó Canainn 1978:49). He then presented an intimidating set of reasons that an aspiring instrumentalist with no knowledge of *sean-nós* could not possibly hope to succeed as a piper. These criteria for appreciating and understanding *sean-nós* singing are well known and frequently echoed among members of the older generation of musicians (singers and instrumentalists alike), to the point that any monolingual English-speaking fledgling instrumentalist has been well warned about the pitfalls of playing an instrumental air based on a *sean-nós* song. The climate in which Ó Canainn wrote those words—in the mid-1970s—was indeed a difficult time not just for understanding *sean-nós* but also for speaking the Irish language, because of the State's ambivalent attitudes toward its maintenance. Links between Irish speakers and supporters of violent Republican extremism also contributed to sentiment against the language.[11] The oil crisis bit hard and Ireland's economic boom, much vaunted in the 1990s, was far in the future. Moreover, the overwhelming success of Irish groups such as the Bothy Band, Planxty, or De Dannan (which became a frequent target of Heaney's wrath) was just beginning to be influential in the burgeoning revival of traditional music. While it is unfair and inaccurate to say that the appreciation of traditional culture was moribund, it is perhaps appropriate to acknowledge some of the potential defensiveness of Ó Canainn's statements.

The evidence of how contemporary Irish and Irish Americans see and understand the image of the traditional singer is far less readily available in popular media (including film and the Internet) than are competing images of the Irish tenor. By way of example, in the film *The Matchmaker* (1997), a number of men on the Aran Islands vie for the attentions of an American (Janeane Garofalo) by singing for her (with the understanding that she will spend the night with the winner). The one handsome and rugged fellow who sings (in English—"On Raglan Road") at a relatively low pitch in *sean-nós* style (complete with standard-issue *báinín* or cream-colored Irish fisherman's sweater)[12] is clearly the best singer in the room, as well as the most emphatically masculine. He has held back during the competition, singing only after everyone else has finished. Yet, entirely in keeping with other popular images of this style of singing, rather than selecting the good singer, Garofalo's character chooses the one Irishman who can sing an American popular song (badly).

Irish films (made either in the States or at home) that include segments of traditional Irish music—and many Irish films do not—tend to use exclusively instrumental music. The timbre of the pipes or the harp, for example, can be instantly evocative to audiences at home and abroad; indeed, for certain Irish audiences, the harp and pipes are every bit as exotic to them as they are to the Americans and other foreigners. Only *The Secret of Roan Inish* (a film by the American John Sayles) includes the *sean-nós* song "An Mhaighdean Mhara," and that occurs only during the closing credits as a near throwaway song in terms of its placement, even as its lyrics mirror the content of the film.

A brief and hardly exhaustive survey of popular Internet sources bears out this claim. In an online interview, the harper Harriet Earis claims, "People seem to either love or hate *sean-nós*. I love it, but some musician friends I've got can't bear to be in the same room as a *sean-nós* singer!"[13] On an online Irish-language teaching site, one of the optional phrases for prospective students to say out loud, repeatedly, is "I do not listen to *sean-nós* because it is boring."[14] Many more examples of this relative degree of marginalization of *sean-nós* specifically, and of the genre of traditional song in general, abound in casual conversation and in media of various kinds. Clearly, for some, the *sean-nós* singer has no place in a modern view of Irish achievement either at home or in the diaspora.

These hints as to the popular reception of *sean-nós* singing (and those who sing it) seem to hit home with some online fans of the genre, who defensively point out that they always have enjoyed *sean-nós* since the time when it was "neither popular nor profitable" (a nod to the Irish satirist Myles na gCopaleen, a.k.a. Brian O'Nolan). The overwhelming contemporary evidence in Ireland points to *sean-nós* as premodern and out of style, like wearing a *báinín* (the sweater/jumper) instead of a suit. In contrast, the image of the Irish tenor appears to continue to be built upon, year after year, from *Riverdance* to musical theater on Broadway. Yet how does this pair of images—the popular Irish tenor and the unpopular *sean-nós* singing male—tally with the increasing popularity of the *gaelscoileanna* (the Irish-medium schools) in Ireland, and demand for Irish Studies courses in both Ireland and North America?

Joining the Image with the Reality

The two images of musically enhanced masculinity are both heavily romanticized and based only partly on reality. Part of the issue rests in the fact that *sean-nós* is an invented category that has taken on a contemporary life of its own. Until it was celebrated on Irish national radio by Seán Ó Riada as one of the heights of Irish musical expression (Ó Riada 1982:23–39), the term *sean-nós* had not taken on the iconic aura of authenticity beyond a small coterie of enthusiasts. Its elevation to the peak of Irish traditional vocal achievement, and the exhortations to appreciate it, resulted from the desire promoted by the Gallic Revival to preserve and promote all older manifestations of traditional culture, and the official support these views enjoyed among enthusiasts in de Valera's Ireland, which continued in its altermath. It was a powerful min.

Privileging *sean-nós* is an attempt to gain recognition and some continuity in the culture of Gaelic Ireland. It makes the claim that the traditional song repertoire and the traditional style of singing are valid forms of artistic expression worthy of attention. Additionally, it posits a claim for the recognition of a Gaelic-speaking nation. The irony here is that the critical mass of Irish people has been English-speaking since well before the Famine, and that the Famine and its aftermath sounded the death knell of any critical mass of Gaelic speakers in Ireland. Although Gaelic Ireland can justifiably claim to exist, that existence for the vast majority is vestigial and Other. A dream of Gaelic revival has at best been only partially achieved, and the powerful image from Nuala Ní Dhomhnaill's poetry

(2007) of the mermaids who flap around on dry land but who no longer recognize water as their true element is a powerful and disturbing one.

Yet Heaney drew upon many of the images of the Irish tenor in his construction of Irishness for his American audiences. Dressed impeccably in suit, tie, and well polished shoes, he spoke in English (even as he harshly criticized his fellow countrymen and women for not speaking Irish), conversed easily and readily with people from all over the world, and served as an intermediary between their late twentieth-century reality and the rural Irish past of the American imagination. Playing on the legendary charm of the Irish tenor, he alternately flattered and dismayed his admirers (sometimes in the same sentence) with his mercurial and unpredictable temper. Bluntly refusing a naive request for "Danny Boy," he would nonetheless humor the children in his audiences, singing a sweet song from his schoolboy days even as he looked sternly at the children. It was a powerful combination, and American children were usually convinced.

To offer a comparison with a contemporary of Joe Heaney, the singer Seán Ó Sé stands as an in-between figure of the Irish tenor and the *sean-nós* singer. With his excellent command of Irish and his knowledge of the song tradition, Ó Sé is easily able to perform traditional unaccompanied songs in Irish, but also performed virtuosically with Ó Riada's orchestrated accompaniments. His performances with Ceoltóirí Chualann (predecessors to the Chieftains) and Seán Ó Riada (for example, the 1970 CD *Ceol na nUasal* [Music of the Nobles]) reveal his rich vibrato and dramatically high tenor voice. In stark contrast to the *basso profundo* sound of Joe Heaney, the Irish-language "Irish tenor" singing of Seán Ó Sé (and the orchestral arrangements of Seán Ó Riada, for that matter), had brought Irish song directly into the parlor by the 1960s and dared the purists of either side to blink. Both men—Joe Heaney and Seán Ó Sé—have performed, recorded, and taught in both Irish and English.

It is worth expanding the collective understanding of *sean-nós* by pointing out that singers of this style come in all ranges. Male *sean-nós* singers are not by any means limited to the bass register. While Heaney was one of the lowest-pitched singers, he was not the only one. Furthermore, a purism that requires its constituencies to blatantly ignore all the new composition taking place in Irish—from country and western to rap—is simply an ineffective response to Ireland's modernization and globalization. Ó Giolláin makes sense of these contradictions in the following passage:

> Are these the uncomfortable compromises with modernity that an ancient folk culture has to make in order to survive in an unsentimental world? Or are they part and parcel of the unavoidable and necessary engagement that every living tradition makes with change? The point is that the continuity of traditional cultural elements is not necessarily compromised by embracing, rather than resisting, modernity, even if the resulting "second life" may not satisfy the purist. (Ó Giolláin 2000:4)

Heaney's world at home and abroad included fellow singers and musicians, academics, folkies, wealthy people, music industry figures, purists, working-class people, cultural nationalists, the avant-garde, hangers-on, writers, and plenty of uncategorizable people who saw both symbol and substance in his work and his songs. He presented, verbally, a path of Irish maleness that simultaneously revered the idealized rural, Irish-speaking, working singer and dismissed as false the urban, English-speaking, elite tenor (as represented by his disdain for songs such as "Danny Boy" and "Mother Machree"). Questioning his words by alerting him to his actions made him fiercely defensive, but it also allowed him the chance to teach something of Irish traditional culture the way *he* wished it to be remembered or conceived.

Perhaps the most important point to hold, in regarding Heaney as part of a continuum of Irish maleness, is that it was a fluid continuum in theory but a richly complicated continuum in practice. He wore work clothes only when he did physical labor as a younger man, but he dressed in a suit and tie from his 1942 Oireachtas victory through most of his later performances. One photograph of him taken in an Aran sweater at Newport is atypical and clearly influenced by the Clancy Brothers' adoption of the garment as a signature emblem. Even as he extolled the virtues of the country roads, he was an urbanite for almost all his adult life, at ease with subways, noisy Brooklyn bars, and crowded city streets. He was bilingual, translating easily, as he often reported, from Irish into English as he spoke. He could just as easily perform for an outdoor crowd of thousands—as at the Newport Folk Festival—as he could perform in a sitting room for five people. He could write the songs out in detail, every verse of them, and was every bit as literate as the *sean-nós* singer of audience imagination might *not* have been. His understated vocal vibrato was audible, even as he denied its existence.

What these apparent contradictions mean for Joe Heaney the singer and storyteller—the presenter of self, region, and nation—is that he had to fight, his entire professional life, the rigid categories that literature, popular media, and audience expectations built up around him. The reality is that he was astute, shrewd, and fluid. He implicitly understood the contradictions, played with them, and effectively created a whole series of personae that continued to evolve even after his passing. Joe Heaney the man became, then, Joe Heaney the culture hero of a thousand faces.

7

Fighting Words, Fighting Music

The Performative Male

Joe Heaney, in contrast to Thomas Moore and his musical descendants, came from farming and fishing stock,[1] raised in the kind of small Irish-speaking agricultural and fishing community that came to represent the epitome of true Irishness for fin de siècle cultural nationalists. This happened precisely because such communities were idealistically viewed as egalitarian, classless havens remote from the corrupting influence of Anglicization prevalent in the rest of the island and because they had retained the Irish language as their ordinary vernacular. The Irish language, in true Herderian fashion, came to represent the symbol of nationhood par excellence for the cultural nationalist movement.[2] Gender divisions in such communities were mirrored in labor and other activities: women predominant in the domestic sphere and farmyard with responsibility for poultry and dairy produce, men on the land and on the sea. A verse from one of Heaney's songs, "Sadhbh Ní Bhruinnealla," states the case well:

> *Fear maith i mbád mé togha fear iomartha*
> *Fear sluasaide is láí ar dhá cheann an iomaire*
> I'm a good man in a boat, a great oarsman
> A man for the shovel and the loy on both sides of the (potato) ridge

In accordance with such community norms, and the hard labor required to make the land and sea productive, physical strength and prowess were the esteemed measure of a man, and indeed to some extent of a woman, since women were also required to do hard physical labor at harvest and other times. Indeed, women were often praised for being able to do a man's share of the heavy work, whereas conversely, men might be ridiculed for undertaking tasks considered as women's work (Ó Giolláin 2005a:108).

Gaisce, (in the older Irish language *gaisged* = arms or weapons) originally a compound of the words *ga* (spear) and *sciath* (shield), is a Gaelic term meaning feats or deeds of achievement or prowess; originally it referred to armed or martial combat, but by extension it came to be applied to any outstanding physical act or other achievement. Furthermore, the term took on a linguistic aspect so that the heroic descriptions of valorous behavior or deeds also came under the semantic scope of the term.[3] This was borne out in a discussion with the late singer Dara Sheáin Choilm Mac Donnchadha (1939–2008), locally known as Dara Bán, a neighbor of Heaney's and his junior by twenty years, who had a favorite song. "Púcán Sheáin Antaine" (Seán Antaine's *púcán*, or sailing boat) lovingly and exuberantly praises the boat and describes how well made she (always she) is, how swiftly she sails in any seas. The song continues as described in the following few sentences: she has traveled to Galway and to Wicklow; had the poet Raftery lived, he would have made a fine eloquent song in praise of her. She was thought to have been past her best, her timbers aged and rotten, but she has been resurrected and is likened to a young woman again. The people of Maighinis miss her and want to see her three snow-white sails among them again. The shipwrights of the Galway coast are all good boat makers, but the palm goes to the Maighinis men, and this is acknowledged by all. When describing what he most enjoyed about this song, Dara Bán answered simply, *gaisce*. He meant the eloquent poetic expression of praise for the boat and its qualities and features, together with the equally fine manner in which the Maighinis shipbuilders are claimed unanimously to be the best, and this is what makes the song so memorable.[4] Consequently, this term expressed a value highly prized in such communities, although it can also express a negative, critical meaning connoting idle, empty boasting.

Such prowess was based on the physical work a person could do in the fields or on the sea and how they were able to provide for their households. Neatness and tidiness were also valued, with skills such as thatching, basket making, spade work, and butter- or dressmaking gaining admiration for men and women, respectively. *Gaisce* also extended to expressive forms, with musical ability, dancing, and singing carrying important symbolic capital, particularly in relation to courtship and marriage. Men and women who danced and sang well performed their gender according to community norms and also showed their physical strength in a sublimated, aestheticized display of skill and deportment, making them more attractive as marriage partners (Ó Laoire 2005). Sexual codes were strict, governed by both church and strong social control (Ó Giolláin 2005). In such communities, a man was admired who "worked to provide for his family, who fulfilled his community obligations, who minded his own business, who did not take advantage of others, but who defended his own rights. He was a strong, resolute figure, because such a character was respected and others did not try to abuse him" (Ó Giolláin 2005:73).[5]

In the same way, social control extended to an egalitarian ethic that kept everyone at about the same level. Those who achieved greater material success than others were regarded with fear and suspicion, since wealth was regarded as finite and the fact that some prospered meant that others must be doing less well. Material assets were regarded as essentially fixed in contrast to the capitalistic notion of unceasing economic growth. A certain religiously inspired fatalism was also characteristic of such communities, by which pain and suffering could be regarded as positive spiritual experience (Ó Giolláin 2005:77). Heaney was raised, and his attitudes were formed, in such a community, and his Gaelic songs in particular reflect such a value system. Examining his songs helps us to appreciate his particular relationship to this general code of behavior.

One way of understanding Heaney's musical masculinity, then, is to look at some of the songs most closely identified with him, those he sang very often and with which he seemed to engage most deeply. James Cowdery notes Heaney's thoughtfulness about his songs and his fondness for them. Such an observation suggests that those he sang often meant the most to him and that they can, accordingly, be regarded as having considerable potential for interpretation (1990:33). Consequently, three songs can offer readings of Heaney's masculinity and its importance for an understanding of the man himself: "Morrissey and the Russian Sailor," "Bean a' Leanna," and "I Wish I Had Someone to Love Me." Choosing these songs excludes others, of course, but these are particularly relevant in his American performance contexts.

"Morrissey and the Russian Sailor"

"Morrissey and the Russian Sailor" (Laws H18)[6] is the song perhaps most emblematic of values comprising the term *gaisce* in its original warlike sense. The song is a mid-nineteenth-century broadside ballad describing a fight between the Irish bare-knuckle boxer Johnny Morrissey (1831–78) and a Russian sailor in Tierra del Fuego.[7] Although there are many records of Morrissey's fights, this one is not among them. However, it is possible that the bout occurred during his sea journey from New York to California in 1851. The oldest broadside specific to this event dates from Dublin in 1860.[8] Johnny Morrissey was born in Tipperary, Ireland, in 1831. His parents emigrated in 1833 and settled in Troy, New York. Morrissey became a strongman and gang member, traveling to California and back and eventually setting up with the Saratoga Springs racecourse in New York. He had a reputation as a tough fighter and fought many illegal prizefights. He was also twice elected a U.S. congressman.[9]

Although it has some bearing on the case, however, Morrissey's historical persona is not our primary concern here. Rather, it is the mythic figure of the Irish fighting man, the underdog who, against all odds, succeeds in defeating his opponents and oppressors by dint of sheer physical stamina and endurance. Read as a broadside, the story progresses predictably enough, with

Morrissey eventually prevailing against his Slavic opponent in the thirty-eighth round (depending on which version one listens to). The fact that the Russian fighter's backers are "Yankees" is significant, referring indirectly to the discrimination experienced by the immigrant Irish in the United States during this period at the hands of the dominant, Protestant class.

In performance, however, the song is transformed by Heaney. His driving voice exudes a relish that implies nothing less than an exultant triumph, entirely appropriate to the song's spirit. It celebrates the physical strength and endurance of the Irishman against what are suggested to be hugely unfavorable odds. In this, the text and its performance represent a heroic ideal that can be traced to the stories of single combat in traditional European folktales, and in Ireland, as far back as Cú Chulainn's defense of the ford in *Táin Bó Cuailgne*. In these stories, the hero uses his wits and initiative as well as his strength to achieve victory, but as Zipes (1979) has noted for traditional folktales, might makes right (Ó Giolláin 2005:107). In the ballad, however, Morrissey appears to have both might and right on his side. The Irishman is specifically called an "Irish hero brave" and is minding his own business. He is not the aggressor and fights only in response to the Russian's challenge, which adds to his moral superiority. Morrissey's character is "stout and true" and refuses to show fear. He trades insults freely with his Russian opponent, calling him a "saucy, beggar bear." This is another performative feature confirming his unbridled masculinity. His bragging is not idle repartee but matches his physical strength in front of the prime arbiters of masculine deportment: the male onlookers.

> Come all you gallant Irishmen, wherever you may be
> I hope you'll pay attention and listen unto me
> I'll sing about a battle that took place the other day
> Between a Russian sailor and gallant Morrissey.
>
> It was in Tierra del Fuego, in South Amerikay
> The Russian challenged Morrissey and these words to him did say
> I hear you are a fighting man and wear a belt I see
> Indeed I wish you would consent to have a round with me.
>
> Then out spoke Morrissey with heart both brave and true
> I am a valiant Irishman that never was subdued
> For I can whale the Yankee, the Saxon, Bull and Bear
> In honor of Ol' Paddy's Land I'll still the laurels wear.
>
> They shook hands and walked around the ring, commencing then
> to fight
> It filled each Irish heart with pride for to behold the sight
> The Russian, he floored Morrissey up to the eleventh round
> With Yankee, Russian, Saxon cheers, the valley did resound.
>
> The Irish offered four to one that day upon the grass
> No sooner said than taken up and down they brought the cash

They parried away without delay until the twenty-second round
When Morrissey received a blow that brought him to the ground.

Up to the thirty-seventh round 'twas fall and fall about
Which made the foreign tyrants to keep a sharp lookout
The Russian called his seconds for to have a glass of wine
Our Irish hero smiled and said, "This battle will be mine."

The thirty-eighth decided on, the Russian felt the smart
And Morrissey with a dreadful blow, struck the Russian on the heart
The doctor, he was called in to open up a vein
He said, "It is quite useless, he'll never fight again."

Our hero conquered Thompson and the Yankee Clipper too
The Buffalo Boy and Sheppard, he nobly did subdue
So let us fill a flowing glass, here is health *go leor*
To noble Johnny Morrissey that came from Templemore.

In some versions of the song, Morrissey wears the "shamrock green,"
an important emblem of nineteenth-century Irishness.[10] Greenery, moreover, was understood as a symbol of "amity, peace and regeneration,"
also symbolizing the "tree of liberty" of Irish political independence
(Owens 1998:252). Consequently, what appears at first glance as the celebration of a mindless brawl turns out upon closer examination to be
also a representation of the Irish struggle for political and cultural recognition, especially in the post-Famine United States, in miniature.
Viewed in this light, it recalls Bakhtin's (1968) grotesque, carnivalesque
renewal of life (and freedom) through the symbolic death of the Russian's
fighter's defeat.

Such a portrayal of ethnic victory epitomizes values of *gaisce* in their
original sense of deeds of prowess in battle. That they contribute to the
Irish American stereotype of the "Fighting Irish" problematizes the uncomplicated straightforward pleasure in victory.[11] This belligerent portrayal of
Irishness was one that many upwardly mobile Irish Americans wished to
cast off in their journey from the shanties to lace-curtain respectability. In
such images, Irish men came across as dangerous and unpredictable, not
far removed from those simian cartoon figures "with crooked limbs and a
villainous face,"[12] so common in the racist anti-Irish press (Curtis 1997).
Heaney's exuberant performance of "Morrissey and the Russian Sailor"
refuses the lace-curtain middle-class pretensions not only of Irish
Americans but also of many urbanized Irish. It is a testament to the raw
energy of vernacular song poetry enjoyed and celebrated by communities
like the one from which Heaney came, regardless of their infringement of
the prescribed mores of respectability. Moreover, as Filene (2000:63) has
noted, the most admired folk performers are those who do not resemble
their usually middle-class audiences too closely. The unruly thrill of the
primitive radiates a compelling allure for such listeners, one that Heaney
could and did use to his advantage.

This conviction is borne out in the melody supporting the lyrics (figure 7.1). The first verse of the song is rich in embellishments (standard practice for Heaney), and as the song progresses it reverts to its melodic bones. Still standing in the final verse is the twisting embellishment at the end of the second line, a melodic turn on the third degree of the scale. It calls attention to what is being said in the words, highlighting both a lyrically unstable point ("and listen unto me," "these words to him did say") and a pause in the melody, indicating important new information to follow. Melodic instability, then, mirrors the textual volatility.

Heaney's use of melodic complexity in the initial verses of his song is interesting because he himself referred to such decoration as similar to the battle dress, the formulaic introductions to international hero tales, favored by older men in his community.[13] Although some women also excelled in telling these tales, the stories themselves were normally regarded as belonging to the male domain, so that his comparison of verbal ornament to musical embellishment specifically invokes the engagement of masculine norms. The term "battle dress," importantly, translates from the Irish terms *cóiriú catha* or *culaith ghaisce*, a testimony to Heaney's own interpretation of his music as part of his distinctive male identity and authority. As a singer and storyteller who had acclaimed performing abilities, who had the right stuff, the *neá* (Cowdery 1990: 38), Heaney performed in such a way as to reinforce a unique, seemingly indomitable projection of masculinity. Deriving from such displays, he also accessed and claimed his didactic authority through singing and narrative.

Heaney's retelling of tales of Gaelic heroes like Fionn Mac Cumhaill or Cú Chulainn links him to these superhuman figures because by narrating these stories of the glorious heroic past, he establishes this connected identity as an authorized narrator and a direct link to the lineage.[14] His work in producing the song—the warrior deed about a warrior deed— evokes an athletic nineteenth-century image in Ireland. Those engaged in cultural revival in the late nineteenth century believed that Ireland's demoralization in the wake of the Great Famine had resulted in the emasculation of males (McDevitt 1997). As an antidote to this, the Gaelic Athletic Association (GAA) was established in 1884; it standardized and

Fig. 7.1: "Morrissey and the Russian Sailor"

nationalized Gaelic games, hurling and football, and produced a newly positive image of the Irish male, fit, lean and athletic, disciplined and stoic. That this image mirrored Victorian ideals of masculinity was precisely the point. It effectively counteracted negative Victorian stereotypes of Irishness and Irish men in particular as feckless drunkards.

This image also had its converse side, where males might work like men on the playing field but play like boys afterward, drinking and enjoying the camaraderie of their teammates in sessions that included singing (McDevitt 1997). The concern with acceptable representations of masculinity was, then, a significant social and cultural concern for the architects of the newly emergent Ireland. Heaney's defensiveness about his own image, and about his sense of authority, projected an irascible, cantankerous attitude called *thumos* by Plato, and considered by him to be one of the defining qualities of manliness. *Thumos* translates as the "snappishness of a dog," which recalls Cú Chulainn, the epitome of Gaelic masculinity.[15]

Heaney's song, then, arguably embodies an older type of masculinity, one that cuts across the image of the sports field, with its gentlemanly British overtones, although the two are related. Heaney's portrayal is sufficiently robust to be attractive to listeners in play mode, presenting, as it were, the untamed red-blooded male beneath the outer veneer of grave and courteous manhood. Morrissey himself portrays an image of the robust, working-class man, performed by an Irishman of rural background, thus providing the song with impeccable credentials for indisputable masculine authenticity and making those values accessible to others when he sang it. Heaney personally liked the song, leading to magnetic performances as his recordings clearly show (see, for example, Rinzler 1961), making the associations all the more convincing and credible.

In this context it is relevant to mention that "Morrissey and the Russian Sailor" was the song Heaney chose to perform at the presentation of the National Endowment for the Humanities award in 1982, the highest honor awarded to a traditional artist in the United States. The award carried, at the time, an honorarium of $5,000, along with the prestige associated with the official recognition. Heaney won the award in such illustrious musical company as bluegrass mandolinist and singer Bill Monroe, fiddler Tommy Jarrell, Georgia Sea Islands singer Bessie Jones, Mexican American singer Lydia Mendoza, Cajun musician Dewey Balfa, and blues musicians Sonny Terry and Brownie McGhee. The award, and the publicity that surrounded it, garnered notice in the Irish press, which generated significant editorial commentary about why Heaney could be honored only in America and not in Ireland. His performance, then, of "Morrissey and the Russian Sailor" clearly foregrounded an explicit symbolic parallel between Morrisey's victory and Heaney's own unequalled *gaisce* in gaining such a prestigious and unprecedented prize on foreign soil.[16] Richard Harrington of the *Washington Post* described Heaney's performance at the award-bestowing ceremony:

Ballad singer Joe Heaney stood like a Prussian and sang about an ancient battle, a round-by-round description of the boxing match between 'Morrissey and the Roosian Sailor.' He also gave a hilarious and tongue-twisted history of one particular Irish tune that led emcee Theodore Bikel to suggest that "history should be taught by folk singers, not historians." (Harrington 1982, cited in Mac Con Iomaire 2007:359)

Performing this song was Heaney's way of taking on the world, proving his mettle as a contender among other world-class performers; additionally, it may be viewed as the apotheosis of all his performances of Morrissey up to that defining moment. Such conviction undoubtedly was also supported by the fact that this song was one he had brought with him from Carna. Others sang it there; although in English, it was part of the local repertoire (Nic Dhonnchadha 1995) and therefore constituted authentic folk material that Heaney could easily feel confident about.

Heaney's original audiences in his native community, invested in *gaisce* as part of a life in which hard labor was a daily necessity, expected no less.[17] His urban-dwelling Irish audiences, still invested in ideas of *gaisce* in a sports context or in the context of leisure and relaxation generally, would appreciate the unrestrained masculinity in the song, while also being familiar with the political message of the Irishman triumphing in adverse circumstances. The song, then, was a popular hit with all sections of Heaney's following.

Likewise, in the United States, left-wing intellectuals imbued with a taste for the authenticity of the folk could read such performances in a positive light by framing them as the epitome of masculine aplomb. The search for such images became popular in the United States through early films. Gerardine Meaney claims:

> The association of Irishness with a lost rural idyll in U.S. popular culture can be traced back to the silent productions of the Kalem Company between 1911 and 1916. Its identification with a form of masculinity threatened by industrial society and recoverable through ethnicity and a return to pastoral values has been a key element of U.S. representations of Ireland since the paradigm-setting Irish American fantasy of Ireland *The Quiet Man* (1952). (2006:255)

The Quiet Man represents an Irishman who was conflicted because he has killed someone in the boxing ring, and who is restored to himself only when he fights again to recover his new bride's dowry. Having done this, he is, for the first time, a full-fledged member of his adopted community (and is able to drink—heavily—with his former adversary). Meaney's comments about the film's plot might be applied equally persuasively to Joe Heaney's performances of Morrissey: "Irishness, then, offers a mode of masculinity which is out of place in industrial and postindustrial societies, but also a narrative of containment of that masculinity within a romantic role" (Meaney 2006:255). Heaney's performances of "Morrissey" and other songs bolstered his authenticity, satisfying among his American audiences a yearning for a simpler, less complicated existence. The fact that at the height of the Cold War, Morrissey's opponent was a Russian is also significant. His American audiences of the 1970s and 1980s, hearing his opening explanation of the song ("...and Johnny Morrissey was fighting...a ROOSHian"), would grin, nudge each other, and lean forward in eager anticipation of a fight that must, by all the laws of folk tradition, result in the glorious defeat of a representative of America's Cold War enemy by one of the Fighting Irish who had never yet let the Americans down.

Cold War–era Americans needed the reassurance of having a hypermasculine representative fighting on their side. The performance of the fight could transform all American listeners into Irish people, whom the listeners seemed to regard as one of the root sources of themselves, except more so, with especially heightened attributes (ethnicized as more earthy, masculine, sexualized, expressive, passionate, and capable). Discussing Irish American song in the late nineteenth and early twentieth centuries, William Williams criticizes the lack of substance of Irish American ethnic symbols, spending an entire chapter on it ("Irish America in Search of an Image," 1996: 200–210).

Arguably, however, the lack of substance is the very point of such symbols because they allow those who are not Irish to connect with and appropriate Irishness on the spot, as it were, when it has been convenient to do so.[18] One could, in fact, take any of those cherished immigrant images of Ireland (the stone cottage, the young lady left behind, the dear elderly mother, the fireplace, the greenness of the countryside) and apply them to Poland, France, Norway, or Russia. Irishness, then, as argued by the writers in *The Irish in Us* (Rains 2006:155), is the most accessible and acceptable white ethnicity of choice for many Americans, regardless of their own (German, Polish, Italian, or other) heritage connections. Such a facility enabled Heaney's already powerful ability to connect and manifest identification with his performing persona of *echt* Irish maleness, particularly in North America.

In terms of the connection here with the great boxing match, it is no coincidence that the Irish word *rince* (dance) derives from the English word "ring" (as in both "boxing ring" and "skating rink"). Modernity feminizes dance and considers male practitioners to be weaklings or homosexuals. In traditional conceptions, however, both dance and fighting were forms of *gaisce*, a choreography of embodied performative action. Dance empowered not just feats of physical prowess but an accomplished style of execution that elicited admiration and even envy from peers and increased the doer's prestige among his social group. Such publicly performed flourishes stimulated narratives in which the action was celebrated again, in suitably hyperbolic terms, losing nothing in the repetition. In Irish narrative tradition, this recitation of the great deeds follows a much older pattern in which the word is more important than the deed, and the powerful are made much more so by celebration in poetry and song. In this way, "Morrissey" fulfills expectations of a collectively constituted masculinity, so that the singer—in this case, Heaney—allows the audience to engage such concepts.

Similarly, a traditional male identity founded on action, or at least a lyricized concept of masculinity, is bolstered and affirmed through the performance of one body affecting others. Such embodied signs are part of a habitus and increase the symbolic cultural capital of performers and auditors alike. Heaney's performances in the United States created a spontaneous traditional community for his audiences. Acting as a medium of the imagined community he had grown up in, he allowed others to access a lost, idyllic time and place that otherwise remained unavailable. Heaney, thus, was the leader of his audiences, a gatekeeper and guide in the foreign country of the idealized Gaelic past.

Drink, Love, and the Lonely Irishman

As much as "Morrissey" reveals about Heaney's masculine aura and the ways in which it was understood and appropriated, other songs also provide insight into his gendered identity. The next two songs, "Bean a' Leanna" ("The Woman of the Beer" or "The Alewife") and "I Wish I Had Someone to Love Me," reveal other aspects of Heaney's presentation of masculinity. "Bean a' Leanna" explores a classic symbol of Irishness: the lonely man, drowning his sorrows in a pub. The lyrics used here represent those on Heaney's recording for Gael Linn in the 1970s. Several other recordings exist, including one from 1957 for Gael Linn and one from 1963 for Topic, all with minor lexical variations from the following text:

> Ó éirigh in do shuí a bhean a' leanna
> Is ná fan le do chaipín a ghléas
> Go bhfagha tú dhom deoch uisce beatha
> Nó cárta de do chuid leanna féin
> Ó beidh muid ag ól go dtí maidin
> Seo sláinte na bhfear uilig go léir
> Ach nuair a fhágfas an mháistreás an baile
> Beidh an cailín is deise agam fhéin
>
> A Dhia céard a dhéanfas mé amárach
> Nuair a fheicfeas mé mo ghrá ag goil aniar?
> Ní fhéadfaidh mé a dhul ina láthair
> Le méid is bhí eadrainn riamh
> Nuair a smaoiním ar a súgradh is ar a gáire
> 'S ar inneach a láimhín a bhí fial
> Ó titim i lionndubh is i ndólás
> Agus goilim féin mórán 'na diaidh.
>
> 'Gus shiúil mise bogaigh agus sléibhte
> Agus cnoic a bhí géar as a mbarr
> Is a lán bealaí eile nach ndéarfad
> Is gan unsa ar bith céille in mo cheann

Ag cur tuairisc mo stáidbheainín bhéasach
Nach sínfead mo thaobh léi go brách
'S go mb'fhearr liomsa codladh taobh thuas di
Ná bheith i gConga dhá uairín roimh lá.

Is fada mo chosa gan bróga
Ach is faide mo phócaí gan pínn
Is fada mé ag ól le mná óga
Ach níor ól mé riamh deoir le mo mhian
Is fada mo chóntra dhá déanamh
Is mo thumba dhá bhreacadh ag saoir
Mo chróchar dhá tóigeál lá an Earraigh
Is na buachaillí óga ag dul faoi.

Is bhí mé oíche is mé súgach
Bhí mé ag triall ar tigh Mhicil sa ngleann
Bhí strioncán de phíobaire sínte ann
Agus jug fuisce líonta aige ar clár
Ó thit muid lag marbh síos ann
Ní raibh preab inár gcois nó inár láimh
Ach seo beannacht shíol Éabha is shíol Ádhamh daoibh
Agus íocfaidh mé féin an reicneáil.

O rise up woman with the beer
And don't wait to fix your cap
Until you serve a drink of whiskey
And a quart of your own beer
O we'll be drinking until morning
Here's a health to the men all around
And when the mistress leaves home
I'll have the prettiest girl to myself.

And what will I do tomorrow
When I see my love coming eastward
I won't be able to approach her
Because of all that has passed between us
When I think of her play and her laughter
And the fairness of her generous beloved hands
I fall into depression and contrition
And I cry profusely because of her

Long are my feet without shoes
Long are my pockets without a penny
Long am I courting young women
But I never had a drink with my own desire
Long is my torment in the making
And my tombstone being printed by the masons
My hearse being raised on a spring day
And the young men going beneath it

And I was one night and I was merry
Heading toward Micil's house in the glen
There was an out-of-tune piper there
And a full jug of *poitín* in his hand
O we fell down dead with weakness
Not a hop in our hands or our feet
But here's the blessings of Eve's seed and Adam's on you
And I myself will pay the reckoning

I traveled bogs and mountains
And peaks that were sharp at their summits
And many other roads that I won't mention
With not an ounce of sense in my head
Asking for news of my gentle, courteous, beloved woman
Whom I'll never lie beside
And how I'd prefer to sleep behind her
Than to be in Cong two hours before day.

Dorian modality (a minor scale with a natural sixth degree) is frequently used in the tonal palate of Appalachian music and all its antecedents across the Atlantic. For American audiences, it evokes a sense of raw, ancient memory. It may also have produced a sense of instability because it freely crosses strict boundaries of major and minor tonalities (figure 7.2). Indeed, audiences who listened to a recording of Heaney singing "Bean a' Leanna" remarked, before knowing the meaning of the lyrics, on the melody's "ineffable sadness," "loneliness," "ancient quality," and "medieval power." Upon hearing the translation, several students said, "You mean it's just a drinking song?"

"Bean a' Leanna," literally, the "woman with the beer", or the "ale wife," is at once drinking song and love song. The speaker is a man who is fond of late-night carousing and socializing. In the first verse he calls for more drink, spirits, and beer and anticipates the landlady's departure, so that he

Fig. 7.2: "Bean a' Leanna"

can have the prettiest girl for himself. The two themes of alcohol and courtship are thus interwoven from the beginning. The second verse shifts the emphasis firmly onto the speaker's troubled relationship with his beloved. What is he to do? He cannot approach her; he muses upon her playful nature, her laughter, the fairness of her two generous hands (all veiled erotic references) and becomes depressed at the thought of his loss. The third verse signals a downward turn in the speaker's economic circumstances. He owns no shoes, his pockets are empty, and despite all his carousing, his heart's desire eludes him. He includes references to the making of his coffin, the printing of his tombstone, and his funeral procession taking place.

In his notes to Heaney's 1963 Topic album, A. L. Lloyd rightly recognizes this as a drinking song and calls attention to the affection lavished on drink. However, he overlooks an important second theme, which is clearly linked to the first, and that is the theme of troubled erotic love from the male speaker's point of view. The speaker in this song is indeed a drunkard and has seemingly fallen on hard times.[19] The fifth verse returns to the love theme; indeed, the way the text swerves between one theme and the other is very interesting. He has traveled valleys and pointed hills, looking for his stately, courteous maiden, with no sense in his head, nearly in a daze (cf. Mad Sweeney and "The Rocks of Bawn"). He wants to sleep beside her rather than reach Cork (also Cong, County Galway) two hours before dawn, suggesting aimless wandering in the darkness.

Drinking has been an important aspect of European culture for centuries. The ability to consume large amounts of alcohol while retaining self-control is historically a mark of aristocratic bearing. However arguably, this behavior underwent subtle but revealing changes in the nineteenth century, which may be linked to patterns of Irish marriage in the post-Famine period. Indeed, some scholars posit a connection between alcohol consumption and the development of the pub as an exclusive male bastion (Stivers 2000). The influence of the reorganized Catholic Church continued to grow throughout the nineteenth century and was an important factor in this development. An interest in celibacy, framed as chastity, became a major focus of clerical attention. Combined with increasingly late marriage in some areas, a culture of bachelorhood came to the fore, centering round the public house as a forum for male social interaction and an escape from domestic responsibilities. Indeed, some argue that pubs acted as a female substitute for working-class men (Malcolm 1998:51). Married men also took part in these male gatherings, often serving as figures of authority within the group, setting standards for alcohol consumption and leading the conviviality (Stivers 2000:83). Regular and heavy drinking, although incurring clerical and social disapproval, served to curb the intensity of intimate male-female relationships, considered the greater sin in this period (Stivers 2000:103).

In the pub, men performed stories and songs for each other, reinforcing socially constituted values of masculinity through the never-ending custom of buying rounds or treating. As Stivers has remarked, "One's ability to drink hard demonstrated great powers of manliness, just as athletic prowess or expertise in storytelling did. The more an individual had proved his manliness, the greater his status within the group" (2000:91). Such values are extolled in one of Heaney's best-known songs in praise of a sailing boat, "Púcán Mhicil Pháidín," where the eponymous hero, Micil Pháidín, is praised glowingly in the following: "bhí sé rímhaith i dteach an óil" (he was really generous in the alehouse) (see Heaney's discography from 2007, CD 1, track 13). Arguably, the burgeoning folk clubs that sprang up all over Britain when Heaney lived there represented another, more organized form of this institution.

In contrast to the heroic ideal of copious consumption and impeccable self-restraint, the representation of alcohol in "Bean a' Leanna" brings up the possibility of its emasculating impact. Alcohol wrecks the suitor's possibilities of success with his lover. The woman is held up as a paragon of good humor, generosity, and sexual desirability, a potential solution to his difficulties, if he could but free himself from his dependence. However, the *buachaill caol dubh* (the dark slender boy, a poetic name for alcohol in Irish) retains the upper hand. To lose control because of drinking is a travesty of ideal masculinity. It is just this transgression that has resulted in the suitor becoming a wanderer vainly hoping to regain his lover.

Consequently, the question arises: Why did Heaney sing this song? Certainly he was aware of how its melody, contained within an aaba structure, appealed to Gaelic Revivalists as among the superior musical forms in the Gaelic folk tradition. This might have been one reason for his choice. However, a second question arises, which is how he related the song to his own experience, since he reinforced connections between song and lived reality. The first recordings of Heaney singing this song date to 1957, when he was a regular guest at the renowned Gael Linn nights of traditional storytelling, music, dance, and song held at the Damer Hall in Dublin (Carolan 2005). The closeness to the date of the ending of his marriage in 1955 is striking. Interestingly, also, this song was recorded from his father, Pádhraic, but with only three verses. Heaney's sourcing and addition of the two extra verses, specifically, "long are my feet without shoes" and "I traveled bogs and mountains," seems to suggest that he worked up this version of the song to answer his own aesthetic needs. Its appearance in his repertoire at this point and its continuance as one of the mainstays of his song store until his death in 1984 further suggest a deep identification with its lyrics:

> I judge a song by the way I feel. Now: do I feel this, or don't I? That's the question I ask myself all the time. Do I feel this song? Do I put myself in the man's name that this particular song was written about? Am I suffering the labors that he did? Can I go through that or have that picture before me? If I can't follow that man, the journey he took, whether he was in bondage or slavery, I don't follow the song, and I don't do it justice. I know I don't if I don't do that.[20]

Consequently, it seems reasonable to argue that this song, with its confusion in regard to a heartfelt relationship, its meditation on the destructive effects of a life lived in the company of alcohol, and its futile longing for some resolution of these two symbiotically linked domains, may be read as a veiled reference to his own solitary situation in the second half of his life. It was the custom of Gaelic poets to compose confessions regretting the wastefulness of their lives, an idea found in another iconic song: "An Buinneán Buí."[21] Although in a conventional sense, Heaney is not the author of these lyrics, it is nevertheless the case that he configured the song in this way for his own reasons.

Oral poetry the world over uses phrases that are repeated exactly or in modified form in different configurations (Foley 2002). Like written texts, then, oral texts inhabit a great echo chamber in which resonant phrases and powerful words recall other similar words. Unlike in written work, where repetition is often considered a fault, orally performed texts avail of such similarities in ways that enhance performance and deepen meaning. This also happens in the case of "Bean a' Leanna," and we draw attention to one small example now as an illustration. The last phrase in the following excerpt is echoed in another important song that Heaney certainly knew:

Shiúil mise bogaigh agus gleannta
Agus cnoic a bhí géar as a mbarr
Is a lán bealaí eile nach ndéarfad
Ní raibh unsa ar bith céille in mo cheann
I traveled bogs and mountains
And peaks that were sharp at their summits
And many other roads that I won't mention
With not an ounce of sense in my head

The song is "An Caisdeach Bán," the lament/confession of a man, Tomás Ó Caiside, or Thomas Cassidy, who had to leave the seminary before ordination because of his involvement with a young woman. In fact, this song is held in the highest regard by singers in Heaney's home region.[22] The phrase "ní raibh unsa ar bith céille" ("with not an ounce of sense in my head") crops up in modified form in Cassidy's song as follows:

Bhí mé seal ag foghaim Béarla is dúirt an chléir go mba mhaith mo
chaint
An fhad úd eile gan unsa céille ach mar na héiníní i measc na gcrann
I spent a spell learning English and the clergy said that my speech was
eloquent
As long again without an ounce of sense but like the little birds among
the trees.

The recurrence in two songs with broadly similar themes is striking and illustrates the word power of Gaelic song formulae. It is also worth noting the second phrase, "like the small birds among the trees." This reminds us of a much older text, the story of Suibhne Geilt, Mad Sweeney, who was driven mad by a saint's curse and also spent his time like a bird among the trees. We are not suggesting that Heaney was aware of this connection. He may certainly have been aware of the similarities between Cassidy's song and "Bean a' Leanna." The echoic phrase "without an ounce of sense" confirms their thematic similarity and adds to our argument that Heaney performed "Bean a' Leanna" as a kind of veiled confession. Another character named Sweeney also appears in "The Rocks of Bawn," a signature tune of Heaney's (see chapter 5). These coincidences are just that—striking similarities with no real link. And yet they belong to the same literary and oral tradition. The unintended correspondences remain impressive, portraying disparate representations of Irish masculinity, with a dark, troubled thread running through all.

Note also that his development of the song "Come Lay Me Down" (see chapter 3) represents a similar lyrical/musical response to an expressed need for a way to construct the Famine for his audiences. Knowing that the image of the lonely Irish man drinking in the pub was current in every audience for which he performed (Irish, English, Scottish, North American), Heaney was responsive to that shared understanding by using a powerful song. In a sense, then, this song may be read as Heaney's confession, his expression of regret at the unhappy end to "all that passed between us." The fact that Heaney does this indirectly and in a way that can be only implicitly linked to him is entirely consistent with a masculine persona in a culture where direct emotional expression is not approved of for males. Heaney had confided in certain people about his personal circumstances, but those who knew never brought up the topic and kept it to themselves (Mac Con Iomaire 2007:261). In 1983 he was asked about whether this song was a reflection of his own circumstance; he laughed, rather grimly, raised his eyebrows, frowned, and said, "Well, that's enough about that."[23]

The fact that Heaney sang this song often leads us to speculate that he identified parallels between the world of the text and the personal circumstances of his own reality, perhaps accessing the therapeutic, cathartic aspects of both words and music. In so doing, he may have been processing his own unarticulated grief in a distanced manner through performance, enabling some degree of release from the conflicted burdens he carried. Furthermore, it does not stretch the point to connect this song with Heaney's other encounters with women. As a charismatic performer and teacher, he could not have been unaware of his effect upon the female members of his audiences and classes, and of his own reaction to their attention. Whatever opportunities he had to form relationships, he never again had a second long-term bond with a woman, choosing instead to live in solitude.[24] Interviews with his children and in-laws for the documentary *Sing the Dark Away* are partially reproduced by Mac Con Iomaire (2007:130–32) and make harrowing reading.

The speaker in "Bean a' Leanna" clearly understands whose is the weakness and the fault, and the remorse in the song is palpable. The dark, turbulent, emotional core of "Bean a' Leanna" suggests that such issues must remain in suspension, never resolving into a calmer, more stable affective situation. "Bean a' Leanna" arguably speaks of a troubled sexuality, consonant with a strict, rural Irish Catholic upbringing, rigid attitudes toward love relationships, and the management and repressive control of sexuality. Although the domestic culture that he embodied also had a bawdy, Rabelaisian side, public norms demanded outward rectitude at all costs (Ferriter 2009:6).[25]

Despite Heaney's chosen solitude, this does not preclude the idea that he might well have desired female companionship. Accordingly, Joe Heaney could also project the image of the lonely male ballad singer in his English-language performances for American audiences. His frequent performances of "I Wish I Had Someone to Love Me" during his time in Seattle endeared him to many people and succeeded in eliciting much sympathy for him. He learned to sing this song from Lucy Simpson, a close friend from Brooklyn who had taken Heaney into her family during the years in which he lived in New York. This song is American, copyrighted by Guy Massey in 1924, but actually composed by his brother Robert with the title "The Prisoner's Song." Vernon Dalhart (1883–1948), a cousin of the Masseys, had a hit with it in 1925–26. "The Prisoner's Song" earned a Grammy Hall of Fame award in 1998 and was named by the Recording Industry Association of America as one of the songs of the century in the same year.[26]

It was a relatively unusual instance of Heaney developing a new song in his later years; he often used it for sing-alongs when he lived in Seattle. It begins with the chorus and follows with verses that use the same melody throughout the song.

Chorus:
I wish I had someone to love me
Someone to call me his own
Someone to sleep with me nightly
I'm weary of sleeping alone.

Tonight is our last night together
The nearest and dearest must part
The love that once bound us together
Has cruelly been torn apart.
(Chorus)
Meet me tonight in the moonlight
Meet me in somewhere alone
I have a sad story to tell you
That I'll tell by the light of the moon.
(Chorus)
I wish I had ships on the ocean

I'd line them with silver and gold
I'd fly to the arms of my true love
A young lad of nineteen years old.
(Chorus)
If I had the wings of a swallow
I'd fly far over the sea
I'd follow the ship that he sails in
And bring him home safely to me.
(Chorus)

It is clear that Heaney became accustomed to American audiences singing along with him, whether he liked it or not. He sang the first several choruses of this song with the words "someone to be with me nightly, I'm weary of being alone." He then switched the lyrics for the final chorus to "someone to sleep with me nightly, I'm weary of sleeping alone." His change of the lyrics was always accompanied by either a meaningfully charming or severe look. The song may be read as a yearning plea for companionship and affection, experienced by someone who was profoundly alone, but—for one reason or another—Heaney never took it beyond that.

Musically, this is quite easy to sing along with, which is precisely what drew American audiences into the overall atmosphere he was trying to create (figure 7.3). He knew well the importance, in the folk world populated by Pete Seeger, the Clancy Brothers, and others, that the audience was primed for a rousing sing-along. He also carefully chose items that were emphatically *not* rousing sing-alongs; he was far more likely to sing "Whiskey, You're the Devil" than the ubiquitous sing-along "Whiskey in the Jar." Thus, while he was certainly a victim *and* a beneficiary of the folk revival (see chapter 9), Joe Heaney engaged it all on his terms.

It is unlikely that Joe Heaney could have—or would have—sung "I Wish I Had Someone to Love Me" in Ireland. Apart from its maudlin sentiment, it would also raise questions about his marital status, something that he deliberately avoided and that could not be discussed publicly. It was for the exclusive consumption of North American audiences and was dramatically in contrast—in its plaintiveness—to the rugged defiance that Heaney often cultivated at home. Like many of the tracks on the album *Say a Song: Joe Heaney in the Pacific Northwest*, this song con-

Fig. 7.3: "I Wish I Had Someone to Love Me"

trasts sharply with those of his two Gael Linn albums. Clearly such material would not reach the standards of authenticity laid down by the norms of the Gaelic Revival in Ireland. In America, however, performing for those who had no such preconceived notions (or, in Irish terms, those who knew nothing), he was freed from these restrictions and could sing what he chose and what met their expectations. An appeal of the song may be a reflection of the warmth and welcome he experienced with his friend Lucy Simpson and her family in Brooklyn. Lucy's loving description of their weekly meetings and friendly repartee (Mac Con Iomaire 2007:319–24) reveals as close to a family connection as Heaney was ever to have in the United States.

That Heaney should have leaned more heavily on plaintive songs like this one (and "Come Lay Me Down") was a direct response to the needs of his non-Irish audience members, as opposed to what he himself might have been expected to sing in an Irish-speaking milieu. It gained him deep sympathy from his audiences (and students), earned him meals and lifts home and shopping errands, and perpetuated the image of the lonely bachelor sitting in a spartan, starkly lit tenement apartment. Indeed, Mick Moloney has described Heaney's Brooklyn apartment in those terms (Mac Con Iomaire 2007:365), and Heaney's Seattle apartment (until two months before he passed away) was dark, damp, and dank, even though less expensive first-rate apartments were available.

The Confluence of Masculinities

Joe Heaney always claimed a connection between life and song. In the three songs examined here, connections are evident between aspects of Heaney's life and the songs he chose to perform repeatedly. In "Morrissey and the Russian Sailor," Heaney accessed the traditional tropes of the male nationalist underdog triumphing in the face of unequal and unjust adversity. The image of single combat links him to traditional folktales and particularly with that of Cú Chulainn, the greatest of the Irish legendary heroes. The connection with the hound, the loyal defender, is not accidental.

Another aspect of masculinity may be interpreted from our reading of "Bean a' Leanna." Here the connections emerge between overconsumption of alcohol and broken romance. The timing of the song, when first recorded by Heaney, suggests that it may refer to his own broken relationship. This is further reinforced by the fact that the text is Heaney's own configuration. Adding a further two verses to those his father sang, these verses specifically underlie the effects of drink on human relationships.

Finally, "I Wish I Had Someone to Love Me," the most American of Heaney's songs, is one he learned from an American while living in America. This song adopts the persona of the female whose mariner-lover is far away, leaving her languishing and pining for his return. It is a simple song, and one that Heaney used to effect for audience participation; it can be seen as an appeal for companionship and friendship by someone whose isolation proved occasionally too burdensome.

There is no definitive authority over the semiotics of Heaney's masculinity or of Irish masculinity in general; this analysis covers several aspects crucial to an understanding of Heaney's performative representations. It is not that he could not present the full range of human emotions; rather, in taking his traditions to American audiences, certain aspects of his identity received more emphasis than others in the contract between performer and listener. This emphasis worked, in part, because of Heaney's desire to assert himself, and because of his audience's requirements and projected desires for an uncomplicated, straightforward, tough-guy-with-culture image, representing "all that is native and fine."[27] And, of course, there is much more to Heaney than he chose to present either at home or abroad. However, as Steve Coleman has remarked about Heaney's understanding of his own songs, "In song, one can say things without telling them" (2004:398).

Judith Butler claims all gender as performative, sustained through acts which constitute its reality (1990:136). The confluence of Heaney presenting himself as a rural, Irish-speaking manly man and his choice of songs to reflect that gendered status are two intriguing aspects of his life that contain revelatory power regarding gender and performance. Heaney's *sean-nós* practice does not specifically define his gender. Instead, it has great interpretive power, showing desire—the way that he desires to be seen, and what others desire of him. He delivers where the audience wants to go and what he wants them to be (see this phenomenon also in his performance of the Famine). His audience expresses a need—for which he supplies the answer—of a more robust, less effete gender, more assertive, less polite, more attention-seeking masculinity. It is a powerful, engaging, rural masculinity extant in a contemporary urban world.

Part IV

✃◎⊙◎◞✃

Joe Heaney in America

In recent years, the human sciences have become increasingly concerned with modes of representation. Beginning in the 1980s, and continuing to the present, the hegemonic, quasi-objective scientific bias previously apparent in much academic writing has partially given way to more humanistic modes of communication. In such innovation, writers are at risk from accusations of confessional sentimentalism. The balance is a difficult one to strike. Writing about Heaney raises many similar dilemmas which are not easily resolved. This final part begins with an exploration of Heaney's work in the United States, from his long tenure as a doorman in a prestigious building on Manhattan's Upper West Side, to his performances at folk festivals, to his work as a university lecturer. Having spent more than half of his life outside of Ireland, it was in the late 1970s and early 1980s that Joe Heaney came into his own as a master teacher and performer, with a full command not only of his extensive repertoire but also of his audiences. He had traveled to work in London between 1958 and 1961, had previously lived in Scotland, and finally came to America for several visits, settling permanently once he found steady employment. His time in London was marked with visits to his wife and children in Scotland, but the folk music scene in London—particularly the Singers Club, in the company of Ewan MacColl and Peggy Seeger and others—was a magnet for him.

The book closes with an examination of Joe Heaney as both culture hero and antihero. The different identities and symbolic attributes ascribed to him by various entities—academic, folkie, and Irish American—were simultaneously true and false, and he engaged and contested with them at each step. A significant part of that engagement had to do with concepts of Irish and Irish American authenticity. Regina Bendix examines the ways in which a sense of authenticity is generated by the development of a comparative relationship between Self and Other. She points out that "invocations of authenticity are admissions of vulnerability, filtering the self's longings into the shaping of the subject" (1997:17). The longing that so many Americans have for a fictive Irish heritage was projected on a near-daily basis onto Joe Heaney, and onto the extensive body of work—songs, stories, anecdotes, sayings, and even his own persona—that he brought to his American audiences. This same longing, however, may characterize the desires of some Irish people as well, particularly those concerned with the development of a wholesome, linear national narrative. This final section of the current work sheds light on his responses to both quests.

8

❧⊙⊙❧

The Irishman at the Threshold

H eaney was invited to perform at the Newport Folk Festival in July 1965, and stayed until the following October. The following year, May 1966, he immigrated to the United States for good (Mac Con Iomaire 2007: 228-9, 244). He arrived at the invitation of an Irish couple in Long Island under conflicted circumstances. He still had family members and friends in Carna as well as in Scotland and England, but by that time he had struck out by himself, forsaking home and relations in the most material and physical ways. He moved into a small below-ground apartment in Brooklyn, New York, where his neighbors described him as a cheerful man, singing constantly. He frequented Manhattan's Eagle Tavern on West Fourteenth Street, a place known for its lively sessions. He also frequented his corner pub, the Green Isle Inn, at 5623 Fifth Avenue in Brooklyn, where several of his recorded songs were in rotation in the jukebox. He was a friend of the Clancy Brothers and other New York–based musicians and folksingers popular in the 1960s. It was from this beginning—in an Irish enclave of Brooklyn—that he took the first of many steps that would carry him across America and around the world as a performer.

It is ironic that Heaney arrived in America just as popular music began to move decisively away from the folk idiom toward an edgier electric rock sound. The popularly remembered watershed for this was the Newport Folk Festival in 1965. At this event, Bob Dylan, one of the most important and influential musicians of the sixties and subsequent decades, and a leading folk performer, went electric. The fallout at the event is still legendary. Much of it never happened in quite that way, although like all good legends, the stories are told as true (Cohen 2002:236; Jackson 2007:139–50). These narratives are relevant to Heaney's story because of the timing. He was a middle-aged man, fairly set in his ways, already an established artist, and was convinced of the validity of his aesthetic, which was a conservative one that resisted change as much as possible. Ironically, Newport '65 is symbolically seen as having sounded the death knell of acoustic folk as a dominant trend in American music. Henceforth the mainstream future would belong unequivocally to rock and other related styles that made maximum use of modern instruments, arrangements, and recording technology. In one very real sense, then, Heaney arrived too late to make the impression he sought.

When Heaney arrived in the United States, he found work as a doorman in one of Manhattan's upscale apartment buildings, the Langham Building at 135 Central Park West. According to all reports, including his own, he sang constantly as he opened and closed the doors for some of New York City's rich and famous.[1] When asked about his singing at the time, he said that all of his singing was in Irish, as it was one of the only ways to remove himself from his circumstances and take him back home. Paradoxically, the home he had quit for America, to advance his career as an artist, was central to his idea of what his performance and singing meant for him. Further, his general response of singing all in Irish effectively defined a type of musical and cultural bubble within which he sequestered himself. It was clearly also a mnemonic technique, to keep his repertoire active and ready for performance in the absence of a community in which he might have practiced regularly.

Even the Irish Americans who lived in the building—Maureen O'Sullivan, for example—would not have been familiar with his repertoire; indeed, she commented on Heaney's modesty about his achievements in her presence (cited in Mac Con Iomaire 1998:243-44). The contrast between Maureen O'Sullivan's career as an actor provides an interesting counterpoint to Heaney's. The daughter of an army officer, she was born in Roscommon and educated in Dublin, London, and Paris. She returned to Ireland and worked with the poor. She got her break as an actor when she met director Frank Borzage in Dublin, who suggested she take a screen test for the film he was making with singer John McCormack, *Song of My Heart* (1930). She got the part and traveled to Hollywood to complete the film. She subsequently enjoyed a long and successful career as an actor. She continued to work all her life, successfully combining her marriages with her career.

Although O'Sullivan's career and Heaney's were different their paths certainly crossed, albeit on the opposite sides of the class divide. Nevertheless, although the job of doorman may seem to have been a menial one, there were doormen and doormen. While it might seem to those unfamiliar with the prestige accorded to New York City's buildings and their addresses that working as a doorman for two decades should have been beneath someone of Heaney's exceptional talents, it is also important to examine just what that kind of work entails. Manhattan, the best-known of the five boroughs of the city, is home to a small number of palatial, exclusive addresses known as "A" buildings. These include, among others, the Dakota (where John Lennon was killed in 1980), the Majestic, and the San Remo. Each of these places comprises a unique microworld of hierarchies in which the doormen watch over and sometimes engage in the minutiae of the lives of the very wealthy.

Once a doorman has a job at one of these exclusive buildings, the job is generally his for as long as he wants it, and includes a lounge and union benefits together with the long hours on his feet. "Especially at the grand 'A' buildings uptown, the conventional wisdom goes, they are totems of discretion, as prudent and solemn, in their shiny-buttoned coats, as judges," writes Adam Platt, adding that doormen are, in fact, excellent resources for celebrity gossip.[2] The question of race served to distinguish Heaney further. That Heaney was a white doorman at an upscale building, with a correspondingly upscale uniform (he is quoted as being thoroughly put off by the brass buttons on his uniform), only added to his status among doormen. In fact, his whiteness and uniform became part of what made that particular address distinctive, given the attention paid to minute gradations of status differentiating one high-end building from another.

The typical tasks of New York City doormen over the past forty years have included much more than opening doors and greeting the residents. Doormen must memorize faces of residents and their friends and family members, receive packages (or groceries or dry cleaning), announce deliveries, connect constantly with the domestic servants of the residents, and help these same wealthy residents to negotiate the perilous territories of their own lives and those of their family members. In Charlie Leduff's poignant short story about the retirement of a New York City doorman, he writes:

Maybe the new guy will make the residents of 801 [West End Avenue] forget that for thirty-three years, Mr. Mitchell was the man who mopped their hallways and shoveled their snow. Or that he was the man who took their children by the scruff of the neck when he saw them doing wrong. Or that he was the man who ran down the wig-wearing mugger who attacked their mother. Or that he was the man who discovered their dead locked away behind the doors. But it seems unlikely, if the card the six-year-old girl gave him the other day is any indication. *I love you. Please don't go, Robert*, it read. (2005:2–3)

A doorman stands as the intermediary—at the threshold—between the rarefied world of the very wealthy and the gritty reality of urban clamor on the streets of New York. As a bilingual immigrant, Joe Heaney himself was between worlds and shifted regularly between his work as doorman and his life's calling as a traditional singer and storyteller. In a climate in which a number of Irish immigrants to the United States were unemployed, Heaney had a steady, meaningful job that paid him a living wage, allowed him a strong measure of self-respect, and gave him the chance to connect with families and coworkers at an immediate, warm, and human level over a period of many years.

As mentioned briefly earlier, the Newport Folk Festival in 1965 marked a crisis as acoustically minded leaders of the folk revival were forced to accept that some of their beloved icons were actually plugging in guitars, not simply using amplification to be better heard (Cohen 2002:236; Jackson 2007:139–50). Into the midst of that shifting terrain came Joe Heaney, who performed with the Clancy Brothers in his *báinín* sweater. He was one of many traditional singers during the four-day festival, and even though he performed for thousands of people (and into a microphone), his performance style was unchanged. For Heaney himself, however, the audience acclaim he received was something of a revelation, and it opened his eyes about the potential opportunities that might await him in the United States (Mac Con Iomaire 2007:241).

Heaney received another career opportunity in the late 1960s when he performed on Merv Griffin's television show. In the liner notes to the 1996 CD *Say a Song: Joe Heaney in the Pacific Northwest*, James Cowdery mentions the following anecdote: "Joe Heaney was fond of telling a story about the time that the American television host Merv Griffin visited Ireland. At a local pub, Griffin was astonished to see a particular photograph on the wall. 'That's my doorman!' he exclaimed. 'That,' the bartender solemnly declared, 'is Ireland's greatest traditional musician'."

At some point in the late 1960s or early 1970s (the year for the actual event varies according to the person relating the anecdote), Griffin invited Heaney, his own doorman, to perform for his late afternoon talk show on Saint Patrick's Day. Basil Rathbone—mentioned as having been one of the residents of 135 Central Park West (see note 1 of this chapter)— also appeared frequently (sometimes monthly) on the show in 1963 and 1965. Maureen O'Sullivan (another resident) was an occasional guest on the show as well. Liam Clancy described Heaney's appearance as follows:

> *The Merv Griffin Show* was on, and they had all these Hollywood stars. And in the midst of all this *glitterati* Joe Heaney was supposed to come on and sing a song, because he was Merv Griffin's doorman. Merv Griffin made the mistake of asking him a question. And Joe answered him, and told him what he thought of all the plastic shamrocks, and the green beer, and the green mashed potatoes. "We don't have anything like *that* in Ireland!" But he started talking, and everybody in the pub started listening, and instead of doing his three minutes, he must have done fifteen or twenty minutes. And they cut to shots of the stars who were taking part in the show, and they were looking in amazement at this incredible man, as if they were watching Stone Age Man come to life in their midst! (from the film *Sing the Dark Away*)

By the late 1960s, Heaney was dividing his time between his job and the folk festivals and song circles of New England and elsewhere in North America. By this time he had made strong connections with other musicians, had begun working with an agent (Josh Dunson), and had made initial connections with American folklorists and ethnomusicologists, who were to provide him with significant employment during his final years.

Roaratorio and the Avant-Garde

The 1939 publication of *Finnegans Wake* by James Joyce was a turning point in Irish literature, and the work was to have a profound impact on English-speaking literary circles for decades. Scholars and performing, media, and visual artists today continue to explore its hidden meanings, thorny lexical issues, and implications for creativity. Its stream-of-consciousness style and its nonlinear exploration of one man's dream—and, by extension, the collective dream (or nightmare) of humanity—was a groundbreaking departure and drew both positive and negative criticism from multiple sources. The man—Humphrey Chimpden Earwicker (HCE, also "Here Comes Everybody")—recurs in hundreds of manifestations throughout the book, representing a kind of Everyman consumed by guilt over a deed that he might or might not have committed. The extraordinary ambiguity of the work allows for significant artistic interpretation.

The avant-garde composer John Cage selected *Finnegans Wake* as the core of a multivalent performance art piece that he began to develop in 1979: *Roaratorio, an Irish Circus on Finnegans Wake*. In the performance, Cage read selections of the text in a kind of *Sprechstimme* style—whispering, shouting, mumbling, drawing out his words—against a backdrop of sound effects (human, animal, natural, man-made, and other), Irish traditional instrumental music (solo and ensemble), classical music, and countless other sounds. Joyce included several thousand different references to sounds in *Finnegans Wake*, and Cage discussed the process of recording some of the sounds:

> "We could use only a fraction of them. We then decided that half of the sounds should be collected in Ireland and half of the Irish half were to be collected in Dublin. We started [to record sounds] in the centre of Dublin and gradually spiraled to the outskirts, where we finished on the 10th day. The rest of the sounds were selected elsewhere, by chance" (*Toronto Globe and Mail*, January 29, 1982, 15).

Joe Heaney's job as the character of Earwicker in *Roaratorio* was to sing, periodically, songs of his choice in Irish and English, and to tell a story or two. In a recorded version of the performance (*Roaratorio: Ein Irischer Circus über "Finnegans Wake,"* WER CD 63032), Cage presented Heaney with a list of items but conceded to Heaney's wish to perform songs of his own choosing (Mac Con Iomaire 2007:334). Heaney is heard to perform, in order, "Dark Is the Color of My True Love's Hair," "Seoithín Seo Ho," "Connla," "Amárach Lá le Pádraig," "Eamonn a' Chnoic," "Maidrín Rua," and "Casadh an tSúgáin." In performance, he chose any song that came into his mind at the moment. He also told a story titled "The Good Day and the Bad Day," recalling pastimes standard at traditional Irish wakes and making a direct and apposite link between his own repertoire and Joyce's work (Mac Con Iomaire 2007:337). The other musicians—flute player Matt Molloy, bodhrán and bones players Peadar and Mel Mercier, *uilleann* piper Seamus Ennis—also played periodically. Merce Cunningham choreographed the piece. Later performances include Seamus Tansey on flute and, for the Canadian performances, fiddler Paddy Glackin and Liam Óg Ó Floinn on the pipes.[3] *Roaratorio* had several performances in Paris, London, and Toronto.

It is worth remembering that Joe Heaney had been an urbanite for decades, and that as a Brooklyn man with a job on Manhattan's upper-crust West Side, he had not been isolated from the currents of the American performing arts scene in the 1960s and 1970s. His work as a doorman, in which he communicated daily with a number of significant performing artists, was only part of what enabled him to cross over into such a scene as the one *Roaratorio* provided. By the late 1970s he had been on hundreds of stages, met with performers from all over the world, received awards, and was something of a star himself, as noted in print by at least one reviewer (Mac Con Iomaire 2007:335). Heaney, then in his early sixties, had the characteristic looks that made him ideal for the part he had to play. He must also have been aware that this music did not compromise him in any way. Although it mixed all kinds of sounds into a seemingly unstructured format, he did not have to compromise. He was allowed to be himself and garnered the added status of working with an acclaimed avant-garde composer. Indeed, Cage deferred to Heaney throughout the preparations, and they always discussed the performance after the show. As Mac Con Iomaire remarks, "If Seosamh [Joe Heaney] was not happy, John Cage was not happy, and if Cage was not happy, Seosamh was not happy" (2007:337).[4] Consequently, the fact that Cage found Heaney's singing "a delightful and positive experience," and sought and heeded his advice regarding the use of traditional instruments in his composition, must have affirmed Heaney's self-esteem and his identity as an artist considerably.[5]

As well as being involved in the preparation, performing in the show was a highly positive experience for Heaney; he not only was valued as an artist but also had the opportunity to spend time with his good friends among musicians who understood him and his milieu. In spite of his frequently expressed opinions on Irish folksingers and their guitars, Heaney himself was not particularly narrow aesthetically; he was very comfortable in an event that was quite avant-garde. Audience members focused considerable attention on him. The performance provided him with a significant forum and enabled him to present traditional Irish culture, as always, on his own terms. Even more important, he was given complete autonomy in his performance choices, and what he did fit in precisely with the aleatoric elements not only of the performance of *Roaratorio* but also of its origins among the pages of *Finnegans Wake*. A further irony suggests itself: that two supposedly opposing strands of the Irish cultural revival, the innovative modernist literary stream in English, and the traditional, allegedly backward-looking Gaelic one, could meet and blend happily without ire in this seemingly chaotic avant-garde work.

The Master Teacher

Joe Heaney's initial experience of teaching at a university occurred at Wesleyan University in the small city of Middletown, Connecticut. He commuted regularly from his apartment in Brooklyn to Middletown in 1979–80 and 1980–81. He gave guest lectures and performances at other universities in the eastern United States, including the University of Pennsylvania and Dartmouth. At the time he built strong friendships among the faculty and graduate students at Wesleyan, most notably with James R. Cowdery, whose book *The Melodic Tradition of Ireland* (1990) bears witness to their close working relationship. Cowdery's chapter on Heaney's style and performance practice (1990:26–42) was the first detailed—if brief—analysis of musical style in *sean-nós* singing since Ó Canainn's 1978 study and the posthumous publication of selections from Ó Riada's *Our Musical Heritage* lectures (1982). Cowdery, unlike his predecessors, and because of his opportunity, worked exclusively with Joe Heaney and held him up as the gold standard. Furthermore, Cowdery included extensive transcriptions of Heaney's own explanations of how and why he did things the way he did.

During a visit to the University of Washington in Seattle in 1978, Heaney spent three intensive weeks discussing various aspects of his life and songs and stories with Esther Warkov, a graduate student at the time who was assigned to him for interviews.[6] The recordings of those interviews, which form the rich backbone of the Joe Heaney Collection in the University of Washington Ethnomusicology Archives, are a candid example of the many ways in which Heaney chose to represent himself, his region, and his nation. He had been invited to the University of Washington in the first place by Dr. Frederic Lieberman, an ethnomusicology professor teaching a course on American music. Lieberman had originally invited Mike Seeger (a member of the famous Seeger clan of musicians and musicologists), and Mike agreed to come only on the condition that Fred also invite "a true folk (rather than folk-revival) artist to either come with him or overlap" (Lieberman, personal communication). Fred Lieberman brought Joe Heaney to Seattle based on the recommendation of Mike Seeger, but also because of his own admiration for Heaney's recordings.[7] Lieberman's message continued: "Mike suggested Joe Heaney, whom Alan Lomax had 'discovered' when Alan was living in England during the McCarthy era. I listened to some records he sent, and immediately agreed; they scheduled three-week visits, overlapping by one week, so we had five weeks of guest artists that term. It was great" (Fredric Lieberman, personal communication).

In 1982 Heaney was hired as a visiting artist in the Ethnomusicology Division of the School of Music at the University of Washington. In view of the previous discussion of Heaney's work as a doorman at one of Manhattan's A buildings, the decision to move to Seattle is crucial to an understanding of Heaney's project. In New York, Heaney had job security, benefits, a certain prestige, and a flexible schedule that allowed him to juggle his many appearances, as well as his regular classes at Wesleyan University. Heaney exchanged that security for a two-year contract with no guarantee of renewal. He certainly must have hoped that the contract might be renewed, but that he gave up the considerable advantages of his doorman's job in order that he might achieve recognition as a full-time professional artist provides eloquent testimony that Heaney's goal was full professional recognition of his art and artistry. It was another Rubicon in Heaney's life.

Heaney's duties were to make himself available to graduate students for private lessons in the *sean-nós* traditions of Connemara, and to perform on occasion. He quickly developed a unique rapport with each student, assessing each one's interests, capabilities, and needs and offering them songs to fit their individual situation. He was easily able to discern, for example, if a student was interested in the Irish-language songs, or (in rather dramatic contrast) whether a student preferred English-language drinking songs. He could also tell whether a student was capable of complex vocal melismas and offered songs accordingly.

In a typical lesson, the student was asked to perform the song from the previous week and go through a meticulous round of corrections, additions, and variations. Heaney usually began with a complete performance of the song, together with a detailed explanation of the story that went with it. On some occasions, that alone would use up the entire lesson time, or his citing of various other songs with similar melodic or thematic parts would cause the lesson to veer permanently away from the intended song. When time afforded it, he went phrase by phrase, using full decoration rather than offering a more bare-bones approach to the melody. He would also use some of the lesson time to offer advice and strongly worded opinions to the student. Sometimes he would express his ideas about musical matters such as whether or not Irish music should be accompanied by the guitar, and sometimes about life matters, from something as seemingly minor as whether a tea bag should ever be used in place of loose tea to bigger issues like getting married or having children.[8]

Once satisfied with the student's progress, Heaney would offer a song with a very different melody and mood, so as to avoid confusing his pupil with tunes from the same tune family. Each student wrote down the lyrics, or—if the song were in Irish—Heaney wrote them down himself, with occasional hints as to phonetic pronunciation of the Irish. At that point the student was encouraged to turn on the tape recorder, and Heaney recorded the new song of the week. He was prone to being testy if a student neglected to bring his or her cassette tape recorder. One song each week was Heaney's standard practice, but at the slightest hint that a student was ready (or eager) for more, Heaney delivered. During one particularly exhaustive session with a graduate student, Heaney taught four lengthy songs in Irish, one after another. During lessons, he often sat with his chin on his fist as he listened, frowning, in concentration.

One of Heaney's greatest gifts to his students, besides the gifts of his complete attention and rigorous discipline, was his emphasis on vocal timbre. He explained it by discussing the concept of *neá*, and is quoted by James Cowdery as follows:

> "The drone, you know, is similar to the human voice, because— 'nature's accompaniment' they call it, you know. This is the way they handed it down, you see, this is the way they used to do it—through their nose mostly, you know, and humming—and slaves working in the fields and all that, this came about: [hums softly on one pitch] hmmmm, hm-hm, like when you start up the bagpipes, that's the first note you'll hear, you know, the first thing you'll hear is that sad lament.... They reckon that droning the pipes and that [the *neá*] is the nearest thing to each other that ever was. And that's how the *neá* came about; it's in the voice, that you're more or less accompanying yourself all the way. That's right.... The old people—oh, honest to God, I mean—in the small places, the country, Gaelic-speaking areas, almost everybody had the *neá*. You know the first time someone starts singing a song, you know has he got it, or does he not." (1990:36–37; cf. Breathnach 1977:101, as well as chapter 2 in the present volume)

Heaney's vocal timbre was instantly recognizable as a marker of authenticity for his students and audience members; it revealed, in the words of Andrew Buchman, currently a professor of music and one of Heaney's UW students at the time, "a modernist aesthetic of originality and primacy" that marked him as the genuine article (Buchman, personal communication). Buchman continued that Heaney's teaching process conveyed a sense of immediacy and presence; his use of timbre, posture, and nasal resonance and his immense reserves of power took his lessons far beyond the idea of merely learning his sung repertoire. Clearly, Heaney's belief was that of complete immersion, that a learner must experience the full physicality and emotionality of a song in order to be able to perform it correctly.

As a visiting artist at the university, Heaney often wore a suit or sport coat to work and bore himself as tall as any tenured professor. He was treated with respect and deep affection, and offered in return first-rate lessons and performances, good-natured ribbing, and camaraderie. He could frequently be spotted conversing in the hallway of the Ethnomusicology Division, chatting companionably with students, professors, staff members, and visiting artists from Zimbabwe, India, or the Philippines. He held a great measure of respect for musicians from every tradition, and it never stopped pleasing him to be able to offer the gifts of his own tradition to interested people.

A memorable example of Heaney's easy ability to read a situation occurred one day when he was standing in the hallway speaking with Sean Williams and Ephat Mujuru, a master *mbira* player and storyteller from Zimbabwe. A graduate student in ethnomusicology came to Ephat Mujuru with deep apologies over missing their planned lesson. He smiled and kindly accepted her apology, but before the conversation could move on,

Heaney jumped in with a voice simultaneously stern and comical. "Ah, now, dear," he said, with his characteristic frown, "you should have seen him, and didn't he have the tears streaming down his face right on the spot where you're standing. You should be on your two knees, begging forgiveness." In his humorous scolding of the graduate student, he accomplished three crucial social goals: he welcomed her directly into the conversation, expressed his inclusion of Ephat Mujuru as a long-suffering fellow visiting artist having to deal with graduate students, and reasserted his own importance in the conversation. With his good-natured teasing, he also reminded the student gently but firmly of her transgression, without conveying any rancor.

In lessons, concerts, interviews, and conversations, Joe Heaney made no secret of his deep scorn for the folk guitar and other instruments used to accompany popular Irish folk songs. The source of his scorn was twofold: he could not bear the fact that, as he claimed, anyone could just pick up a guitar and "knock hell out o' a song" and be paid handsomely for it. His justification for that side of the annoyance with the guitar was that the people who had been singing songs for hundreds of years, as he put it, "never saw a penny out of it." By highlighting this line, he drew a clear distinction between art and popular culture. This illustrates a resentment sometimes expressed by those who gave material to folklore collectors and especially to the Irish Folklore Commission, which was not sufficiently well funded to reimburse its informants for their contributions but relied on their goodwill and interest in having their own material collected and saved for later generations. The project was seen in the cultural terms current at the time as a great national project, a labor of love, and almost as a sacred duty. However, this did not prevent some of those who contributed from viewing the act of collecting pragmatically as a form of exchange, with gratitude and prestige as their chief (and, crucially, in their often straitened circumstances, nonmaterial) rewards. Many of those who gave the material did so selflessly and without expectation of such returns. They accepted the terms under which they were asked to donate their songs, stories, and knowledge.[9]

Added to these layers of complexity about song ownership is the concern about Irish traditional material (particularly the songs and stories) passing from the members of a community into an archive under the control of academic researchers and other professionals. Such a change brings up many ethical issues regarding—in addition to ownership—power, distribution, and repatriation. As Ó Giolláin has remarked, collection itself was a good thing because, without it, the material would have perished (2005a:104). Heaney's own assertion that his recordings should be available to anyone, together with the Ethnomusicology Archives at the University of Washington already having an open access policy in regard to Heaney's recordings, offers an important corrective to these concerns.

Regarding the issue of compensation, whether or not a song was newly composed and the composer was being paid for the composition was irrelevant; according to Heaney, because singers had not been paid in the past, no new singer deserved money for appearing onstage. Two contradictions mar this opinion: first, Ireland's long history of arts patronage is well documented; second, comparing his statement with Heaney's own paid position as a singer was a contradiction he utterly refused to entertain in conversation, becoming quarrelsome and interruptive. As an old-style patriarchal figure of authority, he found it much easier to vigorously defend certain entrenched positions, however contradictory, than to engage in a dialogue that could offer alternative perspectives, possibly enabling some resolution of such intractable impasses. Students, consequently, learned that (conversational) silence was golden if lessons were not to venture into stormy territory.

His objection to payment and his commentary about those who had transmitted this culture without receiving financial recompense deserve attention, drawing on the concept of the subaltern, those subordinated without a voice in conventional discourse. Gayatri Chakravorty Spivak famously doubted whether, in answer to her own question, those in subaltern situations were really able to speak because they did not control the framework of communication (1988:271–314). Hegemonic groups control and decide the elements that will be included in the Great Tradition, and those that will not. Consequently, these same groups determine what the criteria of excellence are, what will be preserved and, crucially, what will not. Subaltern groups may create beautiful things, but it is difficult for them to convert these things into part of a widely recognized heritage. Furthermore, it is difficult for them to convert their understanding into objective knowledge independent of oral tradition and its attendant face-to-face transmission.

Subaltern groups usually do not have access to institutes of education (Ó Giolláin 2005a:130–131). Heaney's interest in recognition for his culture, his struggle to access these resources, his interest in the avant-garde, and his decision to give up his secure job as doorman for a two-year contract giving him artist status indicate strongly that he implicitly understood the terms of the debate, and where the power lay, despite his inability to articulate these concerns in a detached and dispassionate manner. Consequently, in one sense, his career represents the attempt of the subaltern to speak, and the partial success of that attempt. His attacks on the guitar might be interpreted as a critique of homogenization, of corporate takeover and cultural compromise. For better or worse, for him the transformations of the folk revival were suspect, although paradoxically, they provided him with opportunities.[10]

Heaney's other great campaign against the guitar was over aesthetic grounds. He had seen, many times, performing groups using full folk chord accompaniment on the guitar, singing in harmony, and using a steady beat to accompany Irish songs. It would be fair to say that every last one of Heaney's students at Wesleyan University and the University of Washington listened repeatedly to his tirades against the guitar and got an earful of invective if the names of *any* of the popular and successful Irish folk bands of the 1960s or 1970s were mentioned. What his open war with the guitar masked, however, was his own deep uneasiness with the beat of both the guitar and the harmony-laden choruses driving the song at the expense of the breathing poetic rhythm of the lyrics. In one bitter discussion he likened the use of the guitar to drowning: not drowning out the meaning of the lyrics but drowning as in not being able to breathe.

Most of Joe Heaney's students learned the value of keeping their teacher happy and away from the dreaded topics of both tea bags and guitars, because the more involved in the actual songs and stories he was, the stronger he grew as a teacher, his natural charisma overcoming his prickly public mask/persona. During some lessons, songs would simply pour out of him for the pure joy of it, and his students were the beneficiaries not only of his enormous storehouse of material but also of his skills as an effective, sophisticated, and highly prepared teacher. Yet he did not shy away from making ribald jokes and comments on occasion, or referring to anyone who looked or acted different (by virtue of race, clothing, vocal timbre, or even disability) as "the quare one there." Politically correct he was not. He gauged his comments based on how he knew the others in the conversation would react. He would distinguish, for example, between the English and Oliver Cromwell, or the English and his many English friends.

During the time he lived and worked in Seattle, Joe Heaney enjoyed the cool, rainy weather that reminded him of Ireland. He spoke of "running between the drops" of rain and lost many umbrellas. He spent time at a French bakery in Seattle (La Boulangerie), where he was welcomed as a regular, and frequently grilled the workers there as to the possibility of their Irish origins. "Were your people from Cork?" was one of the first questions he would ask.[11] In fact, his engagement in identity politics was his only playful foray into the world of Irish American stereotyping. Asking the home county (Donegal, Kerry, Galway) of anyone with an Irish name was a way of connecting with Americans in a way that they could understand. Those who did not know their home county or, worse, misspoke (as in "our people were from County Cook") received either an admonishment to learn about their heritage as quickly as possible "from the old people" or a swift and stern correction. Such interactions underlined the paradox of the nonassimilating immigrant whose appeal and authority lay in the strict maintenance of his difference.

One of Heaney's important pedagogical moments came when he had all his students give a recital of the songs he had taught them. He selected the songs in advance (one song per student), asked the students to sit onstage in a semicircle facing the audience, and created, to the best of his ability, a traditional event in front of an audience, in which people took turns doing songs. He offered the introductions to the songs for the audience, and his students sang in turn. It was the only time all the students heard each other sing the songs they knew, and a fascinating moment for revealing differences in interpretation. Some of the students, for example, imitated Heaney's strong accent in their singing, while others used their own North American (or other non-Irish) accents.

While it may have been somewhat excruciating for the students in terms of their attempts to publicly do justice to teacher, song, and tradition right in front of Heaney the taskmaster, it was a much bigger event for Heaney the teacher. He spoke proudly afterward of passing on what he knew to others, and asserted firmly and emphatically that "these songs will never die." It should come as no surprise that most of his graduate students still remember the songs he taught them. In all the talk about Heaney as a performer, and therefore as a powerful link to the rural Irish past for Americans (and some Irish themselves), the fact that he was also a master teacher can never be ignored. All rants forgotten, Heaney would beam with obvious pride and pleasure as his students stepped from the sequestered domain of the one-to-one private lesson and ventured to perform what they had learned for their fellow students and for a public audience for the first time. Those who sat in that semicircle participated in a community of which Heaney was the solar focus, and participated in a golden moment of recognition that remains a treasured memory. Hence, it revealed the lasting effect of his teaching strategy; it started from bitterness and ended with sweetness.

In addition to working closely with individual students, he also offered a class in early 1984 through the university extension division, which allows adult members of the Seattle community to participate in evening classes for a nominal fee. Heaney's course was packed with as many as fifty eager adults (primarily professional women). He carefully planned these classes around particular themes, so that each session covered an important topic.[12] These classes occupied an intersection between lesson and performance; he invited the adult students to sing along with the several songs he taught each time, but he also gave detailed lectures as part of the course. Sean Williams was his assistant (and recording engineer) for the classes, discussing items suitable for the various themes. Each class time was given a title, such as Holidays and Rituals, Children's Traditions, Work Songs, Songs of the Supernatural, and Night Visiting Songs. Students in the evening course received collections of typed lyrics, and each class ended with tea and treats.[13]

Yet another form of outreach in which Joe Heaney connected with people in the Pacific Northwest was through his nine-month residency series at individual schools and libraries. The series was funded by a grant from the Folk Arts division of the National Endowment for the Humanities and managed by Jill Linzee, who drove him to each event (he usually traveled on public transport), introduced him, intervened for him with the noisy children, and helped him to plan and carry out the performances.[14] He would confidently enter a room packed with squirming youngsters, wait for his introduction to be completed, fix them in place with his characteristic frown, and proceed to connect with them at a surprisingly human and tender level. He told stories about the leprechaun ("there's only one leprechaun, you know; and he gets two years younger each year"), cats ("The King of Cats"), and hunchbacks ("The Two Hunchbacks"). He peppered his talks with proverbs or sayings ("Do you know why you have two ears and one mouth? So that you will LISTEN twice as much as you speak"), partly as a way to keep the noisy exuberance of the children to a minimum, and also to convey traditional wisdom in age-appropriate ways. The teachers and librarians with whom he worked were enthralled. Each performance in the series took place at a small-town location outside of Seattle (Maple Valley, for example, or Bothell), for the benefit of those who could not attend one of his performances in the city.

One of the reasons he was able to stay in Seattle after his appointment at the University of Washington ended is because, quite simply, almost the entire community of friends that he had developed in the two years of his residency there had become devoted to him. They responded well to him, cared very much about his welfare, and pooled resources to help him continue to make a living as a performer.

The National Heritage Fellowship

The greatest honor of Heaney's American career came in 1982 with the announcement that he was being awarded the National Heritage Fellowship. He was among the first group of artists ever to receive the honor, which has continued to be awarded every year since 1982. Together with such exceptional American performers and artisans such as fiddlers Dewey Balfa and Tommy Jarrell, blues artists Sonny Terry and Brownie McGhee, singers Bessie Jones, Hugh McGraw, and Lydia Mendoza, bluegrass musician Bill Monroe, *tamburitza* musician Adam Popovich, and a carver, saddlemaker, ribbonworker, and ironworker, Joe Heaney represented Ireland from Brooklyn, New York. According to the National Endowment for the Arts Web site (http://www.nea.gov/honors/heritage), the mission statement of the award reads as follows:

> To honor and preserve our nation's diverse cultural heritage, the National Endowment for the Arts annually awards one-time-only NEA National Heritage Fellowships to master folk and traditional artists. These fellowships recognize lifetime achievement, artistic excellence, and contributions to our nation's traditional arts heritage. Nominees must be worthy of national recognition and have a record of continuing artistic accomplishment. They must be actively participating in their art form, either as practitioners or as teachers. Fellows are selected according to criteria of authenticity, excellence, and significance within the particular artistic tradition.

In 1982 the award carried with it a stipend of $5,000, about $11,500 in today's dollars.

The importance of this award, to Heaney personally, has already been discussed in chapter 7 (his singing of "Morrissey and the Russian Sailor," for example); he certainly knew that it was a crowning achievement, and the press on both sides of the Atlantic celebrated it warmly. After earning the award, Heaney returned briefly to Ireland to continue the celebration. A number of his old friends organized a concert for him at the National Concert Hall in Dublin as a means of marking his singular achievement. The concert was held in the John Field Room of the newly opened hall. Other musicians and singers participated in this event, but Heaney was the star of the show. RTÉ, the Irish national broadcaster, recorded him before the concert. In the footage, a white-haired Joe looks distinguished in a dark jacket and open-necked shirt, relaxed and happy to be made so welcome by his friends, and in sterling form, singing old favorites, "Cúnnla" and a moving "Curachaí na Trá Báine" for the cameras.[15] When one considers his failing health leading to his untimely demise less than two years later, it is no wonder that the news came as a shock to many of those who were gathered with him on this occasion.

Returning to Ireland

Joe Heaney was a heavy smoker and drinker for many years. His doctor in New York had told him that he was killing himself, and in one night he quit both smoking and drinking, decisively and permanently. As he later used to say, "I gave up three things fifteen years ago" (leaving it up to anyone's imagination what the third thing was). However, the damage was irreversible. He had developed emphysema, a disease for which there is no cure. Emphysema tends to affect men (more than women) in their fifties and beyond; it comes on gradually as a result of chronic irritation to the bronchial tubes of the lungs.[16] Heaney did not experience frequent colds, but he had a chronic cough that disturbed him when he sang and told stories in performance. His breathing was noisy, and he often paused to catch a breath in the middle of song phrases.

On the whole, Heaney enjoyed reasonable health despite his debility. However, in March 1984, he contracted the flu that was to end his life. In common with many Irish males, Heaney tended to make light of his illness and joke about it as if it was a matter of little concern to him. However, it became increasingly clear that this illness was serious. His students rallied around to help, substituting for him in class and visiting him regularly during the month and a half of his final illness. His community of support was thrown into consternation, many in denial about the fact that he was fading quickly. After his hospitalization, they continued to visit him regularly, and after he was discharged, they arranged that he move into a new apartment, brighter and more comfortable than the dank basement he had lived in previously.[17] The visits continued, but it was clear that recovery would be impossible.

Heaney asked for an Irish-speaking priest two days before his death on May 1, 1984; ironically, it was the festival of Bealtaine, the first day of summer and the return of light in the old Gaelic calendar. His supporters arranged his funeral, adhering as faithfully as possible to their idea of an authentic service. After this, Cáit Callen collaborated with Máire Nic Fhinn on further arrangements, ensuring that the transportation of Heaney's remains to Ireland by Aer Lingus went smoothly. He was subsequently taken to Carna for requiem Mass and burial in Maigh Ros cemetery. His death and requiem services received significant media coverage in both Ireland and America, and large numbers traveled to show their respects, creating a long and impressive cortège on the narrow road west from the village to the graveyard. Music and song marked the official requiem and were central to the subsequent gathering at the hotel in Carna.

The loss of Joe Heaney was a tremendous blow to his communities at home and abroad. He knew songs by heart that few others had even heard of, and his internal storehouse of anecdotes and stories was seemingly endless. It is often somewhat bitterly remarked that Heaney gained more honor and renown from the United States than he had received at home. There is some truth to this. The image of the western, rural, Irish-speaking people had been central to the idealism that led to the foundation of an Irish autonomous state. It is clear, however, that few had seriously thought about the realistic implications of such a trope. Most Irish people were concerned with practical issues such as education, health, and work; the architects of the impoverished new state saw the need for modernization. For all its ideological power, in the common view, folk culture belonged to the past with limited, if any, relevance to modern living. As the Irish language had been abandoned over most of Ireland, people also jettisoned the traditions it carried when it became practical to do so. It was only with the advent of the sixties and the growing prosperity that accompanied that decade that the idea of professional folk artists could become a reality.

It is significant that although many of Heaney's contemporary traditional singers from Connemara and other areas enjoyed artistic status at home in Ireland and occasionally abroad, none of them made their living exclusively from their art. As on many other issues, Heaney was obstinate on this point. Although he dearly wished to return home, he was not prepared to return under just any circumstances. He had given up his job as a doorman, and the considerable security it provided, for the precarious position of a two-year contract as artist in residence and would not resume the menial status he had shaken off. In a letter written in Irish to his friend Máire Nic Fhinn, who had participated in making his recordings for Gael Linn when she worked there, he remarked, "At my age, I wouldn't be expecting a job, but if I had a nice place [back there]—I could do things, and I could take the odd trip to America once a year, to give small concerts and [do] the universities etc." (Mac Con Iomaire 2007:412).

In the early 1980s, despite proposals by Gael Linn executive Roibeard Mac Góráin with the Arts Council of Ireland, to have Heaney recognized as a member of Aos Dána or employed as a teacher of sean-nós songs under an Arts Council scheme, the embargo on new public appointments seems to have prevailed in the recessionary economic climate of the period. Reflecting on these developments in an interview with Liam Mac Con Iomaire, Roibeard Mac Góráin revealed that a situation had been available in which Heaney would have an apartment in Dublin, in exchange for taking care of a building that belonged to the Department of Education.

Heaney declined. A university appointment similar to the one he had had in Seattle was what Heaney wished for. Mac Górain said he believed Heaney had come before his time, pointing to the recent developments occurring in Irish language education, especially at NUI Galway. The first *sean-nós* singer in residence, Dara Bán Mac Donnchadha, Heaney's next-door neighbor, was appointed at the University of Limerick in 1995. The National University of Ireland, Galway followed and has appointed singers on an annual basis since 2002, the first appointee being Bríd Ní Mhaoilchiaráin, a great-niece of Heaney's (Mac Con Iomaire 2007:414, 428).

Mac Górain's mention of Aos Dána, founded in 1981, is significant. A state-supported affiliation that provides artists (*saoithe*) with a basic income (*cnuas*), was then open only to "creative" artists: those who had produced a body of original work. Heaney's folk traditions, as individual performances emerging from a community genre held in common, represented a problematic category, a gray area that did not meet metropolitan assumptions of the artist as individual genius, creating inspired original works of excellence supposedly ex nihilo. The irony of the nomenclature used by the organization is poignant. The term *aos dána* (band or company of artists) derives from preconquest Gaelic Ireland, as do the terms *saoi*, pl. *saoithe* (artistic master) and *cnuas* (a treasure). Artists under the Gaelic system received patronage from chieftains in return for the work, but the foremost modern representative of that tradition, who sang "Seachrán Chearbhaill"—an item that had once been sung in the halls of Gaelic nobility—was not deemed eligible for inclusion. The conundrum certainly highlights the contradictions inherent in the symbolic validation of folk culture, with a simultaneous unwillingness to recognize and reward it as real art. It underlines a profound slippage between the symbolic rhetoric of cultural nationalism and the pragmatic, business-as-usual approach that frequently prevailed in postcolonial reality.

Heaney should have been immediately recognized by dint of his enormous and unique contribution to the development of his heritage as eminently qualified for inclusion; indeed, he was recognized and celebrated in Ireland, during his lifetime, by only a small cadre of aficionados and increasingly by others after he had passed away. He had taken what was his community's artistic heritage and molded it into a distinctive performance genre. He had garnered recognition for that genre globally, in halls and theaters far from the firesides of his youth as no other exponent had done, all the while defending the integrity of what he had absorbed to be received as it was. He had taken advantage of sound recording technology to record a large body of the work, and even on the eve of his death he had plans to make another recording, one that was to contain previously unrecorded material. He had, in short, overseen the change of his folk material from its first life, as a community endeavor where individual ability was held in check by the demands of society, to a world genre that anyone with the wherewithal to acquire one of his recordings could access and learn. Had he enjoyed better health and lived longer, he might well have achieved his wish to return to Ireland as an artist.

Although Mac Góráin remarked that Heaney was a man before his time,[18] one might equally add that he was a man *after* his time, a fact underscored by the contradictory gesture of the Gaelic titles used by the Arts Council that, on one hand, alluded to a connection with the patronage system of Gaelic Ireland while, on the other, refusing to recognize that tradition's most renowned contemporary exponent. When a major conference of political, business, and cultural figures was held in Dublin in 2009, the participants identified culture as one of Ireland's greatest exports and hopes to reverse the catastrophic economic downturn.[19] In hindsight, twenty-five years after his death, Heaney has been vindicated.

9

෴ලෙ෴

The Folk Revival and the Search for Authenticity

Joe Heaney did not enter a vacuum when he arrived in the United States; he arrived through the venue of the Newport Folk Festival and was thoroughly engaged not only in gigs and teaching but also in the surrounding social scene in New York City. Folk culture in the 1950s and 1960s also attracted the notice of journalists and recording companies. The era's name ("The Folk Scare") among the musicians of the folk revival implies that the powerful fusion of "political consciousness, . . . performance style, persona, and repertoire firmly rooted in American folk traditions" (Filene 2000:183) that characterized artists such as Bob Dylan signaled a significant change in that it had the potential to shake music industry executives out of their complacency.[1] In this final chapter, then, we examine Heaney's life in folk revival America as an example of the powerful allure of nostalgia and an idealized premodern, preindustrial past to Americans, and why Heaney's work during this period was so perfectly gauged to his American audiences in the 1970s and early 1980s.

Since the beginning of feudalism, elites have tended to distance themselves from the common people, and, in time, new perceptions and forms of cultural expression accompanied such separation. The advent of modernity from the late eighteenth century accelerated the marginalization of the folk and their culture. In this context, in a concept formed well before Dundes's famous deconstruction (1977:17–35), the folk were those who lived in the country, in small-scale societies where strict social controls prevailed (Ó Giolláin 2005a:iii, 7, 85). To speak of a folk revival, then, is to acknowledge the burgeoning of social change and upheaval, as well as the growth of a desire among some of those who had left the rural and the traditional behind them for a nostalgic return to something viewed as an earlier, uncomplicated simplicity.

With the wave of cultural nationalism that swept much of Europe in the late nineteenth century, the concern for waning folk culture focused on a search for the real (Bohlman and Stokes 2003:5). That is to say, following

ideas emerging from the Romantic reaction to Enlightenment univer-
salism, those involved in such movements were at pains to identify the
true, unadulterated culture of the people, "a matter of separating what is
real from what is not, and of separating those who have been taken in by
the fantasies and fictions of an earlier generation and those who have not"
(Stokes and Bohlman 2003:6).

In practice in Ireland, this meant a rejection of the mistakes that had
been made by pioneering individuals such as Bunting and Petrie and a
return to the field in an attempt to get it right. The interest in music and
song was part of a broad fascination with vernacular rural culture in general, and most especially that of the Irish-speaking regions. In such a climate, gifted performers such as the piper and singer Labhrás Ó Cadhla
(1889–1961), a native Irish speaker with an immense store of songs from
South-East Munster, could be seen as the epitome of an authentic Gaelic
culture and set a standard for others to follow (Browne, Ó Cearbhaill and
Bradshaw 1994; Ó hÓgáin 1994). Forty years Heaney's senior, and a pioneer in the achievement of recognition for Gaelic folk song, Ó Cadhla was
a teacher who, with others like him, established modes of interaction in
sharing songs and stories with students that Heaney was to duplicate later
in his own career. The difference between them was that Ó Cadhla's efforts
were confined to language and cultural maintenance and revitalization in
his own native area of Irish-speaking Waterford, whereas Heaney took his
efforts to an international level, encompassing everything from American
public elementary schools to the cutting edge of the avant-garde.

Interestingly, another older contemporary, and a near neighbor of
Heaney, Sorcha Ní Ghuairim (1910–75), from just east of Carna, also an
excellent singer, storyteller and, additionally an early journalist, teacher,
and language activist (Ó Ciosáin 1993; Ní Ghuairim 2004), recorded songs
and a story for Folkways Records when she visited New York in 1945,
arguably setting a precedent for Heaney. We discussed one of her performances in chapter 4 ("The Religious Laments"); she remains influential
not only in the Carna area but among *sean-nós* singers in other regions of
Ireland. Such individuals possessed the criteria for authenticity that the
new orthodoxy, molded by the ideas current in contemporary academic
folklore, required: a native command of Irish, a tradition absorbed from
family and neighbors by the fireside, and, furthermore, an ability to remold
what they had and present it in an appealing fashion to their audiences.
When Joe Heaney appeared on the scene in 1940, his profile also matched
the ideals of the real so sought after by urban revivalists in the same way
as his antecedents.

It has been established that Joe Heaney came to represent much about
Ireland and Irishness that sectors of both Irish and Irish American society,
respectively, valued or reviled. Heaney's image as an ideal member of the
folk forms part of a historical trajectory that is worth reviewing briefly. Joe
Heaney had antecedents and contemporaries who, in some ways, defined
how he responded to strategies of representation, all of which were—and
continue to be—culturally and politically charged. Issues of the colonial

subaltern, the feminized, subordinate Celtic male, so vividly evoked in the writings of Renan and Arnold (Ó Giolláin 2000:26), are crucial to an understanding of how Heaney represented himself, and were received and interpreted by those who admired him. Such figures include, first of all, Thomas Moore and his cultural descendants (see chapter 6), along with those Irish tenors who represented—and continue to represent today—the aspirations of upwardly mobile Irish people intent on erasing memories of deprivation, material poverty, and ethnic otherness.

Many Irish people accepted such images as necessary in the absence of alternative models, not only as immigrants in the United States but also on the home soil of Ireland. Heaney in many ways stood for the antithesis of such a trajectory; he was a throwback. As long as he remained within the subculture of the nationalist Gaelic folklore movement, he could be celebrated unequivocally, but as he tried to gain wider audiences, complications arose. During the course of his life, he performed his place, his community, his history, and his emotional enmeshment in the local by foregrounding his kinship ties, his linguistic allegiance and his steadfast loyalty to a particular style of singing. Those Anglophone architects of Irish independence—among them, the members of the National Literary Movement like William Butler Yeats and Lady Augusta Gregory—believed themselves to have been separated from such intense attachment by the colonial process and were determined in some ways to valorize and legitimate these aspects of Irishness in an urban, literary, and dramatic milieu.

The spectacular and enduring success of the Anglo-Irish literary and theatrical project highlighted the divisions between the members of the National Literary Movement and the Gaelic Revival, which did not, and arguably could not, achieve the same wide international acclaim. Heaney grew up under the Free State, with its institutionalized promotion of the Irish language as a badge of nationhood and cultural autonomy. His brother had collected selected folk materials for the Irish Folklore Commission's predecessor, the Folklore Society of Ireland. From early childhood, therefore, he was imbued with such cultural values as language rights and the validation of tradition. As someone who was an astoundingly good performer and who enjoyed performing, it was in his interest to promote the folklore of his region.

Ireland's burgeoning interest in folklore paralleled the efforts of folk song collectors in the United States, such as Olive Dame Campbell, who traveled and collected songs in the southern mountains in the early decades of the twentieth century. Interest in the "primitive exotic" represented by Celts on the Anglo-Saxon periphery is linked, paradoxically, by an intense interest in the Anglo-Saxon culture of the mountain regions of the southeastern United States. Though Olive Campbell and Cecil Sharp do not number among those who expressed generally negative attitudes about the people who provided folklore collectors with such rich material, similar attitudes prevailed in both the United States and Ireland, quite often including collectors themselves who were critical of the folk (Whisnant 1983:118).

The folk song revival in both places was popular and socially important; Irish views on the folklore and folk song revival could often be influenced by Victorian conventions, emphasizing the more appealing, sanitized aspects of folk culture, a cleaned-up noble savage, so to speak, while downplaying forms considered coarse or uncouth. What separates the two movements even more, however, is that whereas in the United States those involved in the folklore movement worked in a single language, in Ireland the collectors faced a bilingual situation in the advanced stages of a rapid language shift. Language in Ireland, therefore, was a loaded issue in terms of whether or how it could convey a sense of identity and authenticity on its users, whether in Irish or in English. Joe Heaney, as a native Irish speaker, from a community in which the language and culture remained remarkably stable, was nonetheless fluent in English and not only understood the distinction well at home but also took the opportunity to introduce it in (almost entirely) Anglophone America. For Americans who spoke only English—particularly those for whom Irish had been a heritage language in their family's past—Heaney's selection of occasional Irish-language songs held what they believed to represent their identity tantalizingly within reach. Importantly, that identity was not received by all of his listeners in the same ways. His performances could be perceived as resting virtually anywhere along a continuum, ranging in their evolation of deep feelings from great pride to abject shame.

Heaney as Antihero

Heaney was not welcome, necessarily, among Irish Americans. Irish Americans in Boston, for example, remembered the great times at the dance halls in the 1940s and 1950s with nostalgic affection, but they fled to the white-picket fences of the suburbs at the earliest opportunity (Gedutis 2000:16). Economics became the driving force for the Irish dispersal from the urban enclaves (Miller 1985:523), rather than a particular loyalty to, or a need for, their Irish ethnicity; standard American English became the right language to speak. Speaking of his mother, historian Richard White notes her early experiences as an immigrant from Ireland in the 1930s as she transformed herself to achieve acceptance in an assimilating immigrant society: "She changed to escape the daily doses of humiliation and ridicule. She began to look different, more American. She began to speak differently, modifying her speech, losing the brogue" (1998:178). Heaney, on the other hand, provided a living reminder of the constraining and incapacitating potential of unmodified, unassimilated Irishness.

When speaking English, his second language, Heaney's pronounced West of Ireland accent, strongly influenced by his native ability in Irish, set him apart. To Heaney, his command of Gaelic marked his authenticity and affirmed his right to speak for himself and his own culture. These features marked him as authentic in his own eyes, but for the carefully cultivated, upwardly mobile, East Coast American manners that suppressed the shanty in favor of the lace curtain, his status could be reduced to that of a pariah. The focus of the assimilated immigrants was on advancement and progress, and anything that hindered such progression needed to be jettisoned immediately. Heaney was Irish, but not the "right kind" for some (O'Brien 2004: 43). In Ireland as in the United States, people tended to focus on the family, the home, and the successes and achievements of its members. Heaney, on the other hand, having cut many of his ties, particularly with his family, remained focused on himself and on the search for public recognition of his heritage. For him the journey was a personal and individual mission.

The playing field was decidedly uneven for Heaney to succeed in Irish American circles. Mick Moloney is correct to some extent when claiming that Heaney's Irish-language material deterred Irish Americans, rendering his performances inaccessible to that segment of his audiences (Mac Con Iomaire 2007:364). Although this captures the dilemma to some extent, arguably the question is more complex than simply a lack of comprehension, or the simple inaccessibility of language. Non–Irish Americans sat spellbound through performances where much of the material was in Irish without any difficulty at all. As Mick Moloney remarks (cited in Liam Mac Con Iomaire's biography of Heaney), "And I don't know of any performer in any tradition in America, who could go on stage, and sing unaccompanied and talk unaccompanied in a style that was really arcane, and singing for the most part in a foreign language, and hold an audience absolutely mesmerized and enthralled for the whole time. And Joe did it every single time I ever saw him" (Mac Con Iomaire 2007:364).

For Irish Americans however, the Irish language was more than a mode of communication. Not unlike their fellows in Ireland, Irish Americans were aware that the Irish language came with baggage. It was the sonic symbol of all that upwardly mobile Irish Americans wished to abandon in their adoption of a new hybridized, dual identity. The acceptable mark of Irishness in America, as in Ireland, was the Catholic religion. More than language, and even instead of it, it was through Catholicism that the Irish founded their new American communities—in the church, the schools, the hospitals, the unions. The Irish language was a reminder of the Famine, of want, of the shanty, of low status, in short of the stigma attached to being an outcast, on the lowest rung in a society strongly prejudiced against them. For the majority, as in Ireland itself, the Irish language was a reminder of everything that needed to be discarded to make the transition to full assimilation. Heaney was almost like the specter at the feast: a living embodiment of what Irish Americans thought they had successfully abandoned. Heaney spoke bluntly of the hard times; he deliberately avoided Americanisms in his speech or body language; he was not particularly reverent about mainstream Catholicism; he believed passionately in his traditions, his language, and his songs, and these were anathema to many of the immigrant Irish. Speaking of patterns of Irish assimilation in North America, Stivers points out that: "The Irish desired to be free from English rule; Irish-Americans wished to be accepted into and become part of

Anglo-Saxon America. Middle-class, aspiring Irish-Americans admonished their own to emulate the Yankee virtues of 'hard work, perseverance, frugality, and integrity'" (Stivers 2000:165).

If the Irish became white through their assimilation to mainstream America, it is no exaggeration, then, to regard the Irish language (even English spoken with a brogue) and its attendant traditions as a stigma that remained a cause of shame (Ignatiev 1995:39). Shame and discomfort around the image of Irishness and the strain entailed by reinvention as Irish Americans led to disproportionate numbers of Irish men represented as blackface minstrels (Williams 1996:65), and behaviors that reinforced the distance from stereotypical rural, Gaelic Irish people.[2] Stivers highlights the difficult – liminal – position held by many Irish immigrants at the time:

> The immigrants preferred stage Irish to the vile and brutal ways in which they were often depicted.... But since the immigrant could not preserve and live out his old culture anymore, and was not fully an American (an Anglo-Saxon), he was forced to choose between a romanticized version of his origins or the totally negative ways his detractors had portrayed him. (Stivers 2000:180)

Both William H. Williams and Mick Moloney have documented the rich efflorescence of music hall song that sustained Irish Americans as they adapted to their new environment and came to terms with their processes of assimilation. Many of these songs draw on the stereotype of the Irish American but do so in a positive way, portraying "Pat" as an endearing, lovable rogue or playboy. If this character was the antithesis of the stolid Anglo-Saxon worker, then he was a character that all sought to emulate at a particular liminal moment such as Saint Patrick's Day, when all the world (or at least all of America) could be Irish. In fact, Saint Patrick's Day parades in the United States had their origin when the immigrant Irish put on their very best clothing and went walking through the wealthiest districts of New York and Boston, showing how well they were able to clean themselves up (Dezell 2000:19).

It was into this milieu that Heaney came; the parameters had been long established prior to his arrival in the 1960s. The Irish American song repertoire had taken on its own hybrid character at that point, perhaps most significantly symbolized by now familiar chestnuts such as "Mother Machree" and "Danny Boy,"[3] sentimental songs that were standard party pieces for the east coast Irish-American community, which were consumed by immigrants of all stripes. The stone cottage, the weeping mother, and the sweet colleen were all stand-ins for a generic rural, nineteenth-century, idealized European background (Williams 1996:116). Heaney's audiences, Irish American or not, eagerly sought a confirmation of their understanding of Ireland as it had been presented to them by popular media. When he failed to affirm their fondest expectations of the stage Irishman, some of them pulled back.

In Heaney's adamant refusal to recognize or sing these songs as part of the real, or to engage with that cultural complex of images and ideas, and to insist on presenting himself in the way that he wanted to, he created a conflict with the expectations of Irish American norms. Heaney's Irishman on the stage differed too much from the stage Irishman to which they were accustomed. His challenge to Irish American conceptions of authenticity destabilized their confidence in that identity so that, for many, their response to his challenge was avoidance. As a group, they usually did not invite him to their cultural performances, celebrations, festivals, or other heritage events, a fact remarked upon by folklorist Mick Moloney:

> "Joe's support system was completely outside the Irish-American circle. The Irish-Americans ignored him completely. They didn't realize that they had a genius in their midst. And it was the Irish language too, which made it inaccessible to most of them. But it was a source of fascination to a lot of people in America, people involved in folk music in America, in the urban folk scene, folk revival.... It was very clear to me that his support system, his whole audience, was a non-Irish audience almost exclusively." (Moloney in Mac Con Iomaire 2007:364)

Heaney himself is quoted as saying that he "wasn't invited to any of the Irish clubs" (Mac Con Iomaire 2007:249). The origins of this complex of attitudes go back to Reformation times in Ireland itself. The behaviors characteristic of Irish American assimilation were strikingly similar to those of Irish people who remained and sought social advancement in Ireland. Before independence, legally, Irish had no rights; consequently, ambitious people, or those anxious for the welfare of their families, had no choice but to conform outwardly to the colonial status quo. By the time of the Act of Union in 1800, most of those who were able to had already made that transition. These were newly emergent middle-class Catholics, English-speaking, for whom Thomas Moore (see chapter 6) became the essential symbol of identity.

Until the time of the Famine, significant numbers of Irish speakers were still to be found in most counties of Ireland, and indeed, the early nineteenth century may represent a historical peak for numbers of Irish speakers. However, the language shift had started by the last decade of the eighteenth century. This shift accelerated gradually throughout the nineteenth century, but in the wake of the Famine, it was greatly exacerbated when 1 million died and another million emigrated, many of whom were Irish speakers, the most vulnerable members of society. The Famine served as the final and most devastating manifestation of a link between the Irish language and culture, on the one hand, and want, deprivation, and exclusion, on the other, and was a lesson that the Irish learned well and would not quickly forget. Thus, memories of that time remained strong in the minds of Irish Americans for the very reason that their identity was forged in the crucible of cultural collapse.

Sharon O'Brien points out that when in the 1930s her grandfather, the blackface minstrel "Handsome Dan" Quinlan, sent home an enormous set of repoussé silver tableware to his wife—who did not at that moment have any food to eat with it—he made a powerful statement about the importance of symbolism in the process of becoming an affluent American (O'Brien 2004:57). They might not have had money to put food on the table, but they took great pains to establish themselves as the right kind of Irish people: those who could succeed by becoming entirely disconnected from the reality of contemporary Ireland and its web of difficult memories. The connection between poverty and traditional ways is not unique to the Irish. For example, the English folk song collector Cecil Sharp, who worked with Olive Dame Campbell, saw how quickly the opportunity to distance oneself from one's roots was taken advantage of among the southern mountain people of the United States: "'Primitiveness in custom and outlook is not, I am finding, so much the result of remoteness as bad economic conditions. When there is coal and good wages to be earned, the families soon drop their old-fashioned ways and begin to ape town manners'" (Sharp, cited in Whisnant 1983:121).

For many Irish Americans, although they felt a strong connection with Ireland, they were deeply unaware of the culture (O'Brien 2004:82): no cuisine, no language, no folklore, no reminiscences beyond carefully mediated images and ideas. This lack of culture, according to William H. A. Williams, was actually an effective strategy of creating a nonthreatening identity to which all could belong at certain times, and which no one would fear. As Williams says, "No other ethnic group managed so neatly to turn the hyphen into a bridge. Yet, it was a bridge that went nowhere, or, rather, it went only from one part of America to another" (1996:241). Williams here refers specifically to Irish American song culture, a hybrid American creation promoted through music hall performances and published broadsheets. If the bridge went nowhere—just as the bridges constructed by workhouse labor during the Famine crossed only dry land—it was deliberately calibrated so that it did *not* lead directly back to Ireland.

The world revealed in Heaney's songs—that of heartbreaking emotional language, of evicted tenants, of aristocratic poets who charmed beautiful ladies, of lamenting communities—remained hidden. In America, religion, not language or culture, provided the primary identity. Coming into such a world, it is unsurprising that Irish America failed to understand Joe Heaney, some of whose anecdotes were decidedly anticlerical and who sang at least one song in which the father of an abandoned young woman's child is a priest ("An Sagairtín"). Furthermore, it is not surprising that those who faintly recognized the culture he carried would have chosen to reject it, since they had expurgated it from their own lives deliberately in order to assimilate. Heaney, on the other hand, wore his identity like a badge; it was an essentialized connection between the self and the folk culture. That was his raison d'être, particularly since he had come to America to try to make it as a performer after he saw the available opportunities. In a sense, the move to America clinched the fusion of identity and culture.

By the time Heaney moved to Seattle in 1982, the earlier (nineteenth-century and early twentieth-century) climate of negative attitudes toward Irish people was changing. In the Pacific Northwest, in particular, divisions between the Irish American community and the academics and folk music enthusiasts were somewhat more relaxed because of a greater generational distance among members of the ethnic community. Heaney's classes at the University of Washington included fourth- and fifth-generation Irish Americans who wholeheartedly embraced what they saw as their living thread to the homeland and their unquestioned birthright. Even if they approached him with a set of initial assumptions based on performances by Tommy Makem and the Clancy Brothers, they were easily able to expand their understanding of their own heritage(s) through Heaney's teaching. Clearly, enough time and space lay between these late twentieth-century West Coast Irish Americans and the "No Irish Need Apply" placards of East Coast nineteenth-century America (Moloney 2002:14–17) that Heaney found in Seattle a warm welcome indeed. Considering that so many millions of Americans claim Irish descent (approximately 44 million as of the 2000 census), it is not surprising that diversity of opinion in late twentieth-century America should have become the norm.

The American population also reflects the regional diversity of its people's many origins. The cultural climate between East and West in the United States differs significantly in many respects. Many of the Irish urban communities on the East Coast were well established and self-perpetuating working-class enclaves (Dorchester, Queens) and retained for decades an integrity that has only recently begun to disperse. In the West, the entire social fabric reflects a looser, less constrained sensibility. Stereotypically, the West prides itself on having a more liberal attitude toward difference. Mick Moloney, quoted in Liam Mac Con Iomaire's biography of Heaney, focused on Heaney's audiences in America: "'It was just festivals and concerts, with a listening audience. There was nothing Irish about it....In fact if you were invited by the Irish-American community at that time, they'd stick you in the corner of a bar and that would be the end of it'" (Mac Con Iomaire 2007:339). As an Irish antihero to some, Heaney was unquestionably an Irish hero of a different kind to others.

The "Authentic" Joe Heaney

Joe Heaney's authenticity grew dramatically with his death in 1984. There is mythmaking and legend-making; representing one of two legends of native Irish sons who had made it in the States (the other being John F. Kennedy), Heaney's photograph appeared side by side with Kennedy's in pubs in Ireland where traditional music was revered. Heaney's name in traditional song circles in Ireland has become a byword for excellence and high standards, and indeed had become that way since before his death. New generations discover and absorb stylistic aspects of Heaney's singing not just through the extant recordings but also through conversations with elders who knew Heaney in his prime. His conviction and integrity as a singer and culture-bearer were unquestioned, and the role model he presented—and continues to present to new generations of singers—is one of urging those around him to reach their own highest standard themselves. Indeed, at a recent Oireachtas competition, Heaney's name was evoked, yet again, as *the* standard-bearer for excellence in *sean-nós*. Heaney was never the only *sean-nós* singer, but he was the most public of them. His achieved recognition through the National Heritage Fellowship emphatically and publicly lifted him above any other Irish musician in the United States. This is a country that had provided safe haven for the Irish in desperate times, and whose narratives told them that success could be achieved if they only worked hard enough.

That Heaney found in his Seattle audiences a combination of Irish Americans, academics, and folk musicians is partly a result of historical events, and partly a result of his novelty as "the real thing." No one questioned his authenticity in Seattle; even though Seattle is home to plenty of native Irish people, along with thousands of Irish Americans, few Seattle musicians could lay claim to his credibility, or could command such a profound bilingual treasury of songs and stories. In the following passage from Mac Con Iomaire's biography, Joe Heaney is cited discussing with Mick Moloney precisely the way he plans and executes a typical performance for Americans:

"I explain to them that I'm going to take them around a country fire, maybe a hundred or a hundred and fifty years or two hundred years ago; what used to happen around a turf fire before there was any radio or television, of course. And then I ask them to give me a chance to explain in every detail little bits of everything that happened around that fire on a winter's evening, between stories and songs, and a bit of lilting for people who didn't have musical instruments; they lilted for somebody to dance. And then I tell them the stories of these songs and the way they related to that period of Irish history, especially the emigration songs and how they came about, say something like the American Wake, how it came about. I would explain that to them. I try to mix it by giving them a bit of the serious stuff and the not-so-serious stuff, without ever having to do any 'popular' song. And a nice story that would have a punchline ending, thinking in Irish while I'm telling the story in English, and more or less translating the story. The Irish stories I tell in English. I explain to them in English the song in Irish I'm going to sing, so that they can follow it, but I don't do the translations. I tell them the whole theme of the song, the whole story of the song, verse by verse, and then I sing it for them. And eventually I bring them in with me on something nice, maybe some song that we can all sing together before the end of the evening. And I usually find them very attentive and very nice audiences, most of them anyway." (Mac Con Iomaire 2007:299–300)

In planning out and executing an evening's performance for his American audiences, Heaney fine-tuned his practice. Though he never created a set list for his performances, certain songs and stories garnered a stronger response than others, and those were the ones he chose most frequently. In a performance in April 1983 (which was advertised as "Afternoon Tea with Joe Heaney"), he delivered the following program to the students, staff, and faculty of the University of Washington Ethnomusicology Department, along with community members and friends. Between each song, story, or anecdote, he would offer an introduction to the material or banter with the audience; many of these songs will seem familiar by now to the readers.

"Morrissey and the Russian Sailor"
"Skibbereen"
"By the Banks of the Roses"
"The Old Woman of Wexford"
Story: "The Two Hunchbacks"
"Amhrán na Páise"
"Come Lay Me Down"
"Cunnla"
"The Yellow Silk Handkerchief"
"The Half Door"
"Going to Mass Last Sunday"
Story: "Fionn Mac Cumhaill and the Giant"
"Molly Bawn"
Story: "The American Wake"
Lilting: "My Love Is in America"
Lilting: "Off to California"
Anecdote: "Lilting Contest"
"A Stór mo Chroí"
Story: "I'm a Catholic, Not a Protestant"
"Red Is the Rose"
"Did the Rum Do?"
"Kitty Lie Over"
"I Wish I Had Someone to Love Me"

In his "Afternoon Tea" performance—which was, indeed, accompanied by tea and treats—Heaney drew from his full spectrum of songs, stories, and anecdotes. He sang in Irish as well as in English (though, surprisingly, included only one Irish-language song in this particular performance), and he lilted several songs. He sang one religious lament, not one but two sing-alongs, and half a dozen ballads. Among the stories, two were comic and two were serious. It would be tempting to look at the overabundance of English-language songs and draw the conclusion that he had "given up" on his Irish-language material. However, it is worth referencing Heaney's own words about his American performances: he tries to create a mix of serious and comedic, and he translates from Irish to English. While he meant a literal translation, his words and actions may also be taken to mean a figurative translation: he worked with the audiences he had, translating Irishness at a level they could understand without either dumbing down his performances or resorting to popular images of Irish and Irish American stereotype.

Unlike many of his generation, for whom education beyond the age of fourteen frequently had to be paid for, Joe Heaney received a high school education at Coláiste Éinde, an Irish medium boarding school that functioned as a preparatory college for primary-level teachers.[4] However, this education is not usually considered important in comparison to the material he learned from his relatives and neighbors in Carna. By the somewhat narrow definitions of early folklore scientists with their emphasis on pure orality, the folk do not go to school, and their culture is both unofficial and defined in opposition to education. Heaney's surviving letters reveal that he was highly literate in Gaelic, a standard that he maintained throughout his life, despite many years abroad. In common with other folk artists, however, his education and literacy did not fit the required image. In Ireland, a conflict between education and folk authenticity was not so stark.

In any case, Heaney had left before completing his course of study, a fact that enhanced his reputation as a maverick, something he did not discourage. Likewise, some of the American emphasis on Heaney's rural roots was a result of American discomfort with sophistication in their folk musicians. Pete Seeger's infatuation with the folk led him to change his appearance to reflect his perceived image of what a folksinger *ought* to look like: his uniform was blue jeans and open-collar work shirts with sleeves rolled up (Filene 2000:201–2). The Lomaxes also required Lead Belly to perform in his prison gear, even though he preferred to wear suits onstage. Seeger's surprise upon encountering Lead Belly in a suit and shined shoes might have been echoed by Heaney's similar appearances as a simultaneously authentic but well-dressed member of the folk and a visiting lecturer at universities in the United States. Just as Lead Belly had to leave his suit and polished shoes at home, some of Heaney's audience members were taken aback by his suit and tie. His *báinín* (cream-colored fisherman's sweater) may have been part of his identity, but because of its irrevocable associations with Tommy Makem and the Clancy Brothers, he rarely wore it in performance in his later years.[5]

The Culture Hero

Patterns are invoked to narrate the lives of great achievers, sometimes by themselves. Heaney is no exception in this case. It is striking how the mythical pattern of the hero's journey provides a framework for the stories that surround his life. The life story of Daniel O'Connell ("The Great Emancipator") of nineteenth-century Ireland also took on mythical aspects in the folk tradition (uí Ógáin 1995). Although Heaney comes from a more recent era, and his life can be instrumentally documented, a strong current of oral tradition runs through his life narrative and shapes understanding of that life. Heaney himself, steeped in those narrative patterns from youth, drew heavily upon them for the models that provided a framework for the presentation of self, region, and nation. Far from being ancillary or marginal to Heaney's oral materials, which were what he was known for, the stories of his life, his *dúchas* (heritage, patrimony) were central to establishing his identity and his legitimacy as a consummate exponent of oral Gaelic culture.

When one views Heaney's life journey, one is able to see close parallels between aspects of the mythic pattern of the hero's journey, the heroic biography, and Heaney's life story. Heaney fits this narrative into a traditional framework and, as such, controls the images that his listeners received of him. The typical pattern of a hero's journey is the following: the miracle birth, showing early promise in his training by a master, initial crisis, competitions and triumph, journey from home, marriage abroad, proving oneself abroad, hero's return, crisis, and death. Heaney's life uncannily fits the trajectory in certain aspects, perhaps nowhere more clearly than the chain of events that led up to and followed his greatest achievement, the awarding of the National Heritage Fellowship in 1982. Heaney had left home, as heroes do, according to the pattern, and this was his triumphant moment of acknowledgment. From his early promise as a singer to the initial crisis of his expulsion from school and the death of his father; from his gathering of many songs from his grandmother and neighbors to his winning of competitions (the Feis Charna in 1939 and Oireachtas in 1942); to his departure from home, marriage and successes abroad, triumphant return to Ireland, and abrupt and untimely death, the pattern invites narration according to well-established traditional models current in Irish oral culture.[6]

Most immigrants shed elements of tradition in their quest to assimilate, but Heaney traded on his traditional credentials to function and ultimately to triumph in a modern context. Heaney's life, then, underlines what Ó Giolláin has claimed in regard to the recognition of folklore by outsiders. Modernity defines folk tradition as its polar opposite. Without modernity, then, folk tradition would not be perceived and understood in the same way. Modern understandings of folk tradition and the American folk song revival enabled Joe Heaney and provided him with opportunities. The United States is the modern nation par excellence—a settler society, dating as a sovereign entity from the last quarter of the eighteenth century. It may be said that U.S. understandings of modernity differ considerably from those found elsewhere, and in this case, particularly Ireland. Modernity in the Irish Free State was officially regarded as a corrupting and dangerous force. Arguably, it was partly a fear of the changes brought by modern life that prompted the major interest in cultural nationalism and emphasized folklore as a part of that movement.

The emigrant dream usually concerns material success. Heaney's achievement, conversely, was symbolic and cultural. His financial affluence was negligible, his accumulation of material goods minimal. His greatest reward came in the realm of the satisfaction of being a man who had held to his values steadfastly, who had a mission to increase awareness of his heritage outside his community and outside Irish-speaking Ireland. In the course of his life, he had developed and perfected a polished, professional style of presentation that nevertheless paradoxically rejected the idea of pandering to what he considered were the tawdry values of the market-place. Despite the changes and innovations he had had to incorporate into his performance and delivery, he felt he had never compromised on these core principles. He founded his reputation on this steadfast resolve, and by the end of his career, it had served to connect thousands of people to that *dúchas*, rehabilitating what had been neglected and despised into a recognized art form that *must* be taken seriously.

The Legacy of Joe Heaney

Many in Ireland asked, verbally and in print, why it was that Ireland—outside a small, dedicated group of people—was unable to celebrate Heaney's accomplishments in the way that the Americans had. Indeed, the Irish outpouring of celebratory response in honor of Heaney's death corresponds to the prophet never being welcomed in his hometown (until his death). Such a narrative is attractively seductive in its simplicity, and many have succumbed to that attraction. His friends in Gael Linn, Roibeard Mac Góráin and Máire Nic Fhinn, did try to secure a position for Heaney in Ireland, where he might live rent-free with minimal duties and be largely free to continue his performances and teaching assignments. These must have seemed tempting, but in the end, Heaney rejected them.

To be recognized as an artist and to have achieved the accolade of receiving the National Heritage Fellowship (*an t-aon European*, the only European, as he said himself), meant that to return home to the position of janitor or caretaker would have seemed demeaning and humiliating. It is worth reminding ourselves that Heaney had already left his post as doorman of Central Park West, a position with good hours, flexibility, and presumably health benefits, for a two-year nonrenewable contract in Seattle that conferred on him the coveted title of artist. Consequently, his pride in his achievement, and his belief in himself as a leading artist, would not have allowed him to accept such a low-level position again. There is some truth, therefore, in the narrative of the lack of recognition in Ireland.

Following Heaney's passing, his star continued to rise, and now that more than twenty-five years have passed, he appears to be even more important than he was in 1984. Heaney is the single most important individual artist to have emerged from the Gaelic community in the twentieth century. Because of his recordings, his versions of songs are the ones most frequently heard and are easily recognized. With each competition that engages young Irish children in pursuing *sean-nós* singing (or the increasingly popular *sean-nós* dance, which Heaney often mentioned), and with each new master's thesis or dissertation on *sean-nós*, Heaney's influence continues to grow. Filene's assessment of African American folk hero Lead Belly's achievement is apposite here: "With the 'real' Lead Belly buried in Louisiana, each generation could 'discover' him for itself, much as the Lomaxes had decades before....After his death, then, Lead Belly himself became an authenticating agent, one who could bestow legitimacy on performers and fans searching for a sense of roots in the midst of ephemeral pop culture" (2000:75).

In the wave of attention paid to all things Irish (*Riverdance* being the most obvious manifestation of Ireland's coming-out party in the 1990s and beyond), some members of the current generation of Americans are struggling to regain a lost sense of connection to a homeland, particularly one that has a significant connection to the American past. Rather than looking to Ireland because it is *not* America, though, contemporary Americans interested in Joe Heaney and *sean-nós* tend to appreciate the man and his songs for the perceived integrity of the material. In Ireland, however, the legacy of Irish cultural nationalism demanded a separation from the colonial power. Irish cultural nationalism worked, in fact, because it was defined in opposition to Englishness. It was a way of being not-English. It took Douglas Hyde, a man with an upper-class Anglo-Irish Protestant background, to understand what was being lost. Cultural nationalism was a desirable symbol, but no one really wanted to return to the donkey cart and the creels. Irish people voted with their feet, and they could not differentiate between the legacy of poverty in material goods and the legacy of wealth in tradition and heritage. For most Irish people, those two aspects of traditional Irishness (legacy and poverty) were inseparably fused.

In the mid-1990s the poet and RTÉ producer Mícheál Davitt developed an hour-long documentary of Heaney's life: the first half in Ireland, and the second half in the United States. This documentary, *Sing the Dark Away*, was broadcast only in Ireland and saw limited release after its initial broadcasts. *Sing the Dark Away* featured such luminaries in the folk revival scene as Mick Moloney, Pete Seeger, Ronnie Drew, and others. It also drew from interviews with Heaney's friends, students, and employers in Seattle and New York. As a rather unusual variant of the hagiography, it reveals much about Heaney's personal life that he never discussed either publicly or privately. Yet it draws together old film footage of performances, shows where he lived, allows his friends a voice on his behalf, and genuinely celebrates his achievements.

One of the developments to occur well before Heaney's passing was the gradual creation of the Joe Heaney Collection in Seattle, Washington. The University of Washington's Ethnomusicology Archives[7] is home to a significant recorded collection of Heaney's songs, stories, concerts, lessons, and videotapes. Anyone who had ever made a reel-to-reel, cassette, or other recording of Heaney has been encouraged to deposit their original collection in exchange for a more contemporary version of it (for example, a CD) free of charge. Most of Heaney's students had taped their lessons on cassettes, and all of Heaney's concerts at the University of Washington were recorded and preserved. In addition, significant collections from James Cowdery and Lucy Simpson followed within a few years of Heaney's passing. Copies of all known written materials (newspaper articles, concert posters, etc.) are also housed in the Collection. Although Heaney was known in Ireland as a *sean-nós* singer, his gifts as a storyteller were also heralded in the United States, when he frequently told half a dozen stories in the course of an evening's performance. Laurel Sercombe, director of the Ethnomusicology Archives and a friend of Heaney, fields frequent requests for copies of Heaney's songs, stories, lyrics, photographs, and newspaper or magazine articles about him. Part of the mission of the Joe Heaney Collection is to make available any and all materials from Heaney's life and works, to anyone who requests them. Heaney himself explicitly stated that anyone, from anywhere in the world, was welcome to listen and to learn.

Developed and produced by Micheál Ó Cuaig of Carna, the Féile Joe Énniú (Festival of Joe Heaney) has been celebrated almost yearly since the early 1990s. Held each May in Carna, it draws on the rich community of Connemara singers, instrumentalists, poets, and dancers, not just from within the region but also from elsewhere in Ireland and abroad. The Féile comprises several days of *sean-nós* singing sessions, song teaching, instrumental music, *sean-nós* dancing, evening set dancing, and a children's competition. Special guests are invited to perform. Often a special event will coincide with the Féile, such as a record or book release party or, in one case, the transference of copies of the entire Joe Heaney Collection from the University of Washington to Carna. The Féile concludes with a post-Mass visit to Heaney's grave, at which words are spoken and a tune or a song is performed. Significantly, the printed program for the Féile is entirely in Irish, which is a clear statement that Irish will be spoken and that Irish speakers are very welcome.

Perhaps ironically, Heaney's life pattern follows the American immigrant dream as well, one of modernity's most powerful mythic narratives. Heaney's success was not material; it was largely symbolic. From a small village abroad ("I was born, bred, and buttered in a little village on the coast of Connemara"), he came to the United States with few material possessions retained in one shabby suitcase secured by a rope (according to legend, which he did not discourage), and made his way to his ultimate goal: recognition and acclaim through the achievement of a major award. Part of the required elements of the Irish American dream is the idea of a linear progression from shanty to lace curtain, in Irish terms: from humble ethnic enclaves to the prosperous white suburbs. Heaney's journey differed radically from this; while he would not have been averse to material prosperity, he forsook whatever hold he had on it when he gave up his position as a doorman in order to attain the status of artist. When Heaney sang of Morrissey and the Russian sailor, it was a statement from him that *he*, like the heroic warriors in the folktales that he told, had finally succeeded in fulfilling his quest. Recordings of his own words and transcriptions of them, now available on the website, www.joe-heaney.org, ensure that his voice will be heard by many more people.

Guide to Pronunciation

Readers familiar with I.P.A. are directed to *An Foclóir Póca* Dublin: An Gúm 1986, for a more comprehensive guide to pronouncing the Irish language. Here we give only those words that appear in the text. The velar consonants "d" and "t" are strongly aspirated in a manner similar to Italian.

The "ch" sound in Irish resembles that of German, or the word 'loch' as pronounced in Scotland. It is not a "k" sound. When preceded or followed by the vowels i or e, the sound resembles the one used in the German word "ich." The "kh" below is our attempt to indicate these sounds. Capitals below indicate word stress. Word stress in Irish usually falls on the first syllable; capitals below usually indicate that stress. There is no substitute for acquiring Heaney's available recordings and listening carefully to the sounds of the language. Additionally, those interested may consult the website www. joeheaney.org and listen to the material uploaded there. There is also an abundance of Irish language recorded material available on the internet.

aosdana	EES-dana
Cearbhaill Ó Dálaigh	KYAIR-ull Oh Daw-lee
"An Buachaill Caol Dubh"	An BUAKH-ill kayl duv
cnuas	KNOO-as
Dara Bán Mac Donnchadha	Dara Bawn Mac DUNN-a-kha
Dara Sheáin Choilm	Dara hyawin khelim
dúchas	DOO-khas
"Eileanóir a Rún"	EY-lee-NOR uh ROON
gaisce	GESH-ka
"Johnny Seoighe"	JohnnySHO-ig-ya
Oireachtas	EER-akh-tas
"Seachrán Chearbhaill"	SHAKH-rawn KHYAIR-ull
sean-nós	shan-nos
Seosamh Ó hÉanaí	SHO-sav Oh HEE-nee

213

Notes

Introduction

The chapter title refers to an hour-long documentary film (*Sing the Dark Away*) about the life of Joe Heaney. Produced by Michael Davitt in 1996, it is both illuminating and controversial. It includes interviews with many people who knew Heaney and covers his life in Ireland, England, and the United States.

1. http://www.census.nationalarchives.ie.

2. In bilingual communities, people have at least two names, one in Irish, and one in English, as well as other, less-official sobriquets such as patronymics, nicknames, and so on.

3. Several of Sean Williams's students at the Evergreen State College in Washington State have recalled incidents in which Irish or Irish-descended grandmothers have slapped them for eating potato skins, admonishing them with, for example, "The Famine is over!"

4. For example, Gribben's book *The Great Famine and the Irish Diaspora in America* (Amherst: University of Massachusetts Press, 1999) does a fine job of examining such important topics as music, women, folklore, and journalistic responses to the Famine. Cormac Ó Gráda's book *Black '47 and Beyond* (Princeton University Press, 1999) deals with history and memories of the Famine. Many such resources deserve further exploration.

5. In the twenty-first century, Ireland's population includes people from Brazil, Burma, Poland, Lithuania, Latvia, and many other nations. Polish is, in fact, the third-most-spoken language in Ireland, and many an American tourist has thought he or she was listening to Irish being spoken when, in fact, the language was Polish. The figures for use of Irish are often cited as up to 1.5 million people. However, because Irish is used daily in most of the Republic schools, this artificially inflates the figures for daily usage.

6. A language commissioner has been appointed as a result of the Official Languages Act in 2003. The commissioner's role is to protect and advocate for the constitutionally recognized right of Irish speakers to conduct business with the state and its organs through the medium of the Irish language.

7. The play *Translations* by Brian Friel works eloquently with this exact subject material, but a further resource is Stiofán Ó Cadhla's *Civilizing*

Ireland: Ordnance Survey 1824–1842: Ethnography, Cartography, Translation (2006).

8. Perhaps Cill na mBan ("Church of the Women") and Cill Mhór ("big church") (http://www.mustrad.org.uk/obits.htm). The joke plays on the idea of "killin' a man" and going to "kill more."

9. All of Heaney's quoted words in this chapter are derived from taped interviews and performances from his time in Seattle. The interviews and performances are in the University of Washington Ethnomusicology Archives in Seattle.

10. The transcriptions used in this book are intended to give a general sense of what, and how, Joe Heaney sang. Only a few of the transcriptions include barlines, because of Heaney's use of free meter in many of his songs. In representing the songs of a man with a deep voice and a large range, a truly accurate transcription would place everything in bass clef and use plenty of ledger lines. Our chosen option is to simply present a representation of his songs, more or less centralized in the treble clef, recognizing that no one—particularly the authors—will be entirely happy. However, for the sake of an acceptable visual representation that conveys the musical structure, attempts at strict accuracy have been forfeited. Perhaps Heaney himself would scowl as well!

Chapter 1

1. The term *sean-nós* has recently been extended in public consciousness to cover a traditional type of step dancing, diverging markedly from the norms of the competitive style promoted by Irish dance organizations through competition. Feet remain close to the floor, arms may be moved around, and there is an emphasis on individual interpretation. It is similar in some ways to American clog dancing and to tap. *Sean-nós* dancing is now a major competitive event at the Gaelic League's Oireachtas; the dancing is televised live, and has rapidly become one of the festival's most popular events since its inception in 2000.

2. Whether the term can be applied to singing in English is a matter of disagreement (see Mac Con Iomaire in Vallely, 1999; also McCann and Ó Laoire 2003).

3. According to Ó Canainn: "Seán provided a reasoned and logical framework within which Irish traditional music could be discussed and, to a certain extent, assessed by its devotees and practitioners, as well as by those not directly involved in it" (1982:16). Although Ó Canainn also notes the controversy that greeted Ó Riada's ideas in some quarters, this is a fair assessment of *Our Musical Heritage*.

4. *is acu a fuaireas na ceolta ba chasta a fuaireas ar chósta Chonamara—is mó atá siad cosúil le ceol maith na Mumhan mar atá ag Cáit Ní Mhuimhneacháin agus ag Labhrás Ó Cadhla*. Translation by Lillis Ó Laoire.

5. The term is to be distinguished from the houses of legislature in Ireland, also known collectively as An tOireachtas, which might translate as "Parliament."

6. The historian Kerby Miller, quoting a Gaelic poet's lament, described the seventeenth-century Catholic Irish under English domination as "strangers at home and exiles in Erin" (1985:11).

7. The full text of the interviews that MacColl and Seeger conducted with Heaney is found at http://www.mustrad.org.uk/articles/heaney.htm.

The late Irish scholar Tom Munnelly created a lengthy and informative review of this collection on November 15, 2000, which is well worth reading. (http://www.mustrad.org.uk/reviews/j_heaney.htm).

8. Only some of Heaney's recordings are discussed here. For a full account of his recorded material, the reader is directed to the discography, and to the Joe Heaney Website, www.joeheaney.org.

Chapter 2

1. Irish and English, though they belong to the same broad Indo-European language group, bear little resemblance to each other in syntax, vocabulary, or grammar. Irish belongs to the Celtic subgroup, while English belongs to the Germanic. Ireland's bilingual culture adds an interesting dimension to concepts regarding musical performance.

2. "To Hell or Connacht!" is famously attributed to Oliver Cromwell (1599–1658), regarding the "choice" he offered the Catholic people of Ireland in the nineteenth century.

3. An example of metathesis is the shift of *lucorpán* (little body person) into *leipreachán* (leprechaun). Hugh Shields mentions supplementary syllables in English-language songs only (1973:62–71). However, he does not view the phenomenon as having come from the language. Shields considers the interpolation of supplementary syllables as a way to break up consonant groups. In addition, it is possible that supplementary syllables fill out the meter of certain songs (69).

4. In fact, Heaney was obsessive in his condemnation of the guitar as an instrument for accompaniment. In the chapters on Heaney's work in the United States (chapters 9 and 10), we go into further detail about his opinions on guitars.

5. An earlier version of this section was published in 2004 as "Melodic Ornamentation in the *Sean-nós* Singing of Joe Heaney," *New Hibernia Review* 8, no. 1: 122–45. Many years before that, it formed the centerpiece of Sean Williams's unpublished master's thesis at the University of Washington: "Language, Melody and Ornamentation in the Traditional Irish Singing of Joe Heaney" (1985).

6. In fact, in today's *sean-nós* competitions, entrants must prepare two songs, one in a slow rubato rhythm, a second in a quicker, more regular one. The slow song is usually sung first. If the singer is recalled, the second song is then performed.

7. All song transcriptions in this text have been placed in a readable key rather than adhering to whatever key in which they were sung; Heaney rarely stuck to one particular key. In addition, the transcriptions lack bar lines because of the free-meter nature of the songs.

8. *Ochón* is a word taken from the traditional *caoineadh*, or lament over a corpse; it is used in "Caoineadh na dTrí Muire" at the end of each line.

9. Ó Canainn argues that the length of a stop may have an impact on which word is emphasized: "A long pause seems to draw attention to the preceding note while a short one concentrates attention on the following note" (1978:73).

Chapter 3

An earlier version of this chapter was published as "Singing the Famine: Joe Heaney, 'Johnny Seoighe' and the Poetics of Performance," in *Dear*

Far-Voiced Veteran: Essays in Honour of Tom Munnelly, ed. Anne Clune (Miltown Malbay, Ireland: Old Kilfarboy Society).

1. See Ó Gráda 1994.

2. Our thanks to Peadar Ó Ceannabháin for his careful reading of, and insightful comments on, an earlier draft of this chapter, and for his transcription of the lyrics to "Johnny Seoighe." Thanks also to Micheál Ó Catháin and Johanne Trew for their knowledgable and perceptive input.

3. Pól Ó Ceannabháin is the grandson of Máire an Ghabha bean Uí Cheannabháin, a woman noted for her religious material and especially her singing of "Caoineadh na Maighdine." See Partridge [Bourke] 1983. Her son and Pól's father, Michael Mháire an Ghabha Ó Ceannabháin (d. 2005), was an acclaimed singer and awarded the prestigious Sean-nós Cois Life Award in 1993. Pól's older sister, Caitríona, is also a noted singer, and a brother Josie is an accomplished accordion player. See Bourke 2007.

4. Recorded by Liam Mac Con Iomaire from Éamonn Ó Conghaile, March 1994. See Ó Gráda, *Black 47*, 274n89.

5. Colm Ó Caoidheáin and Pádhraic Ó h-Éighnigh (Joe Heaney's father) were first cousins. Unusually for an Irish marriage, Heaney's father moved to his wife Barbara Mulkerrins's home on their marriage.

6. Cormac Ó Gráda, e-mail communication, October 17, 2005. In a telephone discussion early in the 1990s, Seán 'ac Dhonnchadha revealed details of this incident to Professor Ó Gráda. Peadar Ó Ceannabháin confirmed that some older individuals, well informed about Johnny Seoighe, were angry at the public performance of "Johnny Seoighe" (e-mail communication, November 14, 2005). Thanks to Nicholas Carolan at the Irish Traditional Music Archive for confirming the dates of the Gael Linn nights.

7. A track of "Johnny Seoighe" was included in a compilation of songs and instrumental tunes titled *Celtic Christmas II*, released by the California New Age recording company Windham Hill in 1996. Performed by Maighréad Ní Dhomhnaill, it is one of just two songs that actually reference Christmas on the recording.

8. www.mustrad.org/Heaney/interview (accessed September 10, 2005). See also the booklet accompanying *Joe Heaney/Seosamh Ó hÉanaí, The Road from Connemara*: Fred McCormick, "I Never Had a Steady Job: Joe Heaney, a Life in Song," 16–21, CICD143 (Indreabhán, 2000).

9. This spelling was also favored by Heaney himself well into the 1940s. The now more common Ó hÉanaí seems to have gained precedence in the late fifties, possibly influenced by his involvement with Gael Linn.

10. Dara Bán Mac Donnchadha (1939–98), personal communication to Lillis Ó Laoire. According to Dara, some relatives of the person mentioned in the song "Is Measa Liom Bródach" took offense at his having recorded it and attacked him in England. Dara's own words were "Buaileadh Joe Éinniú i Sasana faoin amhrán sin" (Joe Heaney was beaten in England because of that song). Dara was quite reticent about singing this song publicly himself.

11. Interview with Joe Heaney, February 24, 1978, no. 78–15.1, Ethnomusicology Archives, University of Washington, Seattle.

12. Niall Ó Ciosáin suggests that the silence popularly believed to surround the Famine has not been sufficiently examined and that it may be exaggerated, since the many narratives contained in the Irish Folklore Commission's archives suggest that the Famine was indeed talked about.

Ó Gráda shows, however, that thieves and converts to Protestantism ("soupers"), for example, are rarely named in these accounts. See Ó Ciosáin 1995–96:7–10; 2001:95–117; 2004:222–32).

13. Performance by Joe Heaney, April 1983, at the University of Washington, Seattle. Recorded by Sean Williams. Ethnomusicology Archives, Tape no. 83–1.1.

Chapter 4

1. This particular comment—especially its inclusion of a reference to "mother earth"—reveals one of the ways in which Heaney was a quick study of his audience, adopting popular and timely terminology when it helped him to connect with his listeners.

2. Interestingly, the song is known in the Carna area as "Caoineadh na Páise" ("The Lament of the Passion"). Heaney's chosen title reveals that he was aware of other versions of the song and accepted the more widely known title. Regarding his identification of the three Marys as "Mary the mother of God, Mary Magdalene and Mary the mother of James and John" (the apostles), Partridge believes that Heaney was probably the source of this identification and that it reflects literary influence (1983:31).

3. The singer Sorcha Ní Ghuairim—who also grew up in the Carna area, in Roisín na Mainiach, a few miles east of where Heaney lived—had a different version of the same song. Though the lyrics were similar and the story was the same, her melody bears the marks of the women's keening tradition (Ní Ghuairim 2002, Track 5). Its descending melodic line—a feature included in many laments and in keening itself—is its hallmark. It descends a full octave from its highest point—the very first note—and emphasizes the lower pitch in the latter half of the song. It would be very interesting to do a deeper study of the two singers, but it is beyond the scope of the current work.

4. A common quatrain runs: ceathrar sagart gan a bheith santach, ceathrar Francach gan a bheith buí, ceathrar gréasaí gan a bheith bréagach, sin dháréag nach bhfuil sa tír. (Four priests who are not greedy, Four Frenchmen who are not swarthy, Four cobblers who are not liars, That's twelve you won't find in the country).

5. Heaney is emphasizing his own authority here as the sole custodian of rare spiritual items that were not widespread outside of his parish.

Chapter 5

1. Heaney learned "Dark Is the Color of My True Love's Hair" from his neighbor and friend Seán 'ac Dhonnchadha, who in turn had learned it from the piper Willy Clancy. Clancy, returning from a trip to a folk festival in Eastern Europe, had brought the song home with him after picking it up from the Appalachian family of Jean Ritchie (as described by Heaney in the videotaped collection made by folklorist Kenny Goldstein, VCT ER6 Ireland 90-39.1, Joe Heaney Collection University of Washington).

2. Indeed, in the version of the story that accompanies the "Seachrán" in Carna, the storyteller Cóilín Ó Cualáin, a neighbor of Joe Heaney, consistently refers to Cearbhall as Cearbhallán—Carolan. Clearly, in his conversations with others, Heaney was advised of this conlation, and accordingly amended his title to the historically correct Cearbhall. However, he often still referred to Carolan when telling the story.

3. Ó Dálaigh is most frequently Anglicized O'Daly or Daly in Ireland.
4. As I roved out on a May morning, on a May morning quite early

I met my love upon the way, oh Lord, but she was early
Her hair was dark, her teeth were white and her buckles shone like silver
She had a dark and a roving eye, and her hair hung o'er her shoulder.

First chorus:
   And she sang a liddle-eyedle liddle-eyedle um
   And she eyedle-liddle um and she eydle-liddle doo and she landie.
Who are you my pretty fair maid, who are you my darling?
Who are you my pretty fair maid, who are you my darling?
She answered me right modestly, I am my mammy's daughter

Second chorus:
   With me ro-rum rah, fraddle deedle dah, dye-dee addle-iddle airy-o.
How old are you, my pretty fair miss, how old are you, my darling?
She answered me right modestly, sixteen come Monday morning.

(First chorus)
Do you want a man my pretty fair miss, do you want a man, my darling?
Do you want a man my pretty fair miss, do you want a man, my darling?
She answered me right modestly, I would but for my mammy

(Second chorus)
Will you come up to me mammy's house when the moon is shining brightly
I'll arise and let you in, and the devil o' one will hear me

(First chorus)
I went up to her mammy's house when the moon shone bright and clearly
I went up to her mammy's house when the moon shone bright and clearly
She arose to let me in but her mammy chanced to hear her

(Second chorus)
She took her by the top of her hair and into the parlor brought her
With the end of a hazel stick she was a well-bet daughter

(First chorus)
She took my horse by the bridle and rein and led him to the stable
She took my horse by the bridle and rein and led him to the stable
There's plenty of oats for the soldier's horse as fast as he can take it

(Second chorus)
She took me by her lily-white hand and led me to a table
There's plenty of wine for the soldier lad as fast as he can take it

(First chorus)
Then she went up and dressed the bed, she dressed it soft and easy

She went up and dressed the bed, she dressed it soft and easy
I went up and I rolled her in, oh, my lassie, are you able?

(Second chorus)
It's there I stayed till the break of day and the devil o' one did hear
     me
It's there I stayed till the break of day and the devil o' one did hear
     me
I got up and put on me clothes, oh, my lassie I must leave you

(Second chorus)
When will you return again, and when will we get married
When broken Delft make Christmas bells, it's then we will get
     married

(First chorus)
Now a pint at night is my delight and a gallon in the morning
The old women are my heartbreak, but the young ones are me
     darlings

(First chorus)
—(Roud no. 3479)

5. See the Gael Linn recording of this song on CD 2, track 7 of the 2007 rereleased CD titled Seosamh Ó hÉanaí, *Ó Mo Dhúchas/From My Tradition*, 1 and 2, CEFCD191. Compare Peadar Ó Ceannabháin's version of the same song on his CD, titled *Mo Chuid Den tSaol*, Cló-Iar Chonnacht Recording, CICD131.

6. In Edward Bunting's collection begun at the 1792 Belfast Harp Festival, he notes that this air—transcribed from the playing of Denis Hempson—probably dates to the beginning of the seventeenth century (Bunting 1840:94). The connection to Hempson, one of the last of the professional harpers, and the only one of the assembled company to play with his fingernails in the oldest style, emphasizes Heaney's canniness in using this song as authentic. These three songs, then, are traceable to the very source of authentic Irish music.

7. This line differs on his Gael Linn record. There it is sung as follows: "Bhí bua eile aici go meallfadh sí an éanlaith ón gcrann" – she had another gift that she could charm the birds from the tree.

8. Heaney Collection. UW85-39.7.

9. This might have been acceptable to the Irish Americans because it was in English.

10. Patrick Sarsfield was an Irish leader in two major conflicts with the English: the Battle of the Boyne, and the Siege of Limerick (both of which took place in 1690). He is still considered a hero, and his name is prominent in Limerick.

11. A *gaisce* is a masculine, warrior-like deed; see chapter 7 for more about this specific term.

12. Further discussion of gender issues and the masculine persona in song occurs in chapters 6 and 7.

13. O'Higgins, Brian. 1918. *Glen na Mona. Stories and Sketches*. Dublin: Whelan and Son. See also 1929. *Songs of Glen na Mona*. Dublin: See: http://www.capeirish.com/websongs/sto023.pdf. Accessed, 09/28/2010. The song may have been published earlier than 1918. Undoubtedly its printing

helped ensure its popularity, but this must also be attributed to its modal *aaba* air.

14. It was noted in an earlier chapter that Heaney is likely to have gained a firm understanding of song categories from such colleagues in folk music as Ewan MacColl and Peggy Seeger. Heaney was also a good friend of academic folklorist Kenny Goldstein, who taught at the University of Pennsylvania.

Chapter 6

1. The Blasket Islands, off the Dingle peninsula in County Kerry, rose to prominence in the arenas of literature and anthropology when, due to an influx of scholars from outside, a number of islanders penned celebrated autobiographies in the late nineteenth and early twentieth centuries.

2. Note the reduction of an entire rowdy shebeen in John Ford's film *The Informer* (1935) into helpless, emasculated tearful men and women by the rendition of Moore's "Believe Me If All Those Endearing Young Charms." The one most devastated by the song is none other than Gippo Nolan, the towering tough-guy lead character.

3. Will Crutchfield, in an archived *New York Times* article titled "Recital: Irish Tenor," dated May 25, 1987. Frank Patterson passed away in 2000 at the age of sixty-one.

4. A vibrato occurs in music when an instrumentalist or vocalist slightly increases and decreases the number of beats per second on a sustained pitch, thereby causing said pitch to fluctuate rapidly back and forth across the "true pitch" of the performed note. Enthusiasts of nineteenth-century opera, popular music, and Irish tenors find that the music sounds "sweeter" or more in tune when performed in this manner.

5. http://www.songwritershalloffame.org/artist_bio.asp?artistId=70.

6. When asked about his own light vibrato, Heaney asserted that Ó Riada was correct, and insisted that no *sean-nós* singer, including himself, ever uses a vibrato.

7. The tenor Kevin Moulton makes note of "returning to his Irish heritage" on his own Web site and in so doing gains the stamp of authority from the deceased:

In 1999, Kevin returned to his Irish heritage, studying the career of John McCormack, and putting together a concert program like one John himself might have performed in the early 20th century. Researching in various libraries, Kevin found many beautiful arrangements of such McCormack favorites as "The Harp That Once Thro' Tara's Halls," "The Minstrel Boy," "Macushla," and "I Hear You Calling Me," and he breathed new life into these classic old songs (http://www.kevinmoulton.com).

8. *Dubliners* (London: Penguin, 1914).

9. http://www.joseflocke.co.uk/.

10. http://www.ronantynan.net/news.aspx?bid=10.

11. The 1970s saw the Irish language given only secondary status as a treaty language when Ireland joined the EEC (EU). Passing Irish language exams was no longer deemed necessary to achieve a pass in State examinations, and the status of the Irish language was also downgraded in the Civil Service. While none of these measures in themselves proved disastrous for the language, and while they recognized for practical purposes that Ireland was predominantly English-speaking and would remain so,

the lack of coherently implemented replacement policies, fostering the extension of Irish, was a profound and bitter disappointment to many committed Irish speakers.

12. This seems to be a reference to, and perhaps even a parody of, the Clancy Brothers' trademark sweaters.

13. http://www.rootsmusic.co.uk/HarrietEaris.htm (accessed May 29, 2009).

14. http://www.teachnet.ie/mhearne/aisceol.htm.

15. In his speech "The Undeserted Village Ireland" (1943), Ireland's first president, Eamon de Valera, put forth an image of a Gaelic-speaking Ireland that would include, among other elements, "comely maidens dancing at the crossroads," a catchphrase that has come to represent an Ireland fossilized in time.

Chapter 7

1. We deliberately avoid the sociological term "peasant" here, since it can be considered a slur in Ireland. See Ó Giolláin 2005a.

2. Johann Gottfried Von Herder was the philosopher most associated with ideas connecting the rural culture of the Folk with the nation. He also published a collection of folk songs.

3. According to Dinneen's *Foclóir Gaedhilge agus Béarla* (Irish-English dictionary), definitions of *gaisceadh* (old spelling) and its related words include arms, equipment; valor, feats of arms, heroism, a great exploit; boasting; *ag déanamh gaiscidh*, acting the hero, doing wonderful things. Those who perform *gaisceadh* are "a champion, a hero, a warrior, a knight, a feat-performer; common in folk-tales; applied to an athlete no less than to a warrior" (511–12).

4. Dara Bán's version of "Púcán Sheáin Antaine" may be heard on his CD *Rogha Amhrán* (CICD140), a recording of twelve songs.

5. "Eiseamláir do gach éinne ab ea an tuathánach fir a oibrigh chun a chlann a chothú, a chomhlíon a dhualgaisí sa phobal, a ghaibh lena ghnóthaí féin, nár sháraigh daoine eile ach a chosain a chearta féin. Duine láidir diongbhálta ab ea é mar bhí meas ar an nádúr sin agus níor bhain daoine eile drochúsáid as."

6. The Laws classification scheme is a means by which folklorists and ethnomusicologists can track ballad types. It is similar to the Child ballad numbering system.

7. http://www.mun.ca/folklore/leach/songs.

8. http://www.mun.ca/folklore/leach/songs/NFLD1/15-06.htm.

9. For a colorful description of Morrissey in fiction, see Quinn 1995. See also http:www.cyberboxingzone.com/boxing/Morrissey.htm. Accessed 07-14#2007. Thanks to Micheál Ó Catháin for this reference.

10. They both shook hands, walked round the ring, most glorious to be seen,
When Morrisey put on the belt, bound round with shamrock green.
They both shook hands, walked round the ring, and then began to fight
Which cheered the hearts of those Irishmen for to behold the sight.
(http://sniff.numachi.com/pages/tiMORRRUS2;ttMORRRUS2.html).
See also Bourke 2007:43–58; she prints a version from Máire An Ghabha Uí Cheannabháin (born 1905), an older contemporary of Heaney's from the same place where the "shamrock green" is the preferred variant. Another recorded version by Seán 'ac Dhonncha, Heaney's contemporary,

schoolmate, and lifelong friend, is found on *Columbia World Library of Folk and Primitive Music*, vol. 2 (Ireland).

11. The University of Notre Dame football team (and therefore, everyone associated with the institution) is fondly called "The Fighting Irish." This name has come into casual use in North America – for better or worse – to sometimes refer to any white person with a temper (Irish-descended or not), anyone of Irish descent who becomes angry, and any Irish American.

12. A quote from the song "Do Me Justice," a pointed reply and refutation of such negative stereotypes.

13. The following is an example of a battle dress that Heaney used to introduce some of his stories: "There was here long ago, and long ago it was, if I was there at that time I wouldn't be here now, and if I was there and here now, I would have a long story, big story, short story, bad story, good story, or no story at all. But whatever way I tell it tonight, I hope you don't tell it half as good tomorrow night. I'm talking about the time that the roofs of houses were thatched with buttermilk, and little pigs went down the street with knives and forks stuck in them, saying 'pig me, pig me, pig me'" (Cowdery 1990:40).

14. As Harvey Mansfield has noted: Instead of submerging themselves in the category of humanity, he-men or heroes connect themselves to the gods. They are sons of gods, or they can trace a lineage to a god....Zeus is a father to the he-men, the heroes, but a ruler of human beings, who do not get his individual attention. Human beings suffer neglect and would be excluded from the care of the gods if they did not constitute a kind of audience before which the he-men display their heroism. Thus patriarchy in the style of the *Iliad* is not the fatherhood of god over the brotherhood of men but a compound of fatherly care of heroes and fatherly indifference to human beings outside the family. The gods care for the best men, and the best men seek to resemble the gods; they are even called demigods (2006:55–56).

15. Again from Harvey C. Mansfield in *Manliness*:
Assertiveness has its basis in a *brutish* quality already mentioned, called by Plato *thumos*. In the *Republic* he presents *thumos*, the bristling snappishness of a dog, as the outstanding feature of the guardians or rulers of the just city that he constructs. A dog defends itself, its master and its turf; and *thumos* is a part of the human soul that performs the similar function of defensiveness. As a dog defends its master, so the doggish part of the human soul defends the human ends higher than itself. In this defense the paradox is that the lower defends the higher and thus asserts the value of the higher. Instead of having reason defend itself in the calm statement of principles and the careful progress of an argument, the reasonable person often gets angry as his *thumos* takes over the defense of its supposed master reason. In adding up the characteristics of *thumos* detailed by Plato, one finds oneself on the rough, not the gentlemanly, side of manliness. (2006:206).

16. *Washington Post*, July 5, 1982, cited in Mac Con Iomaire 2007, 359.

17. See, for example, the rousing, exuberant performance by Seán 'ac Dhonnchadha on *World Library of Folk and Primitive Music Vol. 1*, Ireland, by Alan Lomax.

18. Witness the thousands of Americans claiming Irishness for a day every March 17, usually in order to drink heavily and, in doing so, engage in an annual ritual of ethnic stereotyping.

19. The fifth verse does not appear on Heaney's Topic album, but this verse is on his 1957 recording.

20. *The Joe Heaney Collection* JH 78-15.2 (Seattle: Department of Ethnomusicology, University of Washington).

21. "An Buinneán Buí," or "The Yellow Bittern," is a famous song in Irish about drink. The poet finds a dead bird on a lakeshore on a frosty day; he concludes that the bird has died of thirst because it could not reach the water through the ice. His verses meditate on the bird's death, concluding that although he may only live for a short while, it would be worse to die of thirst. He encourages all to drink their fill during their lifetime, for they will not be able to drink after their death. Heaney's performance of this song toward the end of his life, which can be heard on *Say a Song*, is one of his most moving renditions. It is also noteworthy that the recent documentary by Alan Gilsenan about the life and career of the late Liam Clancy is also titled *The Yellow Bittern* (2009).

22. Tomás Ó Canainn also references "An Caisdeach Bán" and offers a more extensive set of lyrics, as well as a deeper analysis (1978:51–53).

23. Sean Williams, personal recollection.

24. The exception to this was his abiding friendship with the late Lucy Simpson, who took him as a near family member during his time in New York.

25. "There was a continued articulation of the myth that anything which tends to keep the Irish together reduces the risk of moral lapse, revealing a striking double standard; the belief that there were no such lapses at home in Ireland. In truth, the Irish solution was to hide and deny those who had lapsed" (Ferriter 2009:6).

26. http://www.bobdylanroots.com/prisoner.html and http://en.wikipedia.org/wiki/Vernon_Dalhart (accessed January 5, 2010). Dalhart's recording of "The Prisoner's Song" may be heard on YouTube.

27. This is a reference to the David Whisnant's book *All That Is Native and Fine* (1983), which discusses the use of southern rural culture as a representation of authentic Anglo-Saxon, and therefore American, purity.

Chapter 8

1. Actors Maureen O'Sullivan (1911–98), who played Jane to Johnny Weissmuller's Tarzan, among many other roles, and mother of the actor Mia Farrow, and Basil Rathbone (1892–1967), a prolific British actor remembered most for his portrayals of Sherlock Holmes, were among the residents of the building; in fact, Heaney was present when Rathbone died of a massive heart attack on June 21, 1967; Rathbone is alleged to have died cradled in Heaney's arms.

2. This is part of a longer online article by Adam Platt, titled "The Doormen: Those Silent Sentries Are Rarely as Buttoned-Down as They Seem," from *New York Magazine* online: http://www.newyorkmetro.com/nymetro/news/classicnewyork/n_8160/.

3. Paddy Glackin vividly remembers Heaney's kindness to himself and Liam Óg in Toronto. When they both became very ill, Heaney insisted that they be reaccommodated from the college dormitories in which they had been billeted to a hotel to help them recover (Mac Con Iomaire 2007:336–37).

4. "Mura raibh Seosamh sásta, ní raibh John Cage sásta, agus mura raibh Cage sásta ní raibh Seosamh sásta."

5. http://www.themodernword.com/joyce/music/cage_roaratorio.html. Excerpts from the liner notes from the Mode CD written by John Cage (accessed June 2, 2009).

6. In Irish documentation concerning Heaney's life in the United States, the University of Washington is often referred to as "Washington University." The University of Washington is located in Seattle, in Washington State; Washington University is located in St. Louis, Missouri.

7. As a side note, when Fred Lieberman met Heaney, he recalled him as the elevator operator from the apartment building of his high school girlfriend.

8. His oft-repeated advice to female students was to have five or six children as soon as possible. When the women objected (often being new graduate students with six more years to go before obtaining the Ph.D.), the full force of Heaney's stern demeanor came to the fore, and he sometimes halted the lesson, switched over to teaching only English-language drinking songs, or suspended communication for a few days at a time as "punishment" for daring to challenge his views.

9. In 1937-38 all Irish secondary school students were asked to spend a full year engaged in collecting fieldwork as part of their school work. As part of an immense project of nation building, students were sent on collecting missions among their family members and neighbors. The result is the largest folklore collection in the world from a single place – over half a million individual items – covering every part of Ireland. It is a priceless legacy that forms the foundation of all Irish folklore collecting having been conducted since the 1930s.

10. Despite his trenchant theoretical opposition to guitars and other modern arrangements of traditional music, Heaney enjoyed cordial relationships with musicians such as the Clancy Brothers, who, according to his own ideals, might have been guaranteed to earn his disapproval. Heaney, of course, received deferential and respectful treatment from the Clancys and most other musicians, allowing him to occupy his contradictory positions without apparent difficulty.

11. He even asked that of a woman who reached his phone with a wrong number.

12. The sessions were recorded and preserved in the Joe Heaney Collection at the University of Washington; some of the songs from this series, in fact, appear on the 1996 CD released by the archives (*Say a Song: Joe Heaney in the Pacific Northwest*, NWARCD 001).

13. Along with a handful of others, Sean Williams had the sad duty of ringing up each student in the course to pass on the news of Heaney's death.

14. Jill Linzee was one of Heaney's graduate students and friends; she developed a master's thesis on variation in his songs and stories (1985).

15. Some RTÉ footage has already materialized on youtube; Heaney singing "Cunnla," for example, is from this performance.

16. According to the Web site of the Mayo Clinic in Minnesota, "Emphysema causes a loss of elasticity in the walls of the small air sacs in your lungs. Eventually, the walls stretch and break, creating larger, less efficient air sacs that aren't able to handle the normal exchange of oxygen and carbon dioxide. When emphysema is advanced, you must work so hard to expel air from your lungs that breathing can consume up to 20 percent of your resting energy. Unfortunately, because emphysema

develops gradually over many years, you may not experience symptoms such as shortness of breath until irreversible damage has already occurred" (http://www.mayoclinic.com/health/emphysema/DS00296).

17. See Mac Con Iomaire 2007, chaps. 21–23 (pp. 379–455), for more details on the events leading up to and surrounding Heaney's passing. Although the main text is in Irish, most of the American testimonies are offered in the original English.

18. "Ach dá mbeadh post ar fail in Éirinn, post ceart, níl aon amhras orm ach go dtiocfadh sé ar ais go hÉirinn. Is é an saghas ruda a d'fheilfeadh dó ná post i gceann de na hollscoileanna, ach faraor tháinig an fear bocht róluath." In translation, "If a proper position had been available in Ireland, I have no doubt that he would have returned to Ireland. The kind of thing that would have suited him would have been a post in one of the universities, but alas, the poor man came too early" (Mac Con Iomaire 2007:428).

19. "Will Farmleigh Make a Difference?" *Irish Times*, September 29, 2009, http://www.irishtimes.com/newspaper/weekend/2009/0926/1224255 265937.html (accessed January 5, 2010).

Chapter 9

1. http://www.zipcon.com/~highroad/folkscare.html (accessed May 28, 2009).

2. When blackface minstrels removed the burnt cork from their faces, they were symbolically able to affirm their whiteness. For a fictionalized account of this idea, see Peter Quinn's *Banished Children of Eve* (1994).

3. The air of "Danny Boy," also known as the "Londonderry Air," was supplied to George Petrie by Jane Ross in that county and published by him in 1855. The lyrics were composed by Englishman Frederick Weatherly in 1913. See Michael Robinson, "Danny Boy: The Mystery Solved," www.standingstones.com/dannyboy/html (accessed May 29, 2009).

4. Free high school education for all was not introduced in Ireland until the late sixties.

5. A notable, but early, exception to this was his performance at the Newport Folk Festival, when his *báinín*'s sleeves were roughly pushed up to his elbows, and his stern comments to the audience about how Oliver Cromwell "wanted us to *die*" put to rest any expectations of "Danny Boy." The late July heat of Newport was sweltering, but the *báinín* was part of the uniform.

6. Our thanks to Micheál Ó Catháin for drawing this aspect of Heaney's life to our attention.

7. The director of the Ethnomusicology Archives may be contacted at the following address: Dr. Laurel Sercombe, Ethnomusicology Archives, School of Music, Box 353450, University of Washington, Seattle, WA 98105, http://depts.washington.edu/ethmusic/archives.html.

References

Anderson, Benedict. 1983. *Imagined Communities: Reflections on the Origins and Spread of Nationalism*. London: Verso.

Bakhtin, Mikhail M. 1968. *Rabelais and His World*. Trans. H. Iswolsky. Cambridge, Mass.: MIT Press.

Barbour, Stephen. 2000. "Britain and Ireland: The Varying Significance of Language for Nationalism." In *Language and Nationalism in Europe*, ed. Stephen Barbour and Cathie Carmichael, 18–43. New York: Oxford University Press.

Behan, Dominic. 1965. *Ireland Sings*. London: Music Sales Corporation.

Beiner, Guy. 2007. *Remembering the Year of the French: Irish Folk History and Social Memory*, Madison: University of Wisconsin Press.

Bendix, Regina. 1997. *In Search of Authenticity: The Formation of Folklore Studies*. Madison: University of Wisconsin Press.

Bergin, Osborne. 1937. "On the Origin of Modern Irish Rhythmical Verse." *Acta Jutlandica* 9:280–86.

Bhabha, Homi. 1994. *The Location of Culture*. London: Routledge.

Bodley, Seoirse. 1973. "Technique and Structure in Sean-nós Singing." *Éigse Ceóil Tíre* 1:44–54.

Bohlman, Philip V. 1988. *The Study of Folk Music in the Modern World*. Bloomington: Indiana University Press.

Bourke, Angela. 2007. "Songs in English in the Conamara Gaeltacht." In *Dear Far-Voiced Veteran: Essays in Honour of Tom Munnelly*, ed. Anne Clune, 43–58. Miltown Malbay, Ireland: Old Kilfarboy Society.

Breathnach, Breandán. 1977. *Folk Music and Dances of Ireland*. Dublin: Mercier.

Breathnach, Pádraig. 1920. *Ceol Ár Sinsear*. Dublin: Browne and Nolan.

Briody, Mícheál. 2007. *The Irish Folklore Commission 1935–1970: History, Ideology, Methodology*. Helsinki: Finnish Literature Society.

Browne Peter, Pádraig Ó Cearbhaill, and Harry Bradshaw. 1994. *Labhrás Ó Cadhla: Amhráin ó Shliabh gCua*. Dublin: RTÉ (CD 234 + Booklet).

Bunting, Edward. 1840 [2002]. *The Ancient Music of Ireland*. Dublin: Walton Manufacturing.

Butler, Judith. 1990. *Gender Trouble: Feminism and the Subversion of Idenity*. London: Routledge.

Campbell, Matthew. 1999–2000. "Thomas Moore's Wild Song: The 1821 Irish Melodies." *Bullán*, v.4, no.2: 83–103.

Carolan, Nicholas. 2003. 'Ceolta Éireann 1-20: Gael Linn's 78 Recordings 1957–1961. *Seolta Séidte/Setting Sail: Ceolta Éireann 1957–1961. Forty three Historic Recordings*. (Dublin: Gael Linn CEFCD 184, accompanying booklet 6–31).

———. 2005. "From 2RN to International Meta-Community: Irish National Radio and Traditional Music." *Journal of Music in Ireland* 5, no. 1 Accessed online: http://journalofmusic.com/article/280.

Carolan, Nicholas 2005 reference Carson, Ciarán. 1996. *Last Night's Fun: A Book about Irish Music*. London: Jonathan Cape.

Cleary, Joe. 2005. "Introduction." In *The Cambridge Companion to Modern Irish Culture*. 2005, ed. Joe Cleary & Claire Connolly, 1-21. Cambridge: Cambridge University Press.

Cohen, Ronald D. 2002. *Rainbow Quest: The Folk Music Revival and American Society, 1940–1970*. Amherst: University of Massachusetts Press.

Coleman, Steve. 1996. "Joe Heaney Meets the Academy." In *Irish Journal of Anthropology* 1:69–85.

———. 1997. "Joe Heaney and Style in Sean-nós Singing." In *Blas: The Local Accent in Irish Traditional Music*, ed. T. M. Smith and M. Ó. Súilleabháin, 31–52. Limerick: University of Limerick.

———. 2004. "The Nation, the State and the Neighbours: Personation in Irish Language Discourse." *Language and Communication* 24:381–411.

Courbage, Youssef. 1997. "The Demographic Factor in Ireland's Movement towards Partition (1607–1921)." *Population: An English Selection* 9:169–90.

Cowdery, James. 1990. *The Melodic Tradition of Ireland*. Kent, Ohio: Kent State University Press.

Cross, Tom Peete, and Clark Harris Slover. 1936 [1969]. *Ancient Irish Tales*. New York: Barnes and Noble.

Curtis, Perry L. 1997. *Apes and Angels: The Irishman in Victorian Caricature*. Washington D.C. Smithsonian Institution Press.

Davis, Leith.1993. "Irish Bards and English Consumers: Thomas Moore's *Irish Melodies* and the Colonized Nation." *ARIEL: A Review of International English Literature*. v. 24/2: 7–25.

———. 2006. *Music, Postcolonialism and Gender: The Construction of Irish National Identity, 1724-1874*. Notre Dame: University of Notre Dame Press.

Davitt, Michael. 1991. "Dán do Sheosamh Ó hÉanaí." In *The Field Day Anthology of Irish Writing*, ed. Seamus Deane, vol. 3, 922. Derry, Northern Ireland: Field Day Publications.

Delargy, James H. [Séamus Ó Duilearga]. 1945. *The Gaelic Story-Teller, with Some Notes on Gaelic Folk-Tales*. Sir John Rhys Memorial Lecture, British Academy. From the Proceedings of the British Academy. Vol. 31. London: Geoffrey Cumberlege.

———.1999. "Irish Tales and Story-Tellers." In International Folklaristics: Classic Contributions by the Founders of Folklore, ed. Alan Dundes, 153–76. Lanham, MD: Rowman & Littlefield.

De Noraidh, Liam. 1965. *Ceol Ón Mumhain*. Dublin: An Clóchomhar.

de Paor, Liam. 1994. *Tom Moore and Contemporary Ireland*. Cork: Irish Traditional Music Society, University College Cork.

De Valera, Eamon. 1943. "The Undeserted Village Ireland." In the *Field Day Anthology of Irish Writing*, ed. Seamus Deane, vol. 3, 747–50. Derry: Field Day Publications.

Dezell, Maureen. 2002. *Irish America: Coming into Clover*. New York: Anchor Books.

Doan James. E. 1980–81. "The Poetic Tradition of Cearbhall Ó Dálaigh." *Éigse 18*, 1–24.

—— 1981. "Cearbhall Ó Dálaigh as Archetypal Poet in Irish Folk Tradition. *Proceedings of the Harvard Celtic Colloquium*, 95–123.

—— 1982. "Cearbhall Ó Dálaigh as Craftsman and Trickster." *Béaloideas* 50: 54–89.

—— 1983. "Cearbhall Ó Dálaigh as Lover and Tragic Hero." *Béaloideas* 51: 11–30.

—— 1985. *The Romance of Cearbhall and Fearbhlaidh: A Medieval Irish Tale Here First Translated into English*. Mountrath, Ireland: Dolmen Press.

—— 1985. "The Folksong Tradition of Cearbhall Ó Dálaigh." *Folklore* 96/1: 67–86.

—— 1990. *Cearbhall Ó Dálaigh: An Irish Poet in Romance and Oral Tradition*. New York: Garland.

Donnellan, Philip. 1988. "We Were the BBC: An Alternative View of a Producer's Responsibility, 1948–1984." Unpublished memoir.

Donnelly, James S., Jr. 1996. "The Construction of the Memory of the Famine in Ireland and the Irish Diaspora, 1850–1900." *Éire/Ireland*, 31 (1-2): 26–61.

Dundes, Alan. 1977. "Who Are the Folk?" In *Frontiers of Folklore*, ed. William Bascom, 17–35. Washington, D.C.: American Association for the Advancement of Science.

Ferriter, Diarmaid. 2009. *Occasions of Sin: Sex and Society in Modern Ireland*. London: Profile Books.

Filene, Benjamin. 2000. *Romancing the Folk: Public Memory and American Roots Music*. Chapel Hill: University of North Carolina Press.

Finneran, Richard J., ed. 1989. *The Collected Poems of W. B. Yeats: A New Edition*. New York: Collier Books.

Freeman, A. Martin. "Irish Songs from Ballyvourney." *Journal of the Folk-Song Society*, 6/23–25: vii–xxviii, 95–342.

Foley, John Miles. 2002. *How to Read an Oral Poem*. Urbana: University of Illinois Press.

Gedutis, Susan. 2004. *See You at the Hall: Boston's Golden Era of Irish Music and Dance*. Boston: Northeastern University Press.

Gillespie, Raymond. 1999. "Popular and Unpopular Religion: A View from Early Modern Ireland." In *Irish Popular Culture 1650–1850*, ed. J. S. Donnelly Jr. and Kerby A. Miller, 30–49. Dublin: Irish Academic Press.

Glassie, Henry. 1982. *Passing the Time in Ballymenone: History and Folklore in an Ulster Community*. Dublin: Indiana University Press.

Gray, Billy. 2005. "'The Lukewarm Conviction of Temporary Lodgers': Hubert Butler and the Anglo-Irish Sense of Exile." *New Hibernia Review* 9/2: 84–97.

Gribben, Arthur. 1999. ed. *The Great Famine and the Irish Diaspora in America*. Amherst: University of Massachusetts Press.

Hall, Reg. 1995. *The Social Organization of Traditional Music-Making: The Irish in London after the War*. Ó Riada Memorial Lecture 10. Cork: Traditional Music Archive, University College Cork.

Hamm, Charles. 1983. "'Erin, the Tear and the Smile in Thine Eyes': or, Thomas Moore's *Irish Melodies* in America." In *Yesterdays: Popular Song in America*. New York: Norton.

Hardebeck, Carl. 1911. "Traditional Singing: Its Value and Meaning." *Journal of the Ivernian Society* 3 (January–March), 89–95.

Harrington, Richard. 1982. "Honoring America's Folk Heritage." *Washington Post*, July 5, 1982.

Harris, Ruth-Ann. 1999. "Introduction." In *The Great Famine and the Irish Diaspora in America*, ed. Arthur Gribben, 1–20. Amherst: University of Massachusetts Press.

Harrison, Alan. 1979. *An Chrosantacht*. Dublin: An Clóchomhar.

Hayden, Tom, ed. 1997. *Irish Hunger: Personal Reflections on the Legacy of the Famine*. Boulder, CO.: Roberts Rinehart.

Henebry, Richard. 1903. *Irish Music: Being an Examination of the Matter of Scales, Modes, and Keys with Practical Instructions and Examples for Players*. Dublin: An Clóchumann.

————. 1928. *A Handbook of Irish Music*. Dublin: Cork University Press.

Henigan, Julie. 1991. "Sean-Nós in Donegal: In Search of a Definition." *Ulster Folklife* 37:97–104.

Hickey, Raymond. 2007. *Irish English: History and Present-Day Forms*. Studies in English Language. Cambridge: Cambridge University Press.

Hoagland, Kathleen. 1999. *1000 Years of Irish Poetry: The Gaelic and Anglo-Irish Poets from Pagan Times to the Present*. New York: Welcome Rain.

Hogan, Jeremiah J. 1927. *The English Language in Ireland*. Dublin: Educational Company of Ireland.

————. 1986. *Language, Lore and Lyrics*, ed. Breandán Ó Conaire. Dublin: Irish Academic Press.

Hyde, Douglas. 1894. *Love Songs of Connacht*. Dublin: Irish Academic Press.

Ignatiev, Noel. 1995. *How the Irish Became White*. New York: Routledge.

Jacobson, Matthew Frye. 1998. *Whiteness of a Different Color: European Immigrants and the Alchemy of Race*. Cambridge MA: Harvard University Press.

Jackson, Bruce. 2007. "Bob Dylan and the Legend of Newport 1965." In *The Story Is True: The Art and Meaning of Telling Stories*, 139–50. Philadelphia: Temple University Press.

James E. 1985. "The Folksong Tradition of Cearbhall Ó Dálaigh." Folklore 96:1.

Joyce, James. [1916] 1968. *A Portrait of the Artist as a Young Man*. New York: Viking Penguin.

Joyce, P. W. [1910] 1991. *English as We Speak It in Ireland*. Dublin: Wolfhound Press.

Kiberd, Declan. 1995. *Inventing Ireland*. London: Jonathan Cape.

Kristeva, Julia. 2004. "Two Irish Addresses." *Irish Pages: A Journal of Contemporary Writing*, 2/2: 201–228.

Ledbetter, Gordon T. 2006. *John McCormack: The Great Irish Tenor*. Dublin: Town House.

Leduff, Charlie. 2005. "Good-bye to Mr. Hello and Good-bye." In *Work and Other Sins: Life in New York City and Thereabouts*, 2–3. New York: Penguin.

Lloyd, David. 2003. "The Memory of Hunger." In *Loss: The Politics of Mourning*, ed. David L. Eng and David Kanzanjian, 205–28. Berkeley: University of California Press.

Lysaght, Patricia. 1996–97. "Perspectives on Women during the Great Irish Famine from Oral Tradition." *Béaloideas* 64/65:63–131.

————. 1999. "Women and the Great Famine: Vignettes from the Irish Oral Tradition." In *The Great Famine and the Irish Cultural Diaspora*, ed. Arthur Gribben, 21–47. Amherst: University of Massachusetts Press.

Mac Con Iomaire, Liam. 2000. "'Where I come from they all sing like that': Seosamh Ó hÉanaí, His Life and Singing Tradition." Accompanying booklet to the CD *The Road from Connemara: Songs and Stories Told and Sung to Ewan MacColl*. Cló Iar-Chonnachta.

———. 2007. *Seosamh Ó hÉanaí: Nár Fhágha Mé Bás Choíche* [Joe Heaney: May I Never Die]. Conamara, Ireland: Cló Iar-Chonnachta.

Malcolm, Elizabeth. 1998. "The Rise of the Pub: A Study in the Disciplining of Popular Culture." In *Irish Popular Culture 1650–1850*, ed. J. S. Donnelly Jr. and Kerby Miller, 50–77. Dublin: Irish Academic Press.

Mansfield, Harvey C. 2006. *Manliness*. New Haven, CT: Yale University Press.

McCann, Anthony and Lillis Ó Laoire. 2003. "Raising One Higher than the Other: The Hierarchy of Tradition in Representations of Gaelic and English Language Song in Ireland." In *Global Pop: Local Language*, eds. H. M. Berger, & M T. Carroll, 233–265. Jackson, MI: University of Mississippi Press.

McCormick, Fred. 2000. *The Road from Connemara*. CD liner notes.

McDevitt, Patrick. 1997. "Muscular Catholicism: Nationalism, Masculinity and Gaelic Team Sports, 1884-1916." *Gender and History* 9/2: 262–284.

McHugh, Roger. 1956 [1995]. "The Famine in Folklore." In *The Great Famine: Studies in Irish History, 1845–52*, ed. R. D. Edwards and T. D. Williams, 391–406. Dublin: Lilliput.

Meade, Don. 2006. "The Life and Times of 'Muldoon, the Solid Man.' www. blarneystar.com/Muldoon.pdf. Accessed September 19, 2006.

Meaney, Gerardine. 2006. "Dead, White, Male: Irishness in Buffy the Vampire Slayer." In *The Irish In Us: Irishness, Performativity and Popular Culture*, ed. Diane Negra, 254–281. Durham: Duke University Press.

Miller, Kerby. 1985. "Conquest: Exiles *in* Erin." In *Emigrants and Exiles: Ireland and the Irish Exodus to North America*, ed. Kerby A. Miller, 11–25. New York: Oxford University Press.

Moloney, Mick. 2002. *Far from the Shamrock Shore: The Story of Irish-American Immigration through Song*. New York: Crown.

Moran, David Patrick. 2000. "The Battle of Two Civilizations: Irish Nationality, Gaelic League, Douglas Hyde." In *Irish Writing in the Twentieth Century: A Reader*, ed. David Pierce, 31-37. Cork: Cork University Press.

Moreton, Cole. 2000. *Hungry for Home: Leaving the Blaskets – A Journey from the Edge of Ireland*. London: Viking.

Munnelly, Tom, ed. 1994. *The Mount Callan Garland: Songs from the Repertoire of Tom Lenihan of Knockbrack, Miltown Malbay, Co. Clare*. Dublin: Comhairle Bhéaloideas Éireann.

Murphy, Tom. 2001. *The Gigli Concert*. London: Methuen.

Nandy, Ashis. 1988. *The Intimate Enemy: The Loss and Recovery of the Self under Colonialism*. Delhi: Oxford University Press.

Negra, Diane, ed. 2006. *The Irish In Us: Irishness, Performativity and Popular Culture*. Durham: Duke University Press.

Ní Dhomhnaill, Nuala. 1997. "Why I Choose to Write in Irish: The Corpse That Sits Up and Talks Back." In *Representing Ireland: Gender, Class, Nationality*, ed. Susan Shaw Sailer, 45–57. Gainesville, FL: University Press of Florida.

———. 2007. *The Fifty-Minute Mermaid*. Loughcrew, Co. Meath: Gallery Press.

Ni Fhlaitheartaigh, Ríonach. 1976. *Clár Amhrán Bhaile na hInse*. Dublin: An Clóchomhar.

Ní Ghuairim, Sorcha. 2004. *Sorcha: Amhráin Shorcha Ní Ghuairim. Traditional Songs from Conamara*. Ed. Ríonach uí Ógáin. Dublin: Gael Linn/Comhairle Bhéaloideas Éireann. CEFCD182. (Collection of 30 songs by Sorcha Ní Ghuairim with accompanying booklet).

Ní Riain, Nóirín. 1993. "The Nature and Classification of Traditional Religious Songs, with a Survey of Printed and Oral Sources." In *Irish Musical Studies 2: Music and the Church*, ed. Gerard Gillen and Harry White, 190–253. Dublin: Irish Academic Press.

Nic Dhonnchadha, Mairéad. 1995. "Seáirse Siar: Carna—mar a bhí." *Journal of the Clifden and Connemara Heritage Group* 2/1: 96–101.

Nic Dhonncha, Róisín. 2004. "An tOireachtas agus an Amhránaíocht ar an Sean-nós: Cruthú agus Sealbhú Traidisiúin." Bliainiris *2004*. Eds. R. Ó hUiginn & L. Mac Cóil, 28–24. Carbad: Ráth Cairn, 28-84.

O'Brien, Sharon. 2004. *The Family Silver*. Chicago: University of Chicago Press.

O'Boyle, Seán. 1976. *The Irish Song Tradition*. Cork: Ossian Publications.

Ó Cadhla, Stíofán. 2002. *The Holy Well Tradition: The Pattern of St. Declan, Ardmore, County Waterford, 1800–2000*. Maynooth Studies in Local History. Dublin: Four Courts Press.

———. 2006. *Civilizing Ireland: Ordnance Survey 1824–1842: Ethnography, Cartography, Translation*. Dublin: Irish Academic Press.

Ó Canainn, Tomás. 1978. *Traditional Music in Ireland*. London: Routledge and Kegan Paul.

———. 2003. *Seán Ó Ríada: His Life and Work*. Cork: Collins Press.

Ó Ceannabháin, Peadar. 1983. *Éamonn A Búrc: Scéalta*. Dublin: An Clóchomar.

Ó Cearbhaill, Pádraig. 1995. "An Amhránaíocht ar an Sean-nós: Conas is Ceart í a Mheas?" (*Sean-nós* Singing: How Should It Be Assessed?) *Oghma* 7: 44–52.

Ó Ciosáin, Éamonn. 1993. *An t-Éireannach 1934-37: Nuachtán Sóisialach Gaeltachta*. Dublin: An Clóchomhar.

Ó Ciosáin, Niall. 1995–96. "Was There Silence about the Famine?" *Irish Studies Review* 13:7–10.

———. 2001. "Famine Memory and the Popular Representation of Scarcity." In *History and Memory in Modern Ireland*, ed. Ian McBride, 95–117. Cambridge: Cambridge University Press.

———. 2004. "Approaching a Folklore Archive: The Irish Folklore Commission and the Memory of the Great Famine." *Folklore* 115:222–32.

Ó Conaire, Breandán, ed. 1986. "The Necessity for De-Anglicising Ireland." In *Douglas Hyde: Language, Lore and Lyrics*, 153-170. Dublin: Irish Academic Press.

O'Crohan Tomás. 1951. *The Islandman*. ed. & trans. Robin Flower. Oxford: Oxford University Press.

Ó Duilearga, Séamus. 1999. See Delargy, James H.

Ó Faracháin, Antaine. 2001. *Where Linnets Sing*. Góilín CD 004. Dublin.

O'Faracháin, Riobeard. 1947. *The Course of Irish Verse in English*. New York: Sheed and Ward.

Ó Flatharta, John Beag. 1993. *Tá an Workhouse Lán*. CICD093. Indreabhán.

Ó Giolláin, Diarmuid. 1998. "The Pattern." In *Irish Popular Culture 1650-1850*, eds. J.S. Donnelly & K.A. Miller, 201–221. Dublin, Irish Academic Press.

———. 2000. *Locating Irish Folklore: Tradition, Identity, Modernity*. Cork: Cork University Press.

———. 2005a. *An Dúchas agus an Domhan*. Cork: Cork University Press.

———. 2005b. "Revisiting the Holy Well." *Éire/Ireland* 40: 1 & 2 Spring/Summer 2005, 11–41.

Ó Gráda, Cormac. 1994. *An Drochshaol, Béaloideas agus Amhráin*. Dublin: Coiscéim.

———. 1999. "Famine Memory." In *Black '47 and Beyond: The Great Irish Famine in History, Economy and Memory*, 194–222. Princeton: Princeton University Press.

———. 2001. "Famine, Trauma and Memory." *Béaloideas* 69:121–43.

Ó hAllmhuráin, Gearóid. 1998. *A Pocket History of Irish Music*. Dublin: O'Brien Press.

Ó hAllmhuráin, Gearóid. 1999. "The Great Famine: A Catalyst in Irish Traditional Music Making." In *The Great Famine and the Irish Diaspora in America*, ed. Arthur Gribben, 104–32. Amherst: University of Massachusetts Press.

O'Higgins, Brian. 1918. *Glen na Mona. Stories and Sketches*. Dublin: Whelan and Son.

Ó hÓgáin, Daithí, Marian Deasy, and Ríonach uí Ógáin. 1994. *Binneas Thar Meon: A Collection of Songs and Airs by Liam de Noraidh in East Munster. Vol. 1*. Dublin: Comhairle Bhéaloideas Éireann.

Ó Laoire, Lillis. 2005. *On a Rock in the Middle of the Ocean: Songs and Singers in Tory Island, Ireland*. Lanham: Scarecrow.

——— 2000a. "National Identity and Local Ethnicity: The Case of the Gaelic League's Oireachtas *Sean-Nós* Singing Competitions." In *Sharing the Voices: The Phenomenon of Singing 2*, ed. Brian A. Roberts and Andrea Rose, 160–169. St. John's, Newfoundland: Memorial (University of Newfoundland).

———. 2000b. "Up Scraitheachaí!" *Aimsir Óg* 2: 66–78.

Ó Madagáin, Breandán. 2005. *Caointe agus Seancheolta Eile/Keening and Other Old Irish Musics*. Indreabhán: Cló Iar-Chonnacht.

Ó Muirithe, Diarmaid. 1978. "An Chaointeoireacht in Éirinn: Tuairiscí na dTaistealaithe." In *Gnéithe den Chaointeoireacht*, ed. B. Ó Madagáin, 20–29. Dublin: An Clóchomhar.

Owens, Gary. 1998. "Nationalism without Words: Symbolism and Ritual Behaviour in the Repeal Movement's Monster Meetings 1843-45." In *Irish Popular Culture, 1650–1850*, ed. J.S. Donnelly and K.A.Miller, 242–269. Dublin, Irish Academic Press.

Ó Riada, Seán. 1982. *Our Musical Heritage*. Portlaoise: Dolmen Press.

Ó Súilleabháin, Donncha.1984. *Scéal an Oireachtais 1897–1924*. Dublin: An Clóchomhar.

O'Sullivan, Donal. 1974. *Irish Folk Music, Song and Dance*. Dublin: Mercier.

O'Sullivan, Seán. 1966. *Folktales of Ireland*. Chicago: University of Chicago Press.

Ó Torna, Caitríona. 2005. *Cruthú na Gaeltachta 1893–1922*. Dublin: Cois Life.

Partridge [Bourke], Angela. 1983. *Caoineadh na dTrí Muire: Téama na Páise i bhFilíocht Bhéil na Gaeilge*. Dublin: An Clóchomhar.

Pettitt, Lance. 2000. "Philip Donnellan, Ireland and Dissident Documentary." *Historical Journal of Film, Radio and Television* 20/3: 351–65.

Póirtéir, Cathal. 1996. *Glórtha ón nGorta: Béaloideas na Gaeilge agus an Gorta Mór*. Dublin: Coiscéim.

Preminger, Alex, ed. 1974. *Princeton Encyclopedia of Poetry and Poetics*. Princeton, N.J.: Princeton University Press.

Quinn, Peter. 1994. *Banished Children of Eve: A Novel of Civil War New York*. New York: Penguin.

Rafferty, Oliver P. 2003. "Catholicism (Devotional Revolution to Twenty-first Century)." In *Encyclopedia of Ireland*, ed. Brian Lalor, 169–71. New Haven, CT: Yale University Press.

Rains, Stephanie. 2006. "Genealogy and the Performance of Irishness." In *The Irish In Us: Irishness, Performativity and Popular Culture*. Durham: Duke University Press, ed. Diane Negra, 130–160. Durham: Duke University Press.

Rees, Alwyn & Brinley Rees. 1978. *Celtic Heritage: Ancient Tradition in Ireland and Wales*, 2nd edition. London: Thames and Hudson.

Rice, Timothy. 1994. *May It Fill Your Soul: Experiencing Bulgarian Music*. Chicago: University of Chicago Press

Ricoeur, Paul. 1984. *Time and Narrative*, Vol. 1. Chicago: University of Chicago Press.

Ryan, Joseph. 1993. "Assertions of Distinction: The Modal Debate in Irish Music." In *Irish Musical Studies 2: Music and The Church*, eds. Gerard Gillen & Harry White, 62–77. Dublin: Irish Academic Press.

Seeger, Peggy. 2000. "Joe Heaney: Assorted Memories." Liner notes to *The Road from Connemara: Songs and Stories Told and Sung to Ewan MacColl and Peggy Seeger*. Topic Records.

Sharp, Cecil J. [1907] 1965. *English Folk Song: Some Conclusions*. 4th rev. ed., ed. Maud Karpeles. London: Mercury Books.

Shields, Hugh. 1973. "Supplementary Syllables in Anglo-Irish Folk Singing." *Yearbook of the International Folk Music Council* 5:62–71.

———. 1993. *Narrative Singing in Ireland: Lays, Ballads, Come-All-Yes and Other Songs*. Dublin: Irish Academic Press.

Slobin, Mark. 2000. *Subcultural Sounds: Micromusics of the West*. Hanover, NH: Wesleyan University Press.

Sommers Smith, Sally K. 2003. "Interpretations and Translations of Irish Traditional Music." In *Language and Tradition in Ireland: Continuities and Displacements*, ed. Maria Tymoczko and Colin Ireland, 101–17. Amherst: University of Massachusetts Press.

Spivak, Gayatri Chakravorty. 1988. "Can the Subaltern Speak?" In *Marxism and the Interpretation of Culture*, ed. Cary Nelson and Laurence Grossberg, 271–314. Urbana: University of Illinois Press.

Stivers, Richard. [1976] 2000. *Hair of the Dog: Irish Drinking and Its American Stereotype*. New York: Continuum.

Stokes, Martin. 1994. *Ethnicity, Identity and Music: The Musical Construction of Place*. Oxford: Berg.

Stokes, Martin & Bohlman, Philip V. 2003. *Celtic Modern: Music at the Global Fringe*. Lanham: Scarecrow.

Tymoczko, Maria, and Colin Ireland. 2003. "Language and Tradition in Ireland: Prolegomena." In *Language and Tradition in Ireland: Continuities and Displacements*, ed. Maria Tymoczko and Colin Ireland, 1–27. Amherst: University of Massachusetts Press.

uí Ógáin. Ríonach. 1995. *Immortal Dan: Daniel O'Connell in Irish Folk Tradition*. Dublin: Geography Publications.

————. 1996–97. "Colm Ó Caodháin and Séamus Ennis: A Conamara Singer and His Collector." in *Béaloideas* 64–65: 279–338.

————. 2006. "A Job with no Clock: Séamus Ennis and the Irish Folklore Commission." *Journal of Music in Ireland* 6, no. 1: 10–14.

————. ed. 2007. *"Mise an fear ceoil": Séamus Ennis—Dialann Taistil 1942–1946*. Indreabhán: Cló Iar-Chonnachta.

————. 2009. *Going to the Well for Water: The Séamus Ennis Field Diary, 1942-46*. Cork: Cork University Press (Translation of uí Ógáin 2007).

Vallely, Fintan. 1999. *The Companion to Irish Traditional Music*. Cork: Cork University Press.

Whelan, Kevin. 1993. "The Bases of Regionalism." In *Culture in Ireland—Regions: Identity and Power*, ed. Proinsias Ó Drisceoil, 5–63. Belfast: Institute of Irish Studies, the Queen's University of Belfast.

————. 2005. "The Cultural Effects of the Famine." *The Cambridge Companion to Modern Irish Culture*, eds. Joe Cleary and Claire Connolly, 137–154. Cambridge: Cambridge University Press.

Whisnant, David E. 1983. *All That Is Native and Fine: The Politics of Culture in an American Region*. Chapel Hill: University of North Carolina Press.

White, Richard. 1998. *Remembering Ahanagran: Storytelling in a Family's Past*. New York: Hill and Wang.

Williams, Sean. 1985. "Language, Melody and Ornamentation in the Traditional Irish Singing of Joe Heaney." Unpublished M.A. thesis, University of Washington.

————. 2004. "Melodic Ornamentation in the Connemara *Sean-Nós* Singing of Joe Heaney." *New Hibernia Review* 8, no. 1: 22–45.

Williams, William H. A. 1996, *Twas Only an Irishman's Dream: The Image of Ireland and the Irish in American Popular Song Lyrics, 1800–1920*. Urbana: University of Illinois Press.

————. 2008. *Tourism, Landscape and the Irish Character: British Travel Writers in Pre-Famine Ireland*. Madison: University of Wisconsin Press.

Winch, Terence. 1999. "In the Band: Five Sessions." *New Hibernia Review* 3/1: 9–18.

Zimmerman, Georges-Denis. 1967. *Songs of the Irish Rebellion*. Hatboro, PA: Folklore Associates.

Zipes, Jack. 1979. *Radical Theories of Folk and Fairy Tales*. London: Heinemann.

Discography

$\mathbb{T}$he selections in this discography are a few among many and represent commercially available recordings for perusal. The first few are recordings referenced in the text, and the rest are recordings featuring Joe Heaney. More recordings will come to light, of course, as further archival collections are digitized and made available. Readers are directed to two other primary resources for study: the Joe Heaney Collection at the University of Washington School of Music Ethnomusicology Archives, and the website dedicated specially to Heaney's artistry as a singer, a storyteller and an interpreter of his tradition: http://www.joeheaney.org. This growing site includes the full text and translations of Heaney's songs, with annotations by Virginia Blankenhorn.

Recordings Featuring Other Singers

Ennis, Séamus. CEF009. 1961. *Ceol Scéalta agus Amhráin*, rereleased as CEFCD009.

Mac Dhonnchadha, Seán. CIC006. 1987. *An Spailpín Fánach*.

Mac Dhonnchadha, Seán, and Máirtín Ó Cualáin. CEF 117. 1987. *Bruach na Beirtrí*.

Ní Ghuairim, Sorcha. CEFCD182. 2004. *Sorcha: Amhráin Shorcha Ní Ghuairim. Traditional Songs from Conamara*. Ed. Ríonach uí Ógáin. Dublin: Gael Linn/Comhairle Bhéaloideas Éireann.

Ó Faracháin, Antaine. Góilín CD 004. 2001. *Where Linnets Sing*.

Ó Flatharta, John Beag. CICD093. 1993. *Tá an Workhouse Lán*.

Recordings Featuring Joe Heaney

Joe Heaney. BBC LP 25570. 1959. Includes "Amhrán Shéamuis Uí Chrochúir," "Caoine na dTrí Muire," "Amhrán na Páise," "Amhrán Rinn Mhaoile," "Caisleán Uí Néill," "Abhainn Mhór," "O'Brien from Tipperary," "The Maid of SweetGoirtín," "The Banks of the Lee," and "An Droighneán Donn."

Irish Music in London Pubs. Folkways FSS 3575. 1965. Includes "The Rocks of Bawn," "Johnny Morrissey and the Russian Sailor," and "An Spailpín Fánach."

Come All Ye Gallant Irishmen [LP]. Philo 2004. 1963. Includes "Johnny Morrissey and the Russian Sailor," "Dark Is the Color of My True Love's Hair," "The Green Linnet," "The Seven Irishmen," "Róisín Dubh," "Did the Rum Do, Daddy," "Johnny Is the Fairest Man," "The Rocks of Bawn," "An Droighneán Donn," "O'Brien from Tipperary," "I'm a Catholic, Not a Protestant [story]," "An Buinneán Buí," and "Cunnla."

Irish Traditional Songs in Gaelic and English. Ossian [originally released as an LP by Topic] OSSCD22. 1963. Includes "The Rocks of Bawn," "One Morning in June," "Casadh an tSúgáin," "The Wife of the Bold Tenant Farmer," "The Trees They Grow Tall," "Peigín is Peadar," "Cunnla," "Caoineadh na dTrí Muire," "An Tighearna Randal," "Bean an Leanna," and "John Mitchel."

Seosamh Ó hÉanaí. Gael Linn CEF 028. 1971. Includes "Currachaí na Trá Báine," "Bean an Leanna," "Caoineadh na dTrí Muire," "Tá na Páipéir a Saighneáil," "Sadhbh Ní Bhruinneallaigh," "Cuaichín Ghleann Néifín," "Eileanóir a Rúin," "An Buinneán Buí," "An Tighearna Randal," "Amárach Lá 'le Pádraig," "Anach Cuain," Neainsín Bhán," and "Púcán Mhicil Pháidín."

Ó Mo Dhúchas. Gael Linn CEF 051. 1976. Includes "Casadh an tSúgáin," "Róisín Dubh," "Peigín is Peadar," "Úna Bhán," "Deoindí," "Donal Óg," "Seachrán Chearbhaill," "Baile Uí Laí," "Cailleach an Airgid," "An Sagairtín," "Contae Mhaigh Eo," "Amhrán Rinn Mhaoile," and "Amhrán na Páise."

Joe and the Gabe. Green Linnet SIF 1018. 1979. Includes "The Widow from Mayo," "Amhrán Muighinse," "The Banks of Sweet Dundee," "Skibbereen," "Bádóirín Tír Níad," and "The Bogs of Shanaheever."

Bloomsday: James Joyce and Nora Barnacle - a Tribute. Aquitaine Records. AQU, AQA16. 1982. "Peigín is Peadar," "Will You Come Over the Mountain," "The American Wake [A Stór mo Chroí]," and "Óró Sé do Bheatha 'Bhaile."

Roaratorio: ein Irischer Circus über Finnegans Wake. Wergo WER 6303–2. 1994. Various songs in Irish and English in a chaotic context.

Say a Song: Joe Heaney in the Pacific Northwest. NWARCD 001. 1996. Includes "A Stór mo Chroí," "Eileanóir a Rún," "The Galway Shawl," "The Wife of the Bold Tenant Farmer," "Róisín Dubh," "An Raibh Tú ar an gCarraig," "Red Is the Rose," "Oíche Nollag," "Seoithín Seo Ho/Óró mo Bháidín/Coochenanty," "Will You Come Over the Mountain," "The Rocks of Bawn," "An Tiarna Randal," "My Love, She's in America/Off to California," "Óró, Sé do Bheatha 'Bhaile," "Bean Dubh an Ghleanna," "I Wish I Had Someone to Love Me," "An Buinneán Buí," "The Claddagh Ring," and "Caoineadh na dTrí Muire."

Joe Heaney/Seosamh Ó hÉanaí: The Road from Connemara, Songs and Stories Told and Sung to Ewan MacColl and Peggy Seeger. Topic Records TSCD518D. 2000. Includes "My Bonny Boy Is Young," "The West of Ireland," "Skibbereen," "Bean Pháidín," "Amhrán na hEascainne (Lord Randal)," "As I Roved Out," "An Droighneán Donn," "Caroline and Her Young Sailor Bold," "Fishing in Connemara," "Amhrán an Bhá (Currachaí na Trá Báine)," "Singing in Connemara," "The Jug of Punch," "The Ferocious O'Flahertys," "The Widow from Mayo," "The Harp without the Crown," "Suantraí/Seoithín Seo Ho," "Advice to Young

Singers," "The Valley of Knockanure," "Whiskey Ó Roudeldum-Row," "Barbary Ellen," "The Two Greyhounds (The Bogs of Shanaheever)," "The Old Woman of Wexford," "The Banks of Claudy," "Éamonn an Chnoic," "My Boy Willie," "Patsy McCann," "Úna Bhán," "Cailleach an Airgid," "The Lonely Woods of Upton," "O'Brien from Tipperary," "Erin Grá mo Chroí," "Cúnnla," "The Tennis Right," "Eanach Cuain," "Beidh Aonach Amárach i gContae an Chláir," "The Glen of Aherlow," "Slán agus Beannacht le Buaireamh an tSaoil," and "The Old Man Rocking the Cradle."

Seolta Séidte—Setting Sail: Forty Three Historic Recordings. 2003. Gael-Linn CEFCD184. Includes "Caoineadh na dTrí Muire," "Neainsín Bhán," "Bean a' Leanna," "Amhrán na Páise," "Sadhbh Ní Bhruinneallaigh," and "Is Measa Liom Bródach."

Nár Fhágha Mé Bás Choíche [May I Never Die]. 2007. CD included with book of the same title by Liam Mac Con Iomaire. Indreabhán, Co. Galway: Cló Iar-Chonnachta. Includes "Amhrán Rinn Mhaoile," "Port na Giobóige," "Oíche Nollag," "Caoineadh na dTrí Muire," "An Buinneán Buí," "The Yellow Bittern," "Amhrán Shéamais Uí Chonchúir," "Eanach Cuain," "Róisín Dubh," "Úna Bhán," "O'Brien from Tipperary," "Seachrán Chearbhaill," "Eileanóir na Rún," "The Bonny Bunch of Roses," "Amhrán Mháire Ní Mhongáin," "Skibbereen," "Amhrán Mhaínse," and "Bean Pháidín."

Tell a Story: Joe Heaney in the Pacific Northwest. CAMSCO-701. 2008. Includes the stories "The Children of Lir," "Stories about Fionn MacCumhaill," "Fionn MacCumhaill and the Giant," "Oisín's Journey to Tír na nÓg," "Fionn MacCumhaill and the Lamb," "Deirdre of the Sorrows," "Stories from the Táin Bó Cuailnge," "The Man Who Married a Seal Woman," "The Woman Who Pulled a Thorn from the Seal's Fin," "Wren Stories," "The Fairies Who Spun the Wool," "How Cearbhall Ó Dálaigh Got the Gift," "The Three Good Advices," "I'm a Catholic, Not a Protestant," "Stories about Boats," "The Woman Who Fooled the Peelers," "The Fairy Greyhound," "The Two Hunchbacks," and "Did the Rum Do."

Index

England 4, 19, 35, 36, 40, 41, 43, 53, 144
English: language 35, 36;
   ornamentation in songs 65–68;
   parlors 144, 146;
   in songs 50, 65, 79, 125, 127–136;
   use in Ireland 50
Ennis, Séamus 31, 35, 55, 72–73, 113, 184
"Erin, Grá mo Chroí" [song] 20–21
ethnicity 165
Ethnomusicology Archives 42, 62, 99, 185, 188, 211–212, 216n., 227n.
exile 127–136

fame 3, 54, 148, 150
Famine: 71–88, 153–154, 162, 203;
   historical context 11–12;
   historiography 73–75, 78, 81;
   memory of 74, 78, 203;
   presence in the Irish and American
      imagination 7–8, 71–72, 79–81, 201;
   Heaney's presentation of 78–82;
   repercussions from 35–36;
   songs about 71–88;
   stories about 79–81, 218n.
Féile Joe Éinniú xii, 11, 212
Féis Charna 40, 209
festivals 10, 11, 35–40
fighting 159–166, 223n.
films 4, 128, 131–132, 148–149
Fínis, Connemara 35
Fionn Mac Cumhaill 162
fishing 10, 17, 79, 157
folk music: collectors 199, 204;
   culture 147, 197;
   enthusiasts 10, 41, 44, 47;
   movement 29, 32, 197;
   performers 161;
   revival 200
folklore 16, 38–39, 73–74, 94, 97, 114–116, 126, 188, 198–200, 208, 226n.
Folkways Records 198
Foster, Stephen 144
funeral: Joe Heaney's 96–97;
   Pádhraic Ó hÉighnigh's 17

Gael Linn 41–44, 166, 170, 175, 194, 221n.
Gaelic Athletic Association 14, 36, 162
Gaelic Ireland 3–4

Gaelic language, see Irish language and
   language issues
Gaelic League 6, 14, 15, 17, 25, 27, 29, 36, 38, 57, 94
Gaeltacht 3–4, 37–38, 40, 41
gaisce 137, 158, 162–163, 221n., 223n.
"Galway Shawl" [song] 81, 83–85
Garofalo, Janeane 152
Gaskin, George 147
gender issues 43, 97, 130, 140–143, 157–158, 166–176, 199
Glackin, Paddy 184, 225n.
glottal stops 59, 61
goddesses 53
"Going to Mass Last Sunday"
   [song] 50, 59–60, 67
"Good Day and the Bad Day, The"
   [story] 183
grace notes [type of ornament] 59–60
"Gráinne Mhaol" [song] 53
grave 11, 212
"Green Linnet, The" [song] 51
Gregory, Lady Augusta 12, 38, 145, 199
Griffin, Merv 5, 182
guitars 181–182;
   Heaney on 10, 22, 184, 186, 188–190

harp 52, 108–109, 140, 221n.
Harrigan, Edward 82
Heaney, Joe: as anti-hero 200–205;
   as culture hero 155, 208–210;
   as a doorman 180–181, 189;
   on guitars 10, 22, 184, 186, 188–190, 217n.;
   about the Famine 78–82;
   about laments 95;
   as mediator 112, 166;
   in New York 179–184;
   about ornamentation 48, 63, 186;
   as a performer 6, 15, 44, 201;
   presentation of self 16, 22, 203, 206–208;
   rejection of, by Irish Americans 10, 200–205;
   song choices 42, 72, 86, 126, 136;
   as a symbol 6, 15, 142, 161–166, 178, 194, 200–205;
   as a teacher 185–192;
   on vibrato 57, 155

ritual 89–91, 105
Riverdance 22, 153, 211
Roaratorio, an Irish Circus on Finnegans Wake 9, 183–184
Robertson, Jeannie 84
"Rocks of Bawn, The" [song] 9, 17, 41, 43, 62–63, 111–112, 128–132, 135, 169, 172
"Róisín Dubh" [song] 34, 53, 126
roll [type of ornament] 59–60, 64
Romantic Nationalism 4, 6, 27–28, 32, 36, 144, 198
rules 31–35, 55, 57, 66
Russian character 159–165

"Sadhbh Ní Bhruinneallaigh" [song] 41, 157
"Sagairtín, An" [song] 77, 204
Saint Patrick's Day 149, 182, 202
salon 140, 147
Samhain 37
Sarsfield, Patrick 128, 221n.
Say A Song: Joe Heaney in the Pacific Northwest [recording] 42, 44, 45, 99, 174, 182, 226n.
schools 17, 42, 44;
    gaelscoileanna 153;
    hedge 92
Scotland 18, 40, 84, 177
"Seachrán Chearbhaill" [song] 9, 114, 116–120, 126, 195, 219n.
sean-nós singing: creativity in 32;
    definitions of 3, 8, 2, 29, 33;
    Heaney's theories about 47;
    language hierarchy of 55;
    regional hierarchy of 31–35, 47;
    history of 28, 49;
    opinions about 22, 152–153;
    ornamentation of 48;
    "rules" of 31–35, 55;
    variation principle in 31–32
Seattle, Washington 173, 175, 185–192, 195, 205–206, 211
Secret of Roan Inish, The [film] 152
sectarianism 37, 108–109, 152
Seeger, Mike 185
Seeger, Peggy 18, 43, 44, 177, 211, 221n.
Seeger, Pete 174, 208
Seosamh Ó hÉanaí: Ó Mo Dhúchas [two-CD recording] 41, 104–105, 221n.

"Seoithín Seo Ho" [song] 183
Sercombe, Laurel 151, 212, 227n.
sexuality 43, 76, 149, 158, 168–169, 173
Simpson, Lucy 125, 173–175, 225n.
shanty Irish 12, 144–145, 161, 200–201, 212
Sharp, Cecil 204
Sing the Dark Away [film] 3, 172, 211, 215n.
singers' clubs 18–19, 170, 177
social control 157–159
song: categories 35, 53–54, 135;
    in English 48, 65–68, 127–136;
    explanations by Heaney 80–81, 96, 100–101, 104–105, 121–123, 129, 133–134, 170;
    hidden meanings in 52;
    hierarchies 111–113;
    iconic 69–70;
    in Irish 48, 63–65;
    macaronic 41;
    music hall 202;
    ownership 188–189;
    religious 89–109;
    "school" 42, 126
Song of My Heart [film] 148, 180
"Souphouse Mhaigh Rois" [song] 80
spailpín 129
"Spailpín Fánach" [song] 129
speaking the final phrase of a song 58
stage Irishman 148, 202–204
"Statues, The" [poem] 12–13
stereotypes 4, 14, 29, 37, 160–161, 163, 190, 202
stories and storytelling 43, 53, 69–70, 75, 78, 115, 126, 162, 206;
    of songs (*see údar*)
style 29–35, 49, 56
Sweeney 111–112, 128–132, 172
Sydney Opera House 90
symbolism: of Heaney himself 6, 10, 15, 88, 198;
    of Ireland 165;
    of Irish America 165;
    of Irish tenors 140, 147, 154;
    of representing the past through song and story 115–116;
    in songs 161
syllables: stressed and unstressed 49, 50, 63–67;
    supplementary in singing 51, 217n.

Synge, John Millington 38
syntax, poetic 49, 50, 66–67

Táin Bó Cuailnge [story] 160
Tansey, Seamus 184
teaching 42, 44, 47, 111–112, 130,
    152–153, 185–192
*Tell a Story: Joe Heaney in the Pacific
    Northwest* 44, 45, 241
TG4 [Irish-language television] 22
tenor, Irish (*see* Irish tenor)
thumos 163, 224n.
"Tighearna Randal, An" [song] 41,
    59–60, 77
timbre 146, 186–187
Tin Pan Alley 202
Tóibín, Nioclás 31
Topic Records 41, 43–44, 166, 168
Tory Island 55
tourism 36, 93, 139
translation 52, 55, 206–207
Translations [play] 215n.
transcription, *see* musical transcriptions
"Trees They Grow Tall, The" [song] 41,
    51, 66
Trinity College 143–144
turns [type of ornament] 59–61, 64
"Two Hunchbacks, The" [story] 191
Tynan, Ronan 149

údar (explanation of the song) 53, 75,
    78, 99–101, 121–123, 129, 133–134
Údarás na Gaeltachta (Irish Language
    Regional Authority) 38
Uí Cheannabháin, Máire an
    Ghabha 91–92, 99, 218n.
Ulster (province) 67
"Úna Bhán" [song] 77
United Kingdom 37
United States 44, 144, 161, 164, 177,
    194, 197–212

University College Dublin 38
University of Washington 5, 42, 45, 62,
    185–192, 211–212, 225n.
upward mobility 144, 161

variation 31–32
vaudeville 148
vibrato 29, 33–34, 56–57, 146–147, 155,
    222n.
Victorian era 162, 200
vocal technique of Heaney 8, 32,
    47–68, 98, 135, 186–187;
    of John Cage 183

wakes 132–134
war: 1916 Uprising 126;
    Cold 165;
    of Independence 3, 40, 126;
    World War I 14;
    World War II 40
Warkov, Esther 185
waver [type of ornament] 59, 61
Wesleyan University 185–186, 189
"Wife of the Bold Tenant Farmer, The"
    [song] 41
Waterford, County 31, 58
"Whiskey in the Jar" [song] 174
"Whiskey Ó Roudeldum-Row"
    [song] 43
"Whiskey, You're the Devil" [song] 174
White, Richard 200
Williams, William H. A. 202, 204
Wings of the Morning [film] 148–149
women, vernacular religious traditions
    of 89, 91–92, 95;
    and love 166–173 (*see also* Mary,
    Mother of Jesus)

Yankees 160
Yeats, William Butler 12–13, 29, 38,
    113, 139, 145, 199